EDUCATION
SUSTAINABILITY

John Huckle is principal lecturer in geographical and environmental education at De Montfort University, and is a consultant to WWF. Stephen Sterling is a consultant in environmental education, a co-director at the Bureau for Environmental Education and Training, and an academic tutor at South Bank University

How do we get from where we are to where we want to be...?

Edited by
John Huckle and Stephen Sterling

EDUCATION FOR
SUSTAINABILITY

Earthscan Publications Ltd, London

First published in 1996 by
Earthscan Publications Limited
120 Pentonville Road, London N1 9JN

Reprinted 1997

A catalogue record for this book is available from the British Library

ISBN: 1 85383 256 1 (Paperback)

Copy-edited and typeset by Selro Publishing Services, Oxford
Printed and bound by Biddles Ltd, Guildford and King's Lynn

Earthscan Publications Limited is an editorially independent subsidiary of
Kogan Page Limited and publishes in association with the International
Institute for Environment and Development and WWF–UK.
Panda device © 1986 WWF.
WWF–UK is a Registered Charity, No. 201707. All royalties to WWF.
In the USA and in Canada, World Wide Fund For Nature is known as World
Wildlife Fund.

◼ Contents

Part IV
Continuing Education

Part V
Making Progress Towards Sustainability

■ *Contributors*

Tony Alabaster is a reader in environmental citizenship at the University of Sunderland. He has been active in promoting and implementing an 'Integrated Model of Environmental Responsibility' for the University, and has developed a new area of applied environmental citizenship research. He has played a key role in bringing the global Talloires Declaration from the USA to the UK and promoting its wider dissemination across the European Union.

Shirley Ali Khan has been centrally involved in 'greening' the UK further and higher education sector since 1990 and has written guidance publications for a number of strategic sector agencies. She was an acknowledged contributor to the Department for Education's *Environmental Responsibility* (Toyne Report) and is currently an associate of Forum for the Future.

Julian Agyeman is an environmental consultant and writer specializing in environmental education, training and communications. He has worked as a geography teacher and local authority adviser and was the founder and first chair of the Black Environment Network. His current research interest is the presentation of urban nature in environmental education at key stage 2 (7–11 years).

Jeff Bishop trained and practised as an architect before widening and developing his environmental interests with a still continuing focus on advancing practice through education, research and action projects. He has worked mainly in the UK but also in the USA, Australia, Italy and Sweden, and since 1987 has run his own consultancy. BDOR Ltd works with the public, private, voluntary and community sectors, particularly on community participation and consensus building.

Derek Blair is a reader in environmental education at the University of Sunderland where he has played a leading role in the innovative development of its environmental courses, policies and practices and championed the extra-mural role of students. He is a council member of the Institution of Environmental Sciences and has long-standing links with the USA and Poland.

Adrian Cleasby is project coordinator of the Third World and Environment Broadcasting Project (3WE). 3WE works for sustained and fair coverage of 'Southern' countries on behalf of the UK's leading development, environment, and human rights organizations including Oxfam, WWF and Christian Aid.

Geoff Fagan trained as a teacher and community worker and worked in Leicestershire Education Authority in these capacities and as a manager for community-based research projects. He was then appointed as a community education lecturer at Jordanhill College of Education in Glasgow. At present he is engaged in full-time research at Strathclyde University as the manager of the CADISPA project (Conservation and Development in Sparsely Populated Areas) which is using community-based learning and co-investigation techniques to identify local interpretations of sustainable development.

Lisbeth Grundy formerly worked as a primary and secondary teacher and part-time youth worker. In the early 1980s, she was involved in the development of the first local authority cross-departmental policy for environmental education, in Wolverhampton and worked towards its implementation for six years. Lisbeth is currently assistant director of the Council for Environmental Education and a member of the IUCN European Committee for Environmental Education.

John Howson is a consultant in environmental communication and education. Formerly a head of department in a secondary school, he was senior education officer at Friends of the Earth from 1989 to 1993 where he worked directly with the media, including television, radio and the national press. He has been involved in writing and editing many environmental education resources, including the media unit for the South Bank University distance learning MSc in Environmental and Development Education.

John Huckle is principal lecturer in geographical and environmental education at De Montfort University Bedford. He is a consultant to the World Wide Fund for Nature and the main author of its Global Environmental Education Programme and its teacher education programme, Reaching Out: Education for Sustainability. He has written extensively on critical approaches to geographical and environmental education and has spoken and run workshops at numerous conferences in Britain and Australia.

Peter Martin taught in schools in the UK for seven years before leaving the formal sector to set up and run a suburban educational nature reserve in the Lea Valley Regional Park and become an education officer for the Royal Society for the Protection of Birds. Since 1981 he has been principal education officer for the World Wide Fund for Nature (UK) responsible for the development of the philosophy and programme of education in the UK.

Jane Morris is the Local Agenda 21 project officer at the Local Government Management Board, working on behalf of the local authority associations in England, Wales, Scotland and Northern Ireland. The project has produced a wide range of guidance on Local Agenda 21.

Andrea Oates has worked on health and safety and environmental issues at the Labour Research Department, an independent trade union research organization since 1990. She recently worked at the Wissenschaftszentrum Berlin (Centre for Social Science Research, Berlin) as part of a network of researchers concerned with worklife and environment issues.

Jonathon Porritt is one of the most influential spokespeople on behalf of the environment and has played a key role in establishing environmental concerns as major items on the political agenda. His most recent book, *Save the Earth*, was produced in the run-up to the 1992 Earth Summit and has been published in 23 countries around the world, selling more than 500,000 copies. The emphasis in much of Jonathon's current work is on solutions rather than problems, encouraging and multiplying examples of the best environmental practice wherever possible. Jonathon was director of Friends of the Earth between 1984 and 1990. Current interests include the Real World initiative and Forum for the Future.

Nigel Roome holds the Erivan K Haub chair in business and the environment in the Faculty of Administrative Studies, York University, Canada. He previously worked at the Manchester Business School and the Universities of Bradford and Cambridge. He has published widely on business, environment and sustainability and has advised government agencies, companies, the voluntary sector and education bodies in the UK, Europe and Canada.

Bud Simpkin qualified as a youth and community worker in 1978, followed by a degree in sociology and psychology and an MA in public and social administration. He has considerable experience of the youth and play work sectors, both voluntary and local authority, and was director of the Westminster Play Association for five years. He is currently national youth programme coordinator at the Council for Environmental Education.

Stephen Sterling is a consultant in environmental education. A former teacher, he was later assistant director at the Council for Environmental Education (CEE) for eight years. He was executive editor of CEE's *Annual Review of Environmental Education* from 1986 to 1994. An extensive publications record includes *Good Earth-Keeping: Education, Training and Awareness for a Sustainable Future*, a report to the 1992 Earth Summit. He is a unit writer and academic tutor for the MSc in environmental and development education at South Bank University, and has had extensive involvement in strategy work in the UK and eastern Europe. He is a member of two IUCN commissions, on education and on strategy. His research interest lies in the interface between environmental education, systemic thinking and sustainability.

Gillian Symons is a freelance writer and trainer specializing in education for sustainable development. She is a member of WWF's Reaching Out teacher education team and her publications include *The Urban Environment*, with Prue Polton, and *Sustainable Development in Action*.

Ken Webster is an associate of WWF–UK's education department and has written widely on economics and business education. He is a member of WWF's Reaching Out teacher education team.

■ *Acknowledgements*

The editors would like to thank WWF–UK for supporting this project, and giving them a free hand; and Ewan McCleish for supplying the frontispiece.

Stephen Sterling would like to acknowledge assistance with supplying information or comments on early drafts from John Baines, Deborah Elton, John Fien, Lisbeth Grundy, Chris Maas Geesteranus, Tuire Nikulainen, John Smyth, IUCN Commission on Education and Communication, IUCN Commission on Environmental Strategy and Planning, UNED–UK.

■ *Foreword*

There is something chilling in the idea of the majority of young people today believing that the future (*their* future) is going to be a worse time to live in than the present. Hope, idealism, great expectations in helping to fashion a better world: how cruel that our current model of 'progress' has managed to deprive young people even of these fittingly youthful attributes.

Yet one cannot help admiring what would seem to be their natural instinct for the truth — even at the expense of optimism. Adults so easily become inured to persistent untruths. We are told, for instance, that to go on getting richer we have no choice but to become ever more competitive in the global company. More competitive means fewer people generating a higher turnover year on year. That means fewer full-time jobs, less purchasing power in the economy, and an ever more unequal and divided society.

We are also told that to protect the environment we have no choice but to ensure the economy grows even faster, simply so that we can spend a higher proportion of our national income on cleaning up the mess generated in the very process of getting richer!

The role of education in exposing the prevailing untruths of the day (let alone the vested interests that depend upon them) has been a source of fruitful controversy for many decades. It is no less controversial today, when it has become blindingly obvious that we are educating young people for a world that has already ceased to exist.

Yet the formal education system today seems hopelessly ill-equipped to respond. Battered by one ideological shoot-out after another, under-resourced schools, demotivated teachers and stripped down local education authorities hardly provide the most conducive context for the kind of transformation that this book appears to be signalling.

Worse yet, much of that educational system has been co-opted by the language, values and practice of the so-called 'free market' meekly renouncing progressive educational values in order to mould young people for induction into today's harsh, unforgiving, competitiveness-at-all-costs economy. An economy that many now believe is already collapsing under the weight of the social and environmental costs it now imposes on people and planet alike.

The irony of all this is that at one level governments, business leaders and establishment pundits know full well that their free market emperor has very few clothes left. If the Earth Summit in Rio de Janeiro in 1992 achieved nothing else, it compelled them to acknowledge publicly and powerfully the self-evident *unsustainability* of the world today.

However, identifying the unsustainability of any system is unfortunately a rather easier exercise than devising a sustainable one to put in its place. Just what is sustainability anyway? Several authors in this collection seek to shed light on the true meaning of this elusive concept, but the theological niceties underlying this debate should not divert our attention from the obvious: if you are heading for the abyss, you first need to stop before deciding which direction to head off in instead. And it is that process (stopping and reorienting) which requires systematic, strategic thinking, with the education system taking the lead. But systematic, strategic thinking is in distressingly short supply at the moment, as was picked up by the government's own Panel on Sustainable Development when its first report recommended in forthright terms that the government should 'develop a comprehensive strategy for environmental education and training to cover both formal and informal education, and to bring in the wide range of related activities, by official and voluntary bodies, industry and commerce, and local communities'.

That is very much what this timely and informative book is seeking to accelerate, simultaneously enabling us to discern the outline of what the strategy might look like in practice. As is often the way, it is already emerging in a host of positive developments both within the formal educational system and beyond.

One thing strikes me above all else. Given the state we are in, education for sustainability is perhaps the *only* way of getting back to those intrinsically liberal, progressive values that once underpinned our education system. It challenges head-on the spurious notion of 'value-free education' (which in reality means little more than condoning the lack of values in today's economic orthodoxy), insisting unapologetically on a moral and ethical base for the process of learning about the world and our role in it.

It is explicitly value-driven, and so much the stronger and more inspiring for it.

Jonathon Porritt
March 1996

■ *Introduction*

This book builds on four assumptions: societies are faced with making an unprecedented and historic change in a short period of time if they are to achieve a sufficiently sustainable form — environmentally, socially and economically; education will have to play a key role in any such transition; education will itself be transformed in the process; and it is necessary and possible to build on the limited progress already made. By education we mean a life-long process of learning, action and reflection involving all citizens.

Governments and non-governmental organizations (NGOs) repeatedly point to education as a key policy instrument for bringing about a transition to sustainable development, but there is little discussion about the radical challenge this poses for education. This is the first book published in Britain to provide an overview of the theory and practice of education for sustainability (EFS). It brings together contributions from environmental educators working in the formal and informal sectors and in continuing education, and provides perspectives on the philosophy, politics and pedagogy of education for sustainability, as well as case studies and pointers towards good practice. These chapters acknowledge the role of education in realizing the agenda agreed at the 1992 Earth Summit (Agenda 21) and suggest ways in which policy-makers might improve strategies for education for sustainability at all levels, from local to global.

This book contains neither an overview of environment and development issues nor comprehensive listings of the curriculum and curriculum management materials that have been produced to encourage educators to address these at all levels of education, in both the formal and informal sectors. There is no shortage of books outlining the need for sustainable development and exploring the forms it might take. Similarly, there is no shortage of curriculum materials and guidelines for educators wishing to explore environment and development issues and the nature of sustainable development with their students. The World Wide Fund for Nature (WWF–UK) has an extensive catalogue of such materials, as do many development education centres and other NGOs. However, while education for sustainability is achieving increasing currency through the use of such materials, there has been little attempt to date to reflect on the underlying and emerging theory and practice. This book is an attempt to clarify this theory and practice, and discuss how it might be improved, spread and enacted further.

It is divided into five parts. Part I establishes some initial perspectives on sustainability, education and the role of NGOs, like WWF–UK, in encouraging social change through education. The potential for education for sustainability in the formal and informal sectors is assessed in Parts II and III, while Part IV examines its development as part of the greening of business and local government. Part V is concerned with ways forward. It includes a chapter on strategy building, invited contributions from politicians and a visionary statement about life and education in the future. The parts are separated by quotations to provoke thinking, and each contributor provides sufficient references to enable the reader to find theoretical and practical ways in to relevant areas of education for sustainability.

Both sustainability and education for sustainability have a range of meanings in theory and practice. We have sought to acknowledge philosophical and political debates from the outset and hope that readers will find the book useful in helping to clarify and perhaps extend their own positions. They are likely to recognize a difference between the political ecology or green socialist position supported by one of the book's editors, and the 'darker' green or systemic view supported by the other. We feel there is a healthy and creative tension between these positions, which informs both, and which needs further discussion beyond this book. Space has not permitted us to explore points of convergence and divergence to the extent we would have liked, but we remain convinced that an emerging postmodern education for sustainability will need to incorporate elements of both positions.

The other contributors also adopt different positions, but they too are united in calling for fundamental changes in our current system of education, which move it in different directions from those in which it currently seems to be heading. The recurring theme is that education for sustainability is essentially process-driven, is participative and empowering, is liberatory and continuous, and that it is necessitated by the possibilities and dangers presented by an emerging 'postmodern' world.

In Chapter 1 *John Huckle* lays some foundations for other chapters in the book by relating debates about sustainability and sustainable development to the changing nature of modern societies, different political ideologies and utopias, and contemporary environmental politics. He suggests that different forms of economic production and social reproduction (political economy) are more or less ecologically and socially sustainable and that education for sustainability is essentially shared reflection and action on forms of political economy that would enable us to live sustainably with one another and the rest of nature. He outlines the transition from organized to disorganized forms of capitalism, or from modern to postmodern forms of political economy, and suggests that this has precipitated a double crisis of environment and development. In the resulting debates and policy proposals sustainability takes on a range of meanings. The core contradiction is between the 'weak' sustainability advocated by liberal and social democratic reformers and the 'strong' sustainability advocated by green socialist and utopian radicals. Environmental politics is dominated by the former and there are strong pressures on education to encourage support for such sustainability while ignoring its stronger variants.

In Chapter 2, *Stephen Sterling* argues that education must itself be transformed if it is to be transforming, and suggests that education for sustainability holds the promise of a new transformative paradigm for education. A number of primary requirements, or qualities of education for sustainability, are outlined. The idea of learning being an intrinsic characteristic of a sustainable society is reviewed, and recent moves to restructure formal education to conform to market ideology are critiqued against the imperative of sustainability. The emergence of education for change is briefly reviewed, but it is argued that stronger forms of education for sustainability are needed. Systemic critical theory is outlined as a contributory basis for the elaboration of these forms. The relation between the emergence of education for sustainability and change in wider society is suggested, along with some detail on the constituents of education for sustainability.

In Chapter 3, *Peter Martin* gives a personal and critical view of the role of NGOs. While high-level rhetoric on the need for changed values through education has been seized on by many NGOs as a way of legitimizing their work, there is a gap between expectations and reality. This is partly due to the nature of the NGO movement, which is made up of organizations with different and specific foci, differing political orientations and which tend to interpret the value change advocated by such documents as the World Conservation Strategy in a limited way. The larger conservation-based NGOs have had some influence, but this tends to be limited to initiation into a conservation and ecology-based environmental education. A more socially critical approach is needed, but there are problems in enacting this too. WWF–UK has sought to develop an approach that is 'not synonymous with nature focus, is not prescriptive and not outside the mainstream' and which balances challenge and security. Peter Martin describes the principles of 'an entitlement curriculum' which has formed the basis of WWF's education work and strategy.

Gillian Symons, in Chapter 4, suggests that primary school teachers should meet the challenge of education for sustainability by combining their long-standing tradition of nature study, which develops an affinity with the rest of nature and an understanding of ecology, with a radical social education tradition which addresses such concepts as equity and social change. She reviews these two traditions and provides arguments to counter those of teachers who suggest that such education is too difficult for young children. There is much evidence to suggest that they are capable of critical reflection and action on environmental issues and some of this is presented in the form of case studies of children's project work, including a project linked to Local Agenda 21. Many teachers also suggest that the national curriculum leaves little scope for education for sustainability, but the chapter demonstrates that there is considerable scope within statutory frameworks and that teachers can develop their own forms of mutual support.

Ken Webster begins Chapter 5 by outlining the predicament of secondary schools as modern institutions in a postmodern world. He urges teachers to assess the extent to which the curriculum is riddled with modernism and schools as institutions filter initiatives, taking from them what they want but generally removing their critical core. Education for weak sustainability is more acceptable than education for strong sustainability and teachers who seek the latter are advised that there is important work for them to do in their everyday interactions with students. Taking examples from economics and business education, and from science, the chapter shows how lesson content and pedagogy can be revised in ways which ensure that they contribute to education for strong sustainability. Postmodernity is eroding the foundations of modern secondary schooling and the teachers who are prepared to promote such critical awareness can now make a real contribution to new kinds of educational arrangements that are more in tune with ecological principles, and more devolved, pluralistic and open.

In Chapter 6 *Tony Alabaster* and *Derek Blair* chart recent progress in the greening of further and higher education (FHE). They suggest there are now opportunities for environmental good practice to yield substantial results but that accelerated progress is threatened by the increasingly competitive and resource-constrained climate in which institutions are operating. Corporate environmental responsibility in FHE is a response to legal requirements, the search for economic savings, the ethics of social responsibility and workforce expectations, and is best realized through a combination of top-down and bottom-up initiatives. They describe many successful initiatives, argue for an integrated approach within institutions, and suggest that declarations of intent and international comparisons are prompting continuing improvement. The greening of FHE remains essentially reformist, but there is some prospect that a culture of environmental responsibility will prevail in colleges and universities by the turn of the millennium.

In Chapter 7 on teacher education, *John Huckle* starts by acknowledging how educational restructuring has affected the work of teachers and made it harder for them to educate for strong sustainability. He suggests they should seek to adopt the role of transformative intellectuals, who help pupils and communities to construct alternative futures, and should look to appropriate areas of critical theory to justify their authority in this role. The development of courses in teacher education for sustainability based on the critical theory of Jürgen Habermas is outlined before some revisions of such courses are suggested. These draw on theories of reflexive modernization, answer criticisms of Habermas, and allow radical teachers to maintain their authority in changing times. John Huckle concludes by suggesting that post modernity holds the promise of more enabling structures and cultures for teaching and that education for sustainability could gain ground as the new right's efforts to establish a conservative radicalism, in education and else-where, are increasingly seen to have failed.

In Chapter 8, *Lisbeth Grundy* and *Bud Simpkin* review the potential of education for sustainability in youth work. While the aims and character of youth work are particularly supportive of the experiential and participatory approach required by education for sustainability, the concept of sustain-ability nevertheless provides a context, collective purpose and stronger learning framework still largely to be realized by the youth service. Three key aspects of youth work — political education, using the outdoors, and personal action and social development — are reviewed, along with case studies, in relation to sustainability. While the authors are positive about the potential of education for sustainability in the youth service, and defin-ite that any overall strategy can ill afford to ignore the youth service, they warn that education for sustainability will only succeed where it creates an image with which young people can align themselves.

Geoff Fagan turns the spotlight on community-based learning in relation to Local Agenda 21 in Chapter 9, arguing that the engagement of local people is the key to education for sustainability because only this approach, and the changes that flow from it, are socially and environmentally sustain-able. Education for sustainability has to build on and from core values in the community — including justice, fairness and equality — and it has to spring from people's concerns. Ownership of the outcome and empower-ment by the process are critical aspects, and action and reflection are the defining elements of praxis. Based on experience gained through the CADISPA (Conservation and Development in Sparsely Populated Areas) project in Scotland and other countries in Europe, the author then discusses critical issues involved in pursuing community education, and outlines techniques that can be employed. Such an education, concludes the author, is moving, exciting and risky, but it is also wanted and needed.

In Chapter 10, *John Howson* and *Adrian Cleasby* take different but com-plementary views of the role of the media in education for sustainability. The conundrum tackled by these two authors revolves around how far the televisual media are necessary to mass education for sustainability, or how far the media-educated critical audience is necessary to move the media in this direction. *John Howson* reviews arguments on both sides regarding the ability of the media to engage in critical reflection and outlines entry points for change. He then reviews briefly the idea of media education and discusses the vital role of an engaged critical audience in shaping output. *Adrian Cleasby* looks at the culture, influence and limitations of the media, and while giving a more negative prognosis than *Howson*, agrees that moving the media towards taking on a sustainability culture will require the development and action of a critical audience. Change, he says, is difficult but not unattainable, and examples of active engagement with media are given to illustrate this theme.

Chapter 11, which is also in two parts, examines the implications of education for sustainability in business and trade unions respectively. In the first part, *Nigel Roome* describes the corporate world's response to Agenda 21, and argues that improving environmental performance is a necessary but insufficient strategy to meet the challenge of sustainable business practice. Continual learning and openness to change is a key characteristic of the sustainable business, and the author discusses the implications this deeper response has for management education. Some progress has been made in this direction, but the application of sustainability principles in the management curriculum is essentially new. In part two, *Andrea Oates* reviews gradual union involvement in environmental affairs, and suggests that the broader concerns of sustainable development have yet to make an impact. While there are some examples of good practice on which to build, unions will need to overcome existing barriers to their participation in company policy if they are to assist in making the sort of transition to sustainable businesses argued for by *Roome*.

The educational role of local government in the Local Agenda 21 (LA21) process is explored by *Julian Agyeman*, *Jane Morris* and *Jeff Bishop* in Chapter 12. They trace the growing confidence of local authorities in their environmental role, despite the weaknesses of national policy, and outline their response to the opportunities presented by LA21. Environmental coordinators in local government play key roles in ensuring that sustainability is integral to the workings of the authority and that its interactions with the community promote sustainable development. They carry out much training and education, but their effectiveness is often compromised by the lack of support from other officers, including education advisers, and a failure to see education for sustainability as a lifelong process for everybody. The authors examine good practice, particularly in Reading, Leicester and Scotland, and conclude by highlighting people's scepticism about sustainability and democracy and listing the concerns that should be addressed if this is to be reduced. There are positive signs for the future and work with Scottish Natural Heritage suggests that it is possible to develop a process-based model of local education for sustainability that combines education for participation with the development of a strong community infrastructure. The authors remain uncertain as to whether such opportunities will be seized by enough people and authorities to shift practice to higher levels.

In Chapter 13 *Stephen Sterling* argues that a strategic approach will be needed at every level and in every sector of society to ensure that education for sustainability makes a significant difference to the prospects of sustainability. While there is a growing international mandate for this approach, there is an often unrealized tension between what are here termed 'instructive' (transmissive) and 'constructive' (transformative) strategy models. While both may be necessary in the short term, the latter is argued as the authentic process of education for sustainability. Strategy theory and critical questions are examined, followed by a review of educational strategies in three European countries.

Chapter 14 contains invited statements on education for sustainability from five politicians representing the three major parties, the Green Party, and the European Union. These statements were written in response to a summary of the book's aims and contents, but the politicians did not have access to the text. They provide readers with an opportunity to assess politicians' growing understanding of the politics of sustainability and education for sustainability and the nature and extent of the gap between professional and political debate.

To close the book, in Chapter 15 *Shirley Ali Khan* envisages a whole picture of an educational institution, its physical environment and its relationship with its community in the future. Her picture of a community learning centre as a key part of a sustainable community is set in the early decades of the next century. The author asserts that sustainability depends on people envisioning their preferred future and says that possibilities such as the twenty-first century community learning centre are entirely realizable if enough people want them and work towards them.

The book is UK centred, though many ideas in it are relevant to other settings, particularly where Western culture is dominant. In compiling it we have attempted to challenge and provoke thought and action. We have tried to avoid easy dismissals of the educational system, to explore the basis and possibility of desirable change and to balance discussion of present realities with a vision of the future role and nature of education. We hope this book is used as a platform for a much broader and extensive debate — to push sustainability to the heart of the education debate, and education to the heart of the sustainability movement. The prospects of a sustainable future depend on increasing integration between these forces for change.

John Huckle and Stephen Sterling
March 1996

Part I

Perspectives on Education for Sustainability

Humanity stands at a defining moment in history. We are confronted with a perpetuation of disparities between and within nations, a worsening of poverty, hunger, ill health and illiteracy, and a continuing deterioration of the ecosystems on which we depend for our wellbeing. However, integration of environment and development concerns and greater attention to them will lead to the fulfilment of basic needs, improved living standards for all, better protected and managed ecosystems and a safer, more prosperous future. No nation can achieve this on its own; but together we can — in a global partnership for sustainable development.

(UNCED, 'Preamble', *Agenda 21*, Regency Press, London, 1992)

Sustainable development means improving the quality of life whilst living within the carrying capacity of the supporting ecosystems.

(IUCN, UNEP and WWF–UK, *The World Conservation Strategy: Caring for the Earth*, Earthscan Publications Ltd, London, 1991)

There are 13 general indicators of a sustainable community: (1) Resources are used efficiently and waste is minimized by closing cycles; (2) pollution is limited to levels which natural ecosystems can cope with and without damage; (3) the diversity of nature is valued and protected; (4) where possible local needs are met locally; (5) everyone has access to good food, water, shelter and fuel at reasonable cost; (6) everyone has the opportunity to undertake satisfying work in a diverse economy; the value of unpaid work is recognized, whilst payments for work are fair and fairly distributed; (7) people's good health is protected by creating safe, clean, pleasant environments and health services which emphasize prevention of illness as well as proper care for the sick; (8) access to facilities, services, goods and other people is not achieved at the expense of the environment or limited to those with cars; (9) people live without fear of personal violence from crime or persecution because of their personal beliefs, race, gender or sexuality; (10) everyone has access to the skills, knowledge and information needed to enable them to play a full part in society; (11) all sections of the community are empowered to participate in decision-making; (12) opportunities for culture, leisure and recreation are readily available to all; (13) places, spaces and objects combine meaning and beauty with utility. Settlements are 'human' in scale and form. Diversity and local distinctiveness are valued and protected.

(LGMB, *Educating for a Sustainable Local Community*, LGMB, Luton, 1994)

Education is critical for promoting sustainable development and improving the capacity of the people to address environment and development issues. . . . it is also critical for achieving environmental and ethical awareness, values and attitudes, skills and behaviour consistent with sustainable development.

(UNCED, *Agenda 21*, Regency Press, London, 1992, Chapter 36)

We see 'easing down' from unsustainability not as a sacrifice, but as an opportunity to stop battering against the earth's limits and to start transcending self-imposed and unnecessary limits in human institutions, mindsets, beliefs and ethics.

(D H Meadows, D L Meadows and J Randers, *Beyond the Limits: Global Collapse or a Sustainable Future*, Earthscan Publications Ltd, London, 1992)

Chapter 1

REALIZING SUSTAINABILITY in CHANGING TIMES

John Huckle

Like liberty, justice and democracy, sustainability has no single and agreed meaning. It takes on meaning within different political ideologies and programmes underpinned by different kinds of knowledge, values and philosophy. Its meanings are contested and a key function of education for sustainability (EFS) is to help people reflect and act on these meanings and so realize alternative futures in more informed and democratic ways. This chapter promotes such reflection by relating debates about sustainability to the changing nature of modern societies, different political ideologies and utopias, and contemporary environmental politics.

If sustainability is socially constructed and contested then so too is nature. While most of us are taught to believe in an external nature separate from society there is today little if any nature which is untouched or unaltered by people. We ourselves are nature and so too are the objects and environments which surround us. Nature does have objective properties and causal powers which limit social development, but these are mediated by social processes. The social use and construction of nature lies at the heart of our environmental predicament and of debates surrounding sustainability, and it is with this process that we begin.

To survive and develop people must work with the human and non-human parts of nature to produce the goods and services they need and to reproduce those things that make this production possible. Maintaining a society in the long term requires not only a secure and continuing supply of the raw materials, human labour and technology used directly in the production process, but also a similar supply of the conditions that make the process possible. These conditions include resources, like clean water and genetic material from the wild, and services such as the climate stabilization and nutrient recycling carried out by forests and wetlands. They also include the health and education of workers and their families, a reasonable level of social stability, and the provision of sufficient well-planned urban and rural space to avoid congestion and promote human wellbeing.

At different times and in different places societies organize people differently to produce goods and services, to reproduce people and to reproduce the conditions of production. The social relations between people, in the workplace, the household, the school and elsewhere generally reflect different patterns of ownership and control of the means and conditions of production. They govern how production and reproduction take place and the kinds of technology that mediate people's relations with the rest of nature. Such relations are more or less harmonious and democratic and therefore more or less conducive to ensuring that prevailing forms of political economy (economic production and social reproduction) meet the common interest in human wellbeing and long-term survival. A sustainable political economy will be both ecologically and socially sustainable. It will protect and enhance the life support systems on which it depends and develop social institutions that generate social harmony and commitment to shared values (Robinson et al, 1990).

Different societies regulate political economy in different ways and these modes of regulation are threatened at times when there are problems of maintaining economic output and/or reproducing the conditions of production. We are currently living through such a time. Dominant forms of economic production and distribution are failing to meet the needs of millions of the world's people and are seriously damaging the conditions of production on which they depend. We have created forms of nature we can no longer regulate and control and there is an urgent need to move towards more sustainable forms of political economy that meet everyone's needs while conserving the means and conditions of production. Education for sustainability is one way of encouraging such change. It helps people and communities to examine critically the technologies, systems of economic production, cultural systems of reproduction, laws and politics, and ideas and ideologies they currently employ for living with the rest of nature. It also helps them to reflect and act on viable alternatives. Such education is far-reaching and should start from an understanding of modernity and the way in which it has changed the way we use and think about nature.

Modernity and our Environmental Predicament

Modernity is the form of social organization that now dominates most societies in the world. It has its origins in seventeenth-century Europe and its evolution involved interrelated economic, political, cultural and social trends (Hall et al, 1992). The end of feudalism and the rise of capitalism saw the enclosure of much common land and the break-up of the social institutions that ensured its cooperative and sustainable use. Land became a source of private wealth and, as production for trade and the market replaced subsistence production, nature was increasingly capitalized and treated as a commodity. Capitalism requires economic growth or capital accumulation and has an inbuilt tendency to discount present and future environmental costs. It has no coordinated internal mechanisms for maintaining the conditions of production; the trend away from organic raw materials and renewable sources of energy to inorganic and non-renewable sources has hastened the arrival of ecological limits to growth.

The rise of capitalism facilitated the rise of nation states and governments to create and protect property rights, enforce contracts and regulate social relations in ways that encouraged capital accumulation. Modern nation states are characterized by centralized and bureaucratic forms of administration and liberal democratic forms of government. They claim to regulate democratically the social use of nature, but environmental politics reveals an uneven distribution of power that favours business interests, the disaggregation of problems that prevents coherent action and a short-term horizon that reflects the electoral cycle. Departmentalism, bureaucracy, instrumental rationality and a lack of information limit the state's response to complex environmental problems; the need to sustain capital accumulation and the living standards of a majority of the electorate often constrains moves towards more sustainable forms of development. At the same time, international environmental politics is dominated by issues of national sovereignty and conflicts over who is to pay for necessary policy changes.

As far as culture is concerned modernity resulted in and was the product of revolutionary change. This involved a break with traditional world views that emphasized the interconnectedness of all living and non-living things, the importance of divine will and provenance, and the virtue of things remaining the same. Greek and Renaissance Europe regarded the cosmos as a living organism with a nurturing female earth at its centre. Such organic world views generate respect for nature and contain much traditional and local wisdom that serves to limit its non-sustainable use. Over the last 300 years they have largely been replaced by a mechanistic and scientific world view which sees the earth as dead and nature as a machine that can be transformed, improved and managed in the human interest. Newtonian science eliminated concepts of hierarchy, value, purpose, harmony, quality and form from older organic descriptions of nature, leaving only matter and force. A cosmos of passive matter and external force then provided a subtle sanction for the domination and manipulation of nature, which is central to modernity's grand narrative of development (Merchant, 1992). This suggests that science is a universal and value-free form of knowledge or rationality and that its application, via technology and bureaucracy, to the transformation of nature and society will bring continuing human emancipation and progress.

The process of modernization also produced new divisions of labour, new social classes and new forms of voluntary association. Numerous groups sprang up to form an increasingly vigorous civil society; some of these promoted private interests and others sought to protect and extend collective rights against individual property rights. Trade unions, amenity groups and other NGOs have long been concerned with people's collective rights to a safe and healthy environment and access to nature; and their work illustrates the role of NGOs in channelling interests and energies outside government and acting as a counterbalance to central state power. Socialism grew within civil society because it promised an alternative modernization that better realized liberty, equality and fraternity. Socialists sought to democratize the social relations of production and distribution so that problems of poverty and alienation could be reduced. When they gained control of government they therefore set about creating municipal water companies and parks, public housing, state-run education and health services, and land-use planning systems. Social democratic and state socialist governments rarely realized socialist goals, however, for they embraced technocracy uncritically and so failed to give people real control over their lives. State socialism was particularly instrumental in its use and construction of nature and generally had profound environmental consequences.

While socialists sought to change the material construction of nature, countercultural movements within modernity focused their attention on the limitations of scientific rationality and its impact on the cultural or existential construction of nature. They recognized that the elevation of positivist science to universal high-status knowledge was serving to separate nature from society, knowledge from values, and politics from ethics. It meant that modernism sought to locate society beyond nature and cultural traditions and this was a major cause of people's separation or alienation from the rest of nature, from other people and from their own inner nature (Eder, 1993). While dominant attitudes to nature were increasingly radical, instrumental and manipulative, countercultural attitudes were conservative and nurturing and retained elements of earlier organic world views. Thomas (1983) traces the cultural history of these opposing attitudes, which underlie what O'Riordan (1989) terms technocentric and ecocentric environmentalism. The latter found its first intellectual rationalization and artistic expression in the Romantic movement of the nineteenth century, which suggested that morality should extend beyond human beings to embrace care and concern for other living things. Such sentiments are strongly reflected in the modern environmental movement and serve to remind us that the social construction of nature remains a field of material and cultural struggle. To understand why it has become more significant in the late twentieth century we need to consider the environment and development in the contemporary world.

The Environment and Development in the Contemporary World

Modernity was a global or universal project from the outset. Recent centuries have seen an increasing number of societies and environments fall under its influence, with the result that the vast majority are now linked by global economic, political and cultural structures and processes.

Understanding issues of environment and development therefore means relating them to the workings of the modern world system while at the same time acknowledging each society's unique history, culture and place within that system. It involves consideration of nature's inherent potential in particular territories and of how this has been developed in ways that are more or less sustainable in the long term (O'Connor, 1989; Swift, 1993). Such accounts relate the use and construction of nature to political economy at local, national and international levels and thereby seek to identify those structures and agents of economic, political and cultural power that prevent or enable the democratic control of development in the common interest.

Central to these accounts is a consideration of the conditions that enabled capitalism's 'long boom' from 1945 to the early 1970s, the reasons why these conditions disappeared, and the alternative forms of development offered by the restructuring of political economy in the 1980s and 1990s (Blackwell and Seabrook, 1988; Lipietz, 1992). During the boom, societies in western Europe followed those in North America in adopting a form of social organization and development which has been labelled organized capitalism (Lash and Urry, 1987). Based on mass production and consumption, a routine and highly organized labour process (labelled Fordism after Henry Ford) and social democratic modes of regulation, it brought much progress but eventually came up against the ecological, economic, political and social limits to growth. As the power of the USA to regulate a stable international financial and trading system declined, organized capitalism was threatened by increased costs of reproducing the conditions of production; capital over-accumulation and falling profitability; increased levels of worker alienation; and citizens' demands for more real democracy. Economic paralysis and competitive stagnation largely resulted from world leaders, such as those in Europe, failing to pursue greater economic and political integration and thereby establishing forms of supranational regulation that could replace those formerly exercised by the USA.

To overcome their 'supply side' crisis the owners and managers of capital in the core states of the world system embarked on a period of restructuring, which introduced a new phase of capitalist development. Disorganized capitalism is characterized by a new labour process (post-Fordism) and new modes of regulation for adjusting the contradictory and conflictual behaviour of individuals to the changed conditions of capital accumulation (Harvey, 1990). Its introduction required the erosion of social democracy, or a shift of social forces in capital's favour, and this was facilitated by the rise of the new right, which based its appeal largely on people's discontent with organized capitalism's technocracy and their desire for greater personal freedom. Deregulation and privatization were used to hasten the introduction of new technologies and work practices designed to obtain greater flexibility with respect to production, labour and markets, and to quicken rates of innovation and capital circulation. The new economy involves a shift from mass production to mass customization and produces a vast array of new products and services. Cultural goods and services become particularly significant and there is a degree of decentralization and democratization as firms reorganize spatially and adopt new forms of labour relations. It also involves accelerating globalization along with a global redivision of labour. More events, decisions and activities in one part of the world come to have significant consequences for individuals and communities in distant locations; in a largely deregulated world fewer states can afford the luxury of high environmental and social standards.

Disorganized capitalism fractures society, bringing new status and class divisions along with new interests and insecurities. Consequently, the nature of politics changes with a decline of the old politics, focused on the state and issues of distribution, and a rise in the new politics, focused on civil society and issues concerning the quality of life. This new politics is the contemporary carrier of countercultural attitudes to modernity that seek 'purity' rather than 'justice' and a moral rather than instrumental relationship with the rest of nature (Eder, 1993). It appeals particularly to a new middle (or service) class that sees its quality of life threatened in an emerging risk society beyond control (Beck, 1992). At the same time the global political order is in flux and the power and legitimacy of the nation state is threatened by growing global integration from above and by pressures for local autonomy from below. People lose faith and interest in conventional politics and are encouraged to rethink their notions of political community and citizenship. Some recognize the need for a multidimensional and multilayered community in which citizenship would provide rights and require duties in all spheres of life, at all levels from the local to the global.

The cultural impact of this change is to produce new aesthetic, cultural and intellectual forms and practices, which are labelled postmodernism (Smart, 1993). This reflects and shapes an economy in which knowledge is power and individuals must make their way amongst a bewildering array of signs and identities in an environment of ideological and scientific uncertainty where the borders between image and reality are increasingly blurred. Postmodernism revels in fragmentation, ephemerality and discontinuity; brings a new sensitivity to difference and subjectivity; replaces highbrow culture with popular culture and consumerism; and denies the existence of universal knowledge, values or grand narratives via which all things can be connected, represented or explained. It can lead in relativist and reactionary directions, but a constructive postmodernism represents modernism coming to terms with the limits of positivism and technocracy and exploring other kinds of knowledge, whereby its excesses (materialism, individualism, patriarchy, scientism, technocentrism, secularism, anthropocentrism and ethnocentrism) can be recognized and overcome (Atkinson, 1991; Orr, 1992). A constructive postmodernism can put society back in touch with nature and cultural tradition and so end the alienation induced by the rise of modernity.

While some consider the changes associated with disorganized capitalism as significant enough to justify the use of the term postmodernity to describe emerging forms of social organization, we should recognize that these show major continuities with the past and have a far greater impact on some people and places than they do on others. What is significant in terms of sustainability is that restructuring has been carried out at the expense of the conditions of production worldwide. New and intensified problems of ecological and social sustainability began to emerge from the mid-1980s and the social construction of nature has become a key site of material and cultural struggle with much attention focused on the meaning and realization of sustainability.

The Ethics and Politics of Sustainability

O'Riordan (1988) and Adams (1991) trace the origins and historical development of the concept of sustainability and link it firmly to the spread of modernity and the growth of environmental science and managerialism. Sustainability provides the mediating bridge between the development and environment lobbies, yet Redclift (1987) suggests the concept is surrounded by contradictions. Natural scientists disagree about what is to be sustained at what levels and over what spatial and temporal scales, while social scientists use the concept both as a methodology for maintaining economic growth and in a normative sense, linking it to human needs or livelihood. The core contradiction is between sustainable development in its weak and strong modes. In its weak mode it represents an emerging mode of regulation, involving forms of techno-managerialism, via which capital seeks to ensure a continued supply of the means and conditions of production on its own terms while maintaining the support of the majority of voters. In its strong form it represents a revised form of self-reliant community development which sustains people's livelihoods using appropriate technology.

While weak sustainability is supported by liberal and social democratic reformers, green socialist and utopian radicals are more likely to urge stronger interpretations. Both groups draw on appropriate ethics, philosophy and social theory, with the radicals and utopians employing a range of critical theory provided by green economists, deep, social and socialist ecologists, ecofeminists, spiritual ecologists, postmodern scientists and others. Dobson (1990), Elliott (1993), Jackson (1991), Rees (1990), Martell (1994), Merchant (1992), and Orr (1992) are among those who have explored the contradiction between weak and strong sustainability, which is best understood in terms of contrasting political ideologies.

Liberal political ideology supports weak sustainability because it is compatible with free markets, individual property rights and a minimum of state regulation. It gives expression to egocentric values and adopts a consumer-based theory of value in which the value of nature is related to the value people derive from its use. While a minority of liberals suggests that markets alone will correct resource scarcity and respond to demands for a clean environment through such innovations as the greening of consumerism, business and education, the majority regards environmental problems as evidence that consumer values are not adequately expressed in markets. Neoclassical environmental economics therefore seeks to correct markets by first inventing 'realistic' or surrogate values for such natural materials and conditions as hardwood forests, rare species or clean rivers, and then incorporating these into markets via such instruments as price rises, environmental taxes and pollution licenses (Pearce et al, 1989). Such methods may entail an extension of property rights to previously free materials and conditions, but by internalizing externalities such as pollution and habitat destruction, liberals hope to quicken the introduction of environmentally benign technologies and energy and materials conservation. Radicals believe that such attempts to 'internalize nature' (ideologically to redefine nature and subsume it within capital as a productive asset henceforth subject to rational management) are compromised by the need for capitalists and nation states to compete internationally. Weak sustainability is therefore likely to be of a limited and largely imagined nature. It will function mainly at the ideological level and we can expect education to be pressed into its service.

Socialist political ideology supports social ownership of the means and conditions of production, and democratically planned development, suggesting that only the state or government can realize sustainability in ways that increase social justice and improve people's welfare and quality of life (Ryle, 1988; Pepper, 1993). It gives expression to homocentric values and increasingly adopts a revised labour (producer) theory of value that sees nature as an integral part of society which should be consciously planned and cared for in the interests of present and future human wellbeing. Socialist environmental economists suggest that individual consumers, firms and investors lack the knowledge to act rationally in markets and that governments should therefore intervene to constrain the economy within ecological limits (Jacobs, 1991 and 1995). This will involve the setting of environmental performance targets followed by the use of market and non-market instruments such as prices, taxes, licences, laws, public expenditure, education, persuasion and the land-use planning system to ensure that targets are met. A socialist transition to sustainable development in its strong mode would involve an ecological modernization of society to develop appropriate technologies, narrow the gap between the rich and the poor, create jobs and develop global citizenship.

Libertarian socialists have long argued that democratic organizations in civil society should play a key role in such a transition. They can defend and extend the rights and responsibilities of workers, consumers and citizens and so create a radical democracy that guards against incursions by technocracy. Some trade unionists, environmental activists, municipal socialists and others have formed 'rainbow alliances' to promote more sustainable forms of political economy from below (Huckle, 1990). Their actions serve to empower people through popular planning and local livelihood development, thus helping them to identify their true needs, develop greater self-reliance and rebuild a democratic public sphere beyond the state. The theory and practice of such alliances draws on constructive post-modernism and is in tune with the needs and sensibilities postmodernity arouses. It is particularly relevant to EFS in that it engages people in a form of critical pedagogy, or participative action research (Burkey, 1993), that combines diverse practical and theoretical knowledge, including that from the borders of mainstream society.

Green politics shares much with the libertarian left, but also displays reactionary and utopian elements. It gives renewed expression to cultural rather than material critiques of modernity and this leads it to discount conventional politics in favour of philosophical argument, education, grass-roots activism and alternative world views and lifestyles. Close affinities with anarchism prompt its advocates to suggest that only people themselves can realize sustainability through personal change and community development (Kemp and Wall, 1990) and to evoke ecology and ecosystems to provide lessons on how we should live. Green ideology reflects ecocentric values which claim that nature has inherent value independent of human valuers. These lead many dark greens to focus on people's lack of ecological consciousness and the need for cultural change. People should develop a personal ecophilosophy and parallel lifestyle, for only by recognizing that 'the personal is political' and 'treading lightly on the earth' will they reunite mind and body, people and nature, and move towards sustainability. Such holism is likely to involve bioregionalism or the development of societies in harmony with their local habitat or biome. Such societies will be more self-sufficient, cooperative and decentralized, practising direct democracy in ways that allow them to evolve alongside nature (Plant and Plant, 1990).

Dialogue between libertarian socialists and greens has been particularly productive; the new left has perhaps done most to combine material and cultural critiques of modernity and to develop the theory and practice of a postmodern green politics which sustains modernity's promise of liberation (Wainwright, 1994). Socialists ask greens to remember that enabling states, or systems of government, are necessary to facilitate livelihood development from below and that cultural conversion alone will not change the world. They remain reluctant to accept an ecocentrism that imagines intrinsic values emanating from a fixed and external nature with its own teleology, and suggest that nature is best viewed not as a resource for our use (technocentric materialism), or as a source of intrinsic worth (ecocentric idealism), but as a social category to be consciously created (historical materialism). Such a view collapses the dualism between technocentrism and ecocentrism and between the modern reductionist and postmodern holistic world views. It allows us to restore a moral and cooperative relationship with the rest of nature, which should guide us to more sustainable futures (Pepper, 1993; Martell, 1994). Sadly there are only glimpses of this new morality in the contemporary politics of sustainability.

The Contemporary Politics of Sustainability

Due to the continuing power of liberal capitalism and its supporters, most of the world currently lacks forms of government that can regulate economic production and social reproduction in ways that ensure that they are ecologically and socially sustainable. Global environmental governance has evolved considerably in recent decades but, despite hundreds of laws, policies and agreements, regulation of the social use of nature remains partial and is often ineffective (Soroos, 1994; CGG, 1995). Numerous world conferences have addressed issues of environment and development and a growing number of international agencies and institutions have evolved to tackle them with limited success. There is still no comprehensive and integrated body of international environmental law and that which exists is often weak and difficult to enforce. A prime role of international environmental NGOs is therefore to monitor global environmental governance and work for its improvement. Such aims inspire the WWF to campaign for the implementation of *Caring for the Earth*, the strategy for sustainable living it published in 1991.

The main debates on global regulation take place in the United Nations. It is the most universal of the transnational political organizations but many now question its potential to realize the aims set out in its charter: to operate a system of collective security and further economic and social progress. Its effectiveness is limited by a democratic deficit, sectoralism, underfunding and the refusal of some member states to abide by its decisions (Brazier, 1994). Since 1948 it has perfected and adopted a large body of international law and the challenge for the UN Conference on the Environment and Development (UNCED), held in Rio de Janeiro in 1992, was to extend this framework to embrace our common rights and duties with respect to the earth's natural resources and services, which we share with present and future generations. The conference issued a declaration setting out the principles defining these rights and responsibilities, agreed legally binding treaties on biodiversity and climate change and endorsed Agenda 21, a comprehensive blueprint for the actions needed by societies, at all levels, to realize the transition to sustainable development. A high-level UN Commission on Sustainable Development now reviews progress in implementing this agenda, which will be further helped by some institutional reform of the UN system.

The Rio conference was convened to examine the issues raised by the Brundtland Commission (the World Commission on Environment and Development) which identified unequal development as the root cause of environmental problems and recommended the revival of economic growth combined with a change in its quality (Holmberg et al, 1991). The commission called for basic needs to be met, for populations to be stabilized, for resources to be enhanced and conserved and for technology to be re-oriented, but its attempts to reconcile the environment and development and the perspectives of North and South had limited success. UNCED turned away from the poor and the need for a new international economic order and, in the view of its critics, represented a success for powerful elites and their brand of weak sustainability. Interests in the North largely succeeded in blocking the South's demands for fairer trade, debt relief, controls on transnational companies and money to pay for conservation and clean technologies. By capturing the debate on sustainable development and turning it to their advantage they were able to maintain their access to the world's resources and waste sinks. Talk of 'common' futures and a 'global' crisis obscured real causes and solutions, while sustainable development risked becoming mere rhetoric to mask the continued enclosure and commodification of nature and a new kind of eco-technocracy which works in the interests of the rich (Sachs, 1993). The Global Forum of NGOs and the People's Forum sought to keep sustainable livelihood development on the agenda, but local and radical voices were largely ignored. UNCED did raise the profile of sustainability and produce a declaration, agenda and treaties that can be used to advantage, but it did not represent a breakthrough in global environmental governance (Holmberg et al, 1993).

By endorsing Agenda 21 leaders of nation states committed their governments to prepare and implement national strategies for sustainable development. The agenda makes it clear that such development is not the concern of central governments alone, but that local authorities, business and industry, trade unions, farmers, NGOs, the scientific and technological community and individuals all have complementary roles to play. The UK strategy was published in 1994 and had to reflect existing international agreements and obligations, including the European Union's Fifth Environmental Action Programme and the Maastricht Treaty. These commit the EU to high environmental standards, sustainable and balanced development, and the improvement of environmental quality (Axelrod, 1994). The attainment of such goals may require the further democratization and reform of EU institutions, which should clarify the meanings of federalism and subsidiarity. Recent Conservative governments have been reluctant supporters of a more integrated and regulated Europe, but NGOs have been able to use European legislation to put pressure on these governments to improve their environmental performance.

Sustainable Development: The UK Strategy expressed a commitment to the market and a preference for economic instruments rather than regulation. It proposed an independent panel of experts to advise on policy, a UK round table to coordinate local government, business and other interests, a citizen's environment initiative and some modest new measures. Its critics suggested that the document was largely a restatement of existing policies and that the gap between generalized rhetoric and specific policy commitments remained as wide as ever. There was an urgent need to reform the structure and workings of government, to integrate and coordinate policies across departments, to develop new targets and policy frameworks, and to extend the public's rights to information and consultation (Pearce, 1993). The government appeared to be committed to only the weakest forms of sustainability and it was left to the opposition parties, pressure groups and NGOs to urge stronger and more radical alternatives.

It is at the local level that programmes of sustainable livelihood development are most likely to emerge and grow. Over two thirds of the statements in Agenda 21 cannot be delivered without the cooperation and commitment of local government and it calls for all local authorities to develop a Local Agenda 21 (LA21) by 1996. In Britain, most will build on their experience with greening initiatives that include recycling, traffic calming, landscaping, pollution monitoring, environmental auditing and other projects. In 1993, a report from the Town & Country Planning Association suggested that sustainability, under different names, is deeply rooted in the history of the British planning system (Blowers, 1993). The current challenge is to widen the scope of land-use planning and strengthen its powers so that an integrated process of environmental planning will ensure that sustainability is a prime objective of policy in all sectors and at all levels. Environmental planning uses market mechanisms and regulation, takes account of future uncertainty by adopting a precautionary approach, reflects the integrated nature of environmental processes and policies, and engages local people in the production and implementation of plans. Such planning and the LA21 process have the potential to educate and empower people as agents of sustainable livelihood development, but local governments lack power and resources and may be too anxious to promote and realize artificial forms of consensus.

Towards Ecological Modernization

At the end of the twentieth century Britain is in a poor position. Its economy has been weakened by lack of investment; its state is incapable of keeping parliament in check and encouraging democracy; its society is divided by new inequalities and insecurities and there is little sign of dynamism or social cohesion (Hutton, 1995). There is an urgent need for the EU to provide new forms of regulation and governance to allow for the coordinated ecological modernization of member states and to demonstrate to the world that there are alternatives to free markets, deregulation and competitive stagnation. As the appeal of the new right declines, a new cooperative postmodern green capitalism is perhaps the first step to postmodern green socialism. We need both realism and vision: the immediate priority is to restore social democracy as a moral economy based on social justice, citizenship and sustainability. Education for sustainability can play a key role in both short- and long-term developments provided it engages people in a realistic appraisal of alternative meanings, values and agendas.

References

Adams, W (1991) *Green Development: Environment and Sustainability in the Third World*, Routledge, London

Atkinson, A (1991) *Principles of Political Ecology*, Belhaven, London

Axelrod, R (1994) 'Environmental Policy and Management in the European Community', in N J Vig and M E Kraft (eds) *Environmental Policy in the 1990s*, Congressional Quarterly, Washington

Beck, U (1992) *Risk Society: Towards a New Modernity*, Sage, London

Blackwell, T and J Seabrook (1988) *The Politics of Hope: Britain at the End of the Twentieth Century*, Faber & Faber, London

Blowers, A (ed) (1993) *Planning for a Sustainable Environment*, TCPA/Earthscan Publications Ltd, London

Brazier, C (ed) (1994) 'Winds of Change: The United Nations at 50', *The New Internationalist*, 262, December

Burkey, S (1993) *People First: A Guide to Self-Reliant, Participatory Rural Development*, Zed Books, London

CGG (1995) *Our Global Neighbourhood*, Oxford University Press, Oxford

Dobson, A (1990) *Green Political Thought*, Unwin Hyman, London

Eder, K (1993) *The New Politics of Class*, Sage, London

Ekins, P (1992) *Wealth Beyond Measure: An Atlas of the New Economics*, Gaia Books, London

Elliott, J (1993) *An Introduction to Sustainable Development*, Routledge, London

Hall, S, D Held and T McGrew (1992) *Modernity and its Futures*, Polity Press, Cambridge

Harvey, D (1990) *The Condition of Postmodernity*, Blackwell, Oxford

Holmberg, J, S Bass and L Timberlake (1991) *Defending the Future: A Guide to Sustainable Development*, IIED/Earthscan Publications, London

Holmberg, J, K Thomson and L Timberlake (1993) *Facing the Future: Beyond the Earth Summit*, IIED/Earthscan Publications, London

Huckle, J (1990) *Environment and Democracy (What We Consume, Unit 10)*, WWF/Richmond Publishing, Richmond

Hutton, W (1995) *The State We're In*, Jonathan Cape, London

Jackson, B (1991) Poverty and the Planet, Penguin, Harmondsworth

Jacobs, M (1991) *The Green Economy: Environment, Sustainable Development and the Politics of the Future*, Pluto, London

— (1995) *Sustainability and Socialism*, Socialist Environment & Resources Association, London

Kemp, P and D Wall (1990) *A Green Manifesto for the 1990s*, Penguin, Harmondsworth

Lash, S and J Urry (1987) *The End of Organized Capitalism*, Polity Press, Cambridge

Lipietz, A (1992) *Towards a New Economic Order: Postfordism, Ecology and Democracy*, Polity Press, Cambridge

Martell, L (1994) *Ecology and Society*, Polity Press, Cambridge

Merchant, C (1992) *Radical Ecology: The Search for a Liveable World*, Routledge, London

O'Connor, J (1989) 'Uneven and Combined Development and Ecological Crisis: A Theoretical Introduction', *Race and Class*, 30 (3) 1–12

O'Riordan, T (1988) 'The Politics of Sustainability', in R Turner (ed) *Sustainable Environmental Management: Principles and Practice*, Belhaven, London

— (1989) 'The Challenge for Environmentalism', in R Peet and N Thrift (eds) *New Models in Geography*, vol 1, Unwin Hyman, London

Orr, D (1992) *Ecological Literacy: Education and the Transition to a Postmodern World*, State University of New York, Albany

Pearce, D (1993) *Blueprint 3: Measuring Sustainable Development*, Earthscan Publications, London

Pearce, D, A Markandya and E Barbier (1989) *Blueprint for a Green Economy*, Earthscan Publications, London

Pepper, D (1993) *Eco-socialism: From Deep Ecology to Social Justice*, Routledge, London

Plant, C and J Plant (1990) *Turtle Talk: Voices for a Sustainable Future*, New Society, Philadelphia

Redclift, M (1987) *Sustainable Development: Exploring the Contradictions*, Routledge, London

Rees, J (1990) *Natural Resources: Allocation, Economics and Policy*, Routledge, London

Robinson, J, G Francis, R Legge and S Lerner (1990) 'Defining a Sustainable Society: Values, Principles and Definitions', *Alternatives*, 17 (2) 36–46

Ryle, M (1988) *Ecology and Socialism*, Century Hutchinson, London

Sachs, W (ed) (1993) *Global Ecology: A New Arena of Political Conflict*, Zed Books, London

Smart, B (1993) *Postmodernity*, Routledge, London

Soroos, M (1994) 'From Stockholm to Rio: The Evolution of Global Environmental Governance', in N J Vig and M E Kraft (eds) *Environmental Policy in the 1990s*, Congressional Quarterly, Washington

Swift, A (1993) *Global Political Ecology: The Crisis in Economy and Government*, Pluto Press, London

Thomas, K (1983) *Man and the Natural World: Changing Attitudes in England 1500–1800*, Penguin, Harmondsworth

Wainwright, H (1994) *Arguments for a New Left*, Blackwell, London

Chapter 2 | # EDUCATION in CHANGE
Stephen Sterling

'We are now training our children to live in a world that cannot be sustained' (Milbrath, 1992) . . . 'Education is critical for promoting sustainable development' (UNCED, 1992, Chapter 36). As these quotes indicate, education is both part of the problem and the solution. Any vision of education for change has to grapple with this paradox. Education is proclaimed at high level as the key to a more sustainable society, and yet it daily plays a part in reproducing an unsustainable society. If it is to fulfil its potential as an *agent of change* towards a more sustainable society, sufficient attention must be given to education as the *subject of change* itself. A society faced with a radical imperative to achieve a socially, economically and ecologically sustainable basis within a historically short time needs to reappraise most aspects of its organization; education — as the main means of social reproduction — has to be at the centre of this task, both as subject and agent.

But the 'reorientation of education' — to borrow a phrase from Agenda 21, Chapter 36 — is itself a major challenge. To begin with, education for sustainability (EFS) begs the question of what is meant by sustainability. A seemingly useful definition like 'sustainable wellbeing', which suggests that both the human condition and the condition of the ecosystem are satisfactory and improving, still leaves room for interpretation. As described in Chapter 1, the dominant technocratic view sees sustainability as a matter of making adjustments to present human activities, to sustain the twentieth century project largely unchanged and unchallenged into the twenty-first. At the other end of the spectrum are those who feel that a radical cultural shift of world view is both beginning and required, one which represents fundamental rethinking of most patterns of human activity, which integrates ecological sustainability with social justice, and which sees sustainability as a promising metaphor for a historic and necessary structural and personal transformation. At the same time, radical educators — those involved in 'education in change' in both senses — must recognize that many people influential in political, economic, social and educational arenas still have little or no interest in or awareness of sustainability issues, or the potential of education to address them.

Given this complex background of differing and contesting interpretations and interests, it is now vital that radical educators clarify the meaning and significance of EFS. The term has only achieved currency since the turn of the decade and the debate, as with sustainable development, is still quite young. Is this a next step in the development of environmental education (EE)? (Tilbury, 1995). Does it represent a fusion of EE and development education (DE)? Or is it a convergence of all those 'adjectival educations' oriented towards social change — citizenship, peace, health, political, human rights, multicultural, futures and others, as well as EE and DE? Is it more than the sum of its parts? Does it hold the seed of a whole new educational paradigm commensurate with the challenge of postmodern conditions and the potential of constructive postmodern thinking? This list perhaps represents an increasing gradation of significance and challenge. The more far-reaching EFS is seen to be, the more we have to face other difficult issues relating to the nature of change in education and the relation between social and educational change.

In this chapter I attempt to introduce some of these issues and suggest in broad terms what a more sustainable cultural paradigm for education might look like and from where it can be derived, one that could better assist the development of more sustainable modes of living. An overview of this kind inevitably involves generalization and simplification, but such visioning is necessary if education is to rise to the fundamental challenge that postmodern conditions now present.

Towards a Postmodern Education

EFS is not an agreed set of ideas educators can tack onto existing thinking and practice to allow them to say 'we are doing sustainability'. At simple levels of implementation, there may be elements of such overlay, but it requires fundamental reorienting of much present thinking, and we are still in the early stages of elaborating what this means.

Some of the complexity, tensions and relationships involved in the whole picture are suggested by Figure 2.1. Like any model, this has its limitations, but has the value of suggesting that the still developing body of thinking that is EFS is influenced by the interplay of many ideas and traditions. These can be broadly grouped into two overall paradigms, the 'dominant social paradigm', which is broadly technocratic, technocentric, materialistic, and reductionist, and what has been termed the 'new environmental paradigm' (Milbrath, 1989), which is broadly democratic, more ecocentric, socially concerned and integrative. The emergent idea of EFS has to be understood in the context of the tensions and dynamics both between and within these overall paradigms.

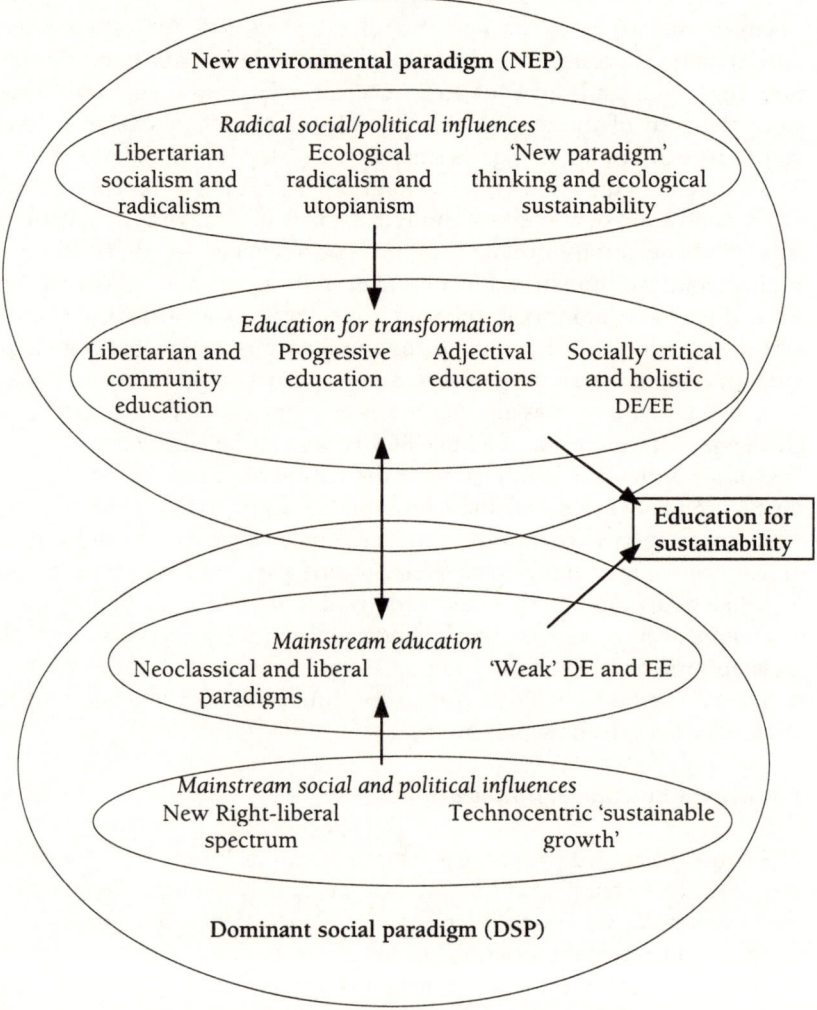

Fig 2.1 Influences on education for sustainability

As all education takes place within a dominant cultural, social and political context, any discussion of EFS — which by implication seeks to influence society — must first recognize the greater influence of the dominant social paradigm upon education. The major part of this paradigm makes little or no acknowledgement of the sustainability challenge, nor of EFS (Smith, 1992). Indeed, over the past decade, much educational debate has taken place within narrow parameters, framed by strongly expressed and implemented political concerns to restructure education to mirror market philosophy and management culture (Ball, 1990; van der Gaag, 1993). The UK and many other societies where this mode of thinking has been similarly influential are pursuing a renewed modernist agenda in their educational systems, underlain by assumptions that have seen little critical debate.

This raises the enduring question of how far education (particularly formal education which is typically less free to innovate than non-formal) can contribute to radical social change, or whether it is necessarily constrained by an encompassing culture. It may be optimistic to expect education to engage with and contribute towards resolving the modern crisis when mainstream culture and values, of which education is both parent and child, largely make an inadequate response. Nevertheless, it is increasingly clear that, in the closing years of the twentieth century, an education that carries on its traditional role of replicating a modernist — or even restructured modernist — society unquestioningly is no longer appropriate, and that we urgently need to find new models and approaches from which to build while retaining continuity with existing good practice.

Education for sustainability appears to hold this potential. As it continues to distil from its many contributory elements, it seems to be more than the sum of its parts — a focus pregnant with a new educational paradigm, which could reflect and contribute to constructive postmodernism in wider society. The latter is most visibly represented through new social movements (Giddens, 1992), which have given rise to the adjectival educations and which are subscribing to and working for a radical rather than cautious and technocratic interpretation of sustainability. In parallel with this struggle, if EFS is to be manifested and meaningful, it has to be clarified and worked for, otherwise a historic opportunity to develop an adequate educational response to postmodern conditions will have been lost or at least delayed.

To many, EFS holds the promise of a more coherent, far-reaching and integrated response than the various adjectival educations, each with their own cultural baggage and supporting interest groups, separately appear to offer. There has been interesting and significant convergence among these areas in recent years, paralleling a similar convergence of interests between social movements. Agyeman (1994) has argued that these educations share 'increasingly common aims and objectives; increasingly common goals; an increasingly common vocabulary and increasingly common educational approaches' and that their defining elements 'should be woven into a core framework utilizing the concept of sustainability to produce an accessible, balanced and empowering "Education for Participatory Democracy".'

However, Agyeman suggests that we have not yet reached this state of integration. At present, environmental and developmental education are in the vanguard of EFS. Even here, however, and running parallel to the fate of sustainable development, the label 'education for sustainability' is in danger of debilitation through being appended to existing theory and practice without sufficient consideration of how it requires an additional or changed response. Partly to address this problem and partly to stimulate debate, the Environment and Development Education and Training Group (EDET) (which later became the Education for Sustainability Forum for DE and EE organizations) offered a definition of EFS (see quotations for Part I) (Sterling and EDET, 1992).

While the EDET definition has been influential in the UK in generating debate, some voices have been concerned to remind proponents of EFS of the need to respect different roots and traditions in moving towards any consensus, and particularly differences both within and between DE and EE (Downs, 1994). At the same time, however, there is an equal need to take the debate forward, to move towards a working (rather than fixed) broad consensus that can make an impact on the wider educational debate.

This involves some examination of the two main influences on the nature of EFS, linked to red/green and dark(er) green critical theory, which may be termed the *radical democratic* and the *radical ecologic*, as well as key thinking on sustainability such as *Caring for the Earth* (IUCN et al, 1991). From these bases, I would argue that the concept of EFS implies some interrelated primary requirements (see Box 2.1).

Box 2.1 *CHARACTERISTICS OF EDUCATION FOR SUSTAINABILITY*

Education for sustainability is:

- Contextual — *fully awake to and engaged in addressing the crises of modernity. Logically, education that reproduces modernism uncritically cannot effectively be engaged in resolving the crises modernism has created. Where possible, EFS should be applied and grounded in the local economic, social and ecological context and community, followed by regional, national, international and global contexts.*
- Innovative and constructive — *drawing inspiration from 'new paradigm' postmodern thinking in a range of fields (including science, ethics, politics, economics, design and psychology) offering insights and ways forward that promise a safe, humane and environmentally sustainable rather than threatened or chaotic future.*
- Focused and infusive — *primarily grounded in, but not limited to,*

---

social development and human ecology, equity and futures, at the centre of a holistic approach which touches all other areas.

- Holistic and human in scale — *recognizing that all educational dimensions, such as curriculum, pedagogy, structures, organization and ethos are mutually affecting and need to be seen as a consistent whole; and that this works best at a scale that relates to the needs of learners and educators. It is also holistic in the sense of being both learner-centred (development of the whole person) and socially oriented (reconstructionist).*

- Integrative — *greater emphasis on interdisciplinary and trans-disciplinary enquiry, reflecting that no subjects, factors or issues exist in isolation. Transdisciplinary means breaking free of disciplinary perceptions and traditions to create new meanings, understandings, and ways of working. Simply putting disciplines together, by contrast, is often no more than the sum of the parts.*

- Process oriented and empowering *rather than product oriented — revisioning and revaluing education and learning as intrinsic to life. Education for sustainability is therefore engaged and participative rather than passive; the emphasis is on learning rather than teaching. In particular, action research with its emphasis on critical reflection, experiential learning cycles and democratic ownership of change is inherent to EFS.*

- Critical — *ideologically aware and socially critical. Recognizing that no educational values are politically neutral, EFS should draw on the body of critical theory associated with deep green and red-green orientations as these constitute the prime challenge to the modernist hegemony. At the same time, it must continuously appraise this theory and its own rationale critically.*

- Balancing — *seeking to rebalance correlated pairs that are dissociated and distorted in the dualistic dominant paradigm. These include personal aspects such as knowledge and values, cognitive and affective learning, rationality and intuition, object and subject, material and spiritual; and collective aspects such as economy and ecology, present and future, local and global, individual and community.*

- Systemic and connective — *putting emphasis on relation and pattern (including dynamics and flows, distortions, feedbacks and causation); encouraging a participative systemic awareness and wisdom in relation to designing sustainable and multilevel physical, environmental, social and economic systems.*

- Ethical — *clarifying ethical issues, but also nurturing normative ethical sensibility that relates and renders seamless the deeply personal and collective, ie it extends the boundary of care and concern*

> *beyond the immediate and personal to a participative sense of solid-*
> *arity with others, distant people, environments, species and future*
> *generations — what Fox (1992) calls 'transpersonal ethics'. This is*
> *neither monist, nor relativist, but reflects an ecological pluralism.*
> ■ Purposive — *exploring, testing, criticizing and nurturing sustain-*
> *ability values and alternatives, with an explicit intention to assist*
> *change.*
> ■ Inclusive and lifelong — *not selective, but for all persons in all*
> *areas of life, and extending throughout their lifetimes.*

These foundational qualities in turn give rise to more detailed characteristics, which are suggested towards the end of this chapter. The next section
interprets the current shift from modernity to postmodernity in terms of
learning imperatives, which further underline the character of and need for
an education which is both transformed and transforming.

Contemporary Change and Learning

If, as Milbrath suggests at the beginning of this chapter, we are educating
(or worse, only training) for a world that cannot be sustained in the future,
we are also largely educating for a world that no longer exists, such is the
inertia in the whole system. That world, of sovereign nation states and
superpower stability, of expanding economies, of full employment and jobs
for life, of global development, of limitless environmental resources and
sinks, of scientific and moral certainty has virtually disappeared in recent
decades. Traditional assumptions and expectations that central governments are able to provide a whole range of services, that personal economic
security can be maintained, or that nature and environmental systems can
go on providing and absorbing unimpaired, are crumbling.

A controllable world of apparent predictability and security is visibly
being replaced by a world characterized by complexity, interconnectedness,
uncertainty and insecurity. These characteristics can be observed at every
level and in every sphere — from local to global economies, and from
personal values to new scientific views of indeterminacy and chaos in
natural and human systems. Old certainties are withering in the face of the
global problématique they helped create — the set of closely interconnected
problems that characterize this period and that, because of their systemic
nature, fail to respond to technical fixes (King and Schneider, 1991). While
postmodernity poses complexity and uncertainty, sustainability presents the
challenge of urgency and the direction of necessary and far-reaching change
(Ekins, 1993; Brown, 1990). Meanwhile, the old paradigm still exerts a
strong influence on thinking, policy and practice in most areas of life.

Meadows et al (1992) and Henderson (1993) suggest that, like any system under stress, global societal and environmental systems are faced either with *breakdown* or *breakthrough*. Whereas breakthrough implies controlled and intended change, unsustainable practices (ie doing more of the same) are likely to lead to dysfunctional and dystopian breakdown through human rigidity and the inability to learn and change course. There are now sufficient indications in social and natural systems to suggest that the disorder and entropy associated with such breakdown has already arrived.

By contrast, positive breakthrough to a new structural state results from learning — changing thinking and practice to live within the limits that ecological, social and economic sustainability requires. Further, a sustainable society will incorporate learning in relation to sustainability as an intrinsic and continuous part of the social process. There are encouraging indications that such learning is taking place in many fields, which are reflecting the diversity, integration and holistic approach demanded by sustainability (although the credit for such learning cannot be given to formal education). For example:

- new economics emphasizing such directions as local economic cycles rather than global linear expansionist economies; sustainable welfare indicators and social justice, as opposed to GNP; and full cost accounting;
- ethical consumerism, investment and fair trade;
- sustainable agriculture and rural regeneration schemes;
- primary focus on energy conservation rather than supply;
- ecological design principles in planning, architecture and ecotechnology;
- industrial ecology and eco-efficiency concepts in industry;
- adoption of the precautionary principle in environmental policy; and
- rejuvenation of local partnerships and participation through self-help groups, Local Exchange Trading Systems (LETS) schemes, Local Agenda 21 (LA21) and so forth.

At the same time, the environmental debate has been on a learning curve, having evolved from single issues to complexes of environmental issues and, in recent years, to encompassing related areas such as economics, development, social, justice and futurity. Meanwhile, new thinking in such fields as science (such as complexity theory) (Waldrop, 1992) and ethics (particularly transpersonal and autopoetic ethics) (Fox, 1992) are supporting a postmodern participative, non-deterministic and interdependent view of the world, which points to a complementary philosophical, ethical and scientific basis for sustainability. In particular, the idea of self-organizing and self-renewing nesting systems has direct implications for designing self-sustaining economic and social structures and systems, as well as for decentralist and participative politics.

Self-organization or relative autonomy is a fundamental characteristic of sustainability, and learning — in a broad sense — is inherent to self-organization. Physical and social systems which are adaptable, resilient, participative, self-renewing and flexible, and which can adjust and respond to mistakes and external forces, exhibit learning. At the same time, there must be a balance between the self-assertive tendencies or relative autonomy of the unit and its relation within the system of which it forms a part if the whole is to be sustainable. Awareness and maintenance of this dynamic relationship, for example between a community and the environment that supports it, is also a continuous learning process. This ecological model of integrated networks can be applied at every level from the individual, to community, to society as a whole.

Such ideas are already being used in parts of the business world and they represent the beginning of a change of thinking and practice from a mechanistic to a systemic view of the world (Callenbach, 1993). At the political level, this model requires greater self-determination, a regeneration of empowering participative democracy — or 'capacity building' in the language of Agenda 21 — in the place of the passive dependency, isolated individualism, sense of powerlessness and loss of faith in provision from government (Macnaghten, 1995), which currently works against sustainability. In sum, there is an inevitable and strong correlation between learning, relative autonomy, integrity and sustainability in human systems.

Sustainability presents a learning imperative that challenges — rather than rejects outright — the adequacy of many established goals and educational processes, as well as the common perception of education as something that is limited to schooling and formal provision. Whether the future holds breakdown or positive breakthrough scenarios — or, as seems likely, some of both — people will require flexibility, resilience, creativity, participative skills, competence, material restraint and a sense of responsibility and transpersonal ethics to handle transition and provide mutual support. Indeed, an education reoriented towards sustainability and nurturing these qualities would help determine a positive and hopeful breakthrough future. Meanwhile, in the shorter term, people require a much better understanding of (and a closer engagement with) sustainability issues to allow or persuade authorities to enact radical environmental policy (Macnaghten, 1995).

Mainstream Education and Building Education for Sustainability

In this context, the current mainstream orientation of education seems singularly inappropriate and inadequate. As Smyth (1995) remarks, 'It is difficult to avoid the conclusion that many have reached, that education should be largely recast.' Whether the emphasis is on academic or vocational achievement, the current emphasis in the formal sector is on selecting and preparing individuals for an expanding market economy, based on specialization at all levels. Dominant values of egocentricism and instrumental rationality underpin the idea that the individual is freed from ties of family, community or natural environment to pursue personal economic security by competing in the market (Smith, 1992). The influence of such thinking is evident in the growth of the use of the management culture's language in education (Bowe et al, 1992). The restructuring of education to conform to market ideas that echo the economic restructuring of the global economy has made this instrumentalist value more overt in recent years, and has suppressed the intrinsic educational values many progressive and liberal educators have upheld for years.

The market view of education takes little account of current issues such as endemic unemployment, increasing gaps between rich and poor, population growth, loss of community, impending resource scarcity, the ending of cheap energy and indicators of deteriorating environmental quality, all of which are feeding back into the modernist scenario and making it increasingly unsustainable. Neither does it appear to have much collective sense of urgency (Barber, 1995), or awareness that options for the future are becoming fewer the longer that significant change for sustainability is delayed (WCED, 1987). One way of interpreting this situation is that the crisis is in no small measure a product of a failed education system (Orr, 1992).

Restructuring, as exhibited in the English and Welsh national curriculum, may be interpreted as a response to postmodernity and particularly post-Fordism and disorganized capitalism (see Chapter 1), but at the same time it adapts and reaffirms the neoclassical view of education, emphasizing subjects, knowledge attainment, didactic methodology, selection and so on (Kemmis et al, 1983).

However, it would be wrong to infer that there is no potential for EFS within the education system, whether formal or non-formal. There has been a response, however insufficient and constrained, which can be and is being built on. The nature of the task of building EFS, and progress made to date, is now briefly reviewed.

Building EFS: Educational Developments and Systemic Theory

Reformulating educational thinking and practice in the light of the challenge of sustainability is a formidable task and one that the educational community is only just beginning to recognize and address. Education for sustainability as an emerging body of thinking has to rise to several challenges including:

- exploring and clarifying the meaning or meanings of sustainability;
- providing a critique of education for *un*sustainability;
- clarifying the philosophical roots and issues underpinning desirable change in educational theory and practice; and
- suggesting alternative pedagogic, curriculum and structural modes.

The first objective might be seen as the 'external' or social/environmental focus, and the rest as the 'internal' or educational focus of EFS. Neither focus is generated in a vacuum, but respectively has to build on radical and new thinking in wider society and the many strands of education for personal development and social change which already exist (see Figure 2.1).

There have long been counter movements in education, which have attempted to influence the debate in favour of intrinsic values and transformational education. Progressive, learner-centred, socialist, community-based and ecological traditions have asserted an alternative view, which has found expression, particularly over the last two decades, in the adjectival educations. Of these, DE and EE have played a prominent role, which has partly been embraced and partly marginalized by the mainstream.

Theory and practice in EE has evolved over some 30 years from a rural studies and science base to a complex of emphases that have increasingly stressed aspects of participative, holistic and political education (Sterling, 1992). However, to use Lucas's (1991) seminal description of forms of environmental education as 'education *in*, *about* and *for* the environment', the first two forms still prevail, as they relate to rather than challenge the dominant liberal/progressive and neoclassical education paradigms. Downs (1992) has traced a similar tension between development education '*about*, *for* and *as* development', the latter being the most radical and least practised form.

Meanwhile, discussion of EFS has emphasized the meaning and development of education *for* the environment — corresponding with a reconstructionist and transformative educational paradigm (Fien, 1993), while Gough (1987) has argued for education *with* the environment as the key to any ecological educational paradigm. At the same time, this debate has criticized the limitations of education *in* and *about* the environment, which it equates with interpretivism and positivism (Robottom and Hart, 1993), and 'education for environmental awareness' and 'education for environmental management' respectively (Huckle, 1993). These might best be described as 'weak' education for sustainability, or education *about* sustainability. While they have some value, through lack of critical reflection, these forms tend to support technocratic approaches to sustainability and an unproblematic view of sustainable development.

If we are to go beyond these 'weak' forms, it is first necessary to review and build on existing transformative practice in education — and there is a wide range of experience here, relating for example to progressive, experiential, human-scale, gender and critical education. In addition, we need to gain new ideas and inspiration from radical roots, and 'new paradigm' thinking in relation to sustainability. A wealth of thinking has arisen, particularly in the last two decades, which seeks to counter and offer alternatives to the dominant social paradigm (see references in Chapter 1 and Merchant, 1994). As noted above, the two main roots are red/green or eco-socialist thinking, and deep green or systemic thinking, and the suborientations identified with these emphases. The former, which I have called *radical democratic*, emphasizes social justice, equity and structural change (particularly with regard to power and wealth), the democratizing duty of government and the importance of mutual relations and community. The latter, which I have called *radical ecologic*, emphasizes the integrity of the environment as both a micro and an encompassing metasystem (Gaia), the necessity of seeing all human activities as having an impact within this system, working within carrying capacities, seeing ecology as design, and the importance of personal change and transformation. There are differences and tensions between (and within) red and green views, and a healthy debate continues. However, there is sufficient common ground and mutual learning to argue that a coherent if not finally agreed postmodern critical paradigm is beginning to emerge from these orientations. In particular, while these views start from different points, their practical visions of social order and educational change have much in common. Some theorists maintain incompatibility, but I would argue that in terms of implications for EFS, the democratic or participatory emphasis of the red/green view, and the ecological or systemic perspective of the deeper green view, are necessary and complementary. John Huckle gives an account of the red/green view and associated critical theory in Chapters 1 and 7.

The radical ecologic or systemic view focuses on what sustains people and communities. For thousands of years, and even into this century, the sustaining foundations have been local links and networks — a complex of integrated and synergetic bioregional, ecological, cultural, economic and community factors which have co-evolved. Progressive modernization, powered by fossil fuels, has replaced this local connectivity with dependence on exogenous and global links, with ensuing effects on distant environments and people, and even future generations, exacerbated through uneven distribution of costs and benefits. In the process, local diversity, connections and references in many areas of life — for example, from architectural styles to genetic bases, from language to belief systems — have been weakened and replaced with a dependent and increasingly homogenous global materialist culture. As a result of such trends and pressures, local economic cycles, employment and resource bases, and social fabrics have experienced weakening systemic links and undergone progressive disintegration and dislocation. In short, there is a progressive loss of what has been termed social and environmental capital, yet also a generation of high entropy in social, economic and environmental systems.

By contrast, the systemic view attempts to foster interdependence and connectedness, particularly at a local level, in contrast to the global management view of technocracy (Sachs, 1993). For communities, it is a matter of regenerating networks of belonging and mutual support, and countering widespread alienation, isolation and survivalism, particularly as experienced by a growing underclass in all societies. In economic and ecological terms, such regeneration of local integration begins to counter and check the vulnerability that the global system has brought about and in which most societies are enmeshed. In cultural terms, it is a matter of rediscovering and rebuilding the connection between culture and environment in a form suited to a globally connected world, and to move towards a participative 'biospheric culture' (Rifkin, 1992). In ethical terms, it is a matter of extending the boundaries of concern and realizing transpersonal solidarity.

The challenge is to work towards physical and social systems and arrangements where costs and benefits are more equitably shared; where it is evident that individual and group interest converges with the wider collective and ecological interest through internalization of these costs and benefits; where positive synergies, or 'win–win' situations, are created; where more is done with less; where resource flows are cyclical rather than linear; and where citizens can gain more control over their lives and living environments. People will need to be able to think more critically, systemically and skilfully to imagine, create, nurture and support more sustainable, less entropic systems and forms of organization, whatever the area of concern — whether housing, farms, communities, cities, energy, transport, industry or trade — against a background of resource depletion and sink overload. They will need to be global citizens, involved locally, but responsible globally. As argued above, this emphasis on working towards more self-sustaining (but not closed) systems at all levels from micro to macro is lent weight by new thinking in areas such as science and ethics, which stress a participative and ecological rather than an objectivist and mechanistic view of the world (Berman, 1981; Macy, 1991).

This discussion illustrates that critical theory is not only critical in the sense of 'deconstructive' in relation to dominant thinking, but also 'constructive' in the sense of exploring alternatives to it. The 'external focus' of EFS has to encompass both these aspects. At the same time, critical theory extends to the 'internal focus' of education itself, and again is both deconstructive and constructive. In both these respects, the democratic critique is perhaps more established than the ecological, but I attempt to reflect both below.

As suggested above, EFS may be an emerging new paradigm for educational thinking and practice on the grounds that it is sufficiently different to qualify as a paradigm in the making. In contrast with the education of modernity, it is broadening, inclusive, participative, critical, integrative, ethical and essentially concerned with the quality of the interrelationship and process. In essence, it is 'connective education' (Orr, 1992). An EFS critique (particularly of formal education) might therefore point to:

- the idea that education is only something that happens in schools and colleges;
- vertical fragmentation of knowledge into subjects, and their associated defences;
- the predominance of decontextualized and abstract knowledge — valuing the map (abstract knowledge) far more than the territory (particularly local, global and future contexts) to which it often bears little relation;
- the assertion of instrumental rationality as the only valid way of knowing, and the devaluation of personal and community knowledge;
- economic and technical instrumental values nurtured in the guise of 'value-free' learning;
- utilitarian and anthropocentric values reflected in curriculum and teaching approaches;
- the predominant didacticism and 'empty vessel' view of the learner;
- the predominance of academic and vocational modes in relation to education for selection;
- the marginalization of environment, development and related issues;
- lack of attention to the hidden curriculum and to community links;
- lack of human scale; and a
- lack of attention to the institution as an entire system expressing prevailing educational values (for example, physical environment, purchasing policy and management styles).

Clearly, this is a characterization, and it does not suggest that all education conforms to these patterns. But these are broad tendencies consistent with modernist philosophies. Characteristics of EFS are indicated in the converse of these tendencies, and in basic form, are suggested above in Box 2.1.

While the radical democratic underpinning for and elaboration of such a view stems from socially critical education and critical pedagogy (see Chapter 7), the ecologic underpinning of this view fundamentally stems from holistic thinking. It therefore has links with progressive and learner-centred traditions in education, with holistic views of knowledge and education (Reid, 1986), with global education (Pike and Selby, 1988) and, more recently, with transformative education of the type represented by Joanna Macy (1991) linked with deep ecology. In particular, the systemic ideas of self-organization and balance between self-assertive and integrative tendencies in systems have profound implications for the organization and nature of education, including the 'whole' development of the critical and autonomous learner, the relation between personal and cultural knowledge, the dynamics between individual and group, action research as fundamental pedagogy, the integrated and whole curriculum, the facilitative role of the educator, the institution as a whole system, interaction and integration with community and so on. These ideas and their relation to modern and post-modern changes in education and society are now explored further.

Towards 'Strong' Education for Sustainability

At this point it is perhaps useful to map the emerging EFS paradigm in relation to social and cultural change and to suggest its constituents in more detail. Like any model, this one is limited and simplifies a complex reality (including under-representing the red/green position), which is why Table 2.1 is called a 'rough map'. It attempts to clarify further the context of the EFS debate by suggesting the predominant relationship between different cultural and educational orientations and their sub-elements. It suggests that EFS may be part of a move away from the values and norms associated with modernity towards the alternatives associated with constructive postmodernity.

I am not suggesting exclusive, polarized paradigms here; rather a series of horizontal spectra along which a variety of positions may be reflected. In reality, often a mix of positions is held by individuals and groups. (For example, it would be simplistic to suggest that all traditional science belongs to positivism and cannot make any contribution to EFS, or that greens do not often think analytically, or that political positions fit quite as neatly as the model suggests.) However, the vertical association between the descriptors shown is strong, reflecting that collectively there is fundamental tension between world views operative in Western and westernized societies. One aim of this chapter, indeed of this book, is to suggest that understanding this tension — which affects us all and all relevant debate — is both liberating and vital to realizing effective change.

The table indicates that a technocentric interpretation of sustainability, reflecting the predominant culture and with a corresponding form of weak EFS or 'education for environmental management and control' (Huckle, 1993), is likely to predominate in the short term. This may be necessary to address technical issues relating, for example, to efficiency of resource use and greening technology. In many respects, this education already exists in many examples of environment and development education and related areas. However, this is essentially a depoliticized instructive strategy (see Chapter 13), which does not go far enough.

Table 2.1 Rough Map of Orientations and Associations

Cultural aspects	Modernity			Postmodernity
Political orientation	New Right Centralist democracy	Liberal	(eco)Socialist	Green Participative democracy
View of focus of change	Technical	Social	Political	Personal
Social environmentalism	Non-green or technocentric			Deep green, ecocentric
Personal environmentalism	Egocentric			Ecocentric, transpersonal
Environmental awareness	Eco-detachment	Eco-awareness	Eco-literacy	Eco-empathy/ participation
Cultural metaphor	Machine/mechanistic			Gaia/systemic
Values/ethics	Instrumental/ utilitarian, individualistic			Intrinsic/instrumental balance, transpersonal; solidarity
Effect on people/nature	Fragmentation, homogeneity, uniformity, dependency			Diversity in unity, relative autonomy
Epistemology	Knowledge as information			Knowledge as wisdom
Thinking	Reductionist, analytic, instrumental rationalist, abstract, dualistic			Holistic, systemic including non-rational, contextual, personal
Development model	Dependency	Inter-dependence		Autonomy/ integration balance
Sustainable development	Growth-centred development			People/eco-centred development
Educational aspects				
Educational orientation	Vocational/classical, positivist	Liberal/ progressive, interpretivist		Socially critical/ transformative
Education and environment	Education for environmental management: add on to existing educational structures	Education for environmental interpretation		Education for sustainability: change in educational paradigm

The table also indicates that a more critical, ecocentric and holistic form of EFS is needed to encourage a deeper response to sustainability over the longer term. Such a deeper form cannot develop widely in isolation from parallel changes in society, but would draw on and support constructive postmodernist changes already under way, such as deepening environmentalism. It is important to note that in this process of social change, the left hand descriptors would not be abandoned so much as gradually transformed as the locus shifted across the spectra. Indeed, the integrative nature of sustainability and sustainability thinking requires a bringing together of what have long appeared disparate polarities, such as analytic and synthetic thinking, qualitative and quantitative measures, objective and subjective stances and so on (see Box 2.1) — a shift from dualistic to pluralistic thinking, or bivalent to multivalent thinking (Kosko, 1994). There are some indications that this is already happening.

Some Suggested Constituents

The primary requirements and some of the background thinking to a stronger form of EFS have been suggested above. Elaborating the detail of EFS is more difficult for several reasons:

- the debate is still young;
- EFS is purposive and indicative, but not prescriptive; and
- it needs to be negotiated according to local environmental and community conditions, needs and perceptions.

Yet, if research bodies at a generic level and communities at a local level can and need to develop indicators of sustainability (MacGillivray and Zadek, 1995; Deelstra, 1995) as signposts and milestones in the process of change and as contributions 'to the self-regulating sustainability of integrated environment and development systems' (UNCED, 1992, Chapter 40), it is likewise necessary to outline indicators of sustainable education. What follows is not a blueprint for a total educational paradigm, but a possible focus for EFS, which in turn suggests changes in educational thinking and practice as a whole.

Let us examine briefly five key dimensions: sustainability values; personal and community values; pedagogy; curriculum; and structure and organization. A defining characteristic of EFS (and of contributory approaches such as EE and DE) is that such dimensions should be regarded as mutually affecting and, as such, need to be considered and intentionally connected in order to maximize positive synergy.

Sustainability Values Macleod (1992) lists a number of values associated with ecologically sustainable development that should be reflected in education. These include ensuring intergenerational equity; conserving bio-diversity and ecological integrity; preserving natural capital and sustainable income; supporting an anticipatory and precautionary policy approach; ensuring social equity; limiting natural resource use; qualitative development; pricing environmental values; ensuring efficiency; ensuring resilient economy; and community participation.

Similarly, Meadows et al (1992) call for 'sustainability, efficiency, suffi-ciency, justice, equity, and community as high social values'.

Logically, most of these can only be enacted and made meaningful in relation to real conditions and existing values, and their implications will vary with locality.

Personal and Community Values The key will be to link these worthy sustainability values to personal and community values, needs and percep-tions through working to extend the boundary of care and concern. Evidence suggests there is already a good deal of latent resonance between personal and sustainability values (Macnaghten et al, 1995). A UNEP–UK document (Sterling and EDET, 1992) suggests that EFS should strive to nurture or bring out eight qualities:

- a sense of responsibility to the environment, to other people and to the future of both;
- the will, knowledge and skills to translate this responsibility into action in both personal and public life;
- the ability to respond positively to change and uncertainty;
- a capacity to see the links between individual and group actions, exter-nal events, and other factors;
- an interdisciplinary and holistic outlook;
- a healthy scepticism alongside the ability and freedom to be creative;
- a balance of rationality with feeling and intellect with intuition; and
- a sense of self-worth combined with a respect for other individuals and cultures.

We might also reiterate here an inclusive environmental and social ethic, and the concept of global citizenship. How far these are possible will depend crucially on the strategy and pedagogy used.

Pedagogy The pedagogic approach or strategy should itself be socially sustainable in the sense that it is based on meaningful rather than token empowerment, participation and ownership. Specifically, the action research approach (Elliott, 1991) is the embodiment of both the systemic and socially critical views of pedagogy. The primary aims should be to develop and link systemic and critical thinking and environmental and social action, or in other words, develop ecoliteracy and political literacy for full and active citizenship.

Specific methodologies employed might include or emphasize experien-tial and cooperative learning; systemic thinking, patterns, soft boundaries and 'fuzzy logic'; the clarification and judgement of values; ideology critique; critical reflection and creative thinking; the envisaging of sustainable futures, sensory and empathetic exercises; communication skills; learning as a continuous process for all; and work outdoors and in the community.

These values and pedagogies imply a holistic approach to the curriculum.

Curriculum Sustainability suggests that attention should be paid to vertical progression in curriculum and horizontal integration (inter- and trans-disciplinarity). Whereas process is more important than content, and the relation between areas more important than decontextualized studies, sustainability does suggest themes that should be *reflected* in any general curriculum, whether or not it retains a subject basis. These might include some or all of the following: political education and political ecology; natural history, environmental science, ecology and biodiversity; systems theory and systemic thinking; social relations, conflict resolution, equity and social justice; local and bioregional studies and local distinctiveness; community building and citizenship; global environment and development issues; transpersonal ethics; cultural studies including southern, indigenous, and traditional views; ecological design including aesthetics, permaculture and sustainable systems; new economics; humanistic psychology and interpersonal relationships; health and the environment; modernity, science and technology; futures studies; and practical capabilities in a number of areas. Implementing anything like such a curriculum will depend on institutional structures.

Structures How people, institutions and communities interact — the hidden and operational curriculum — is all important and should engender a sustainability ethos that is both lived and critically reflected upon. Its characteristics include democratized classrooms and decision-making; greening the physical and management environments of institutions; using institutions as learning centres for the whole community; establishing networked links between all formal and non-formal local educational facilities; teachers and leaders being facilitators rather than authorities; and education for life.

Strategy and Change

Setting out such an outline schema has value, not least as a vision, as a means of stimulating discussion and as a way of encouraging progress already made. Yet there is a tension here: EFS implies an emerging body of values, content and methodology — albeit an alternative one — that needs to be 'sown and grown', but it also implies a participative, learning culture where meaning emerges from a community-based 'constructive' rather than 'instructive' strategy (see Chapter 13).

If sustainability requires urgent wholesale reorientation of educational

systems (UNCED, 1992), and education is difficult to change (given investment in current structures, systems and ideologies), then it seems that we
need some element of 'instructive' strategy based on such schema,
particularly in the short term, and particularly aimed at policy makers. Yet
it is still necessary to work in a more organic, constructive way in building
on existing work and, importantly, on existing perceptions and values.
Here, the highly systemic nature of sustainability and EFS, where all issues
connect and impact on each other, can be seen as an advantage rather than
a problem. By working on one specific issue in one area, it is often possible
to show links with and make a positive impact on other connected issues —
to promote positive synergies intentionally. The other aspect of this
potential is the need to create alliances with and between complementary
movements throughout society, so that synergies are realized (Smith, 1992).

How will we know how far EFS has any influence on progress towards
sustainability? One way is through education's involvement in generating,
monitoring and assessing sustainability indicators on a participative basis,
though it is difficult to infer direct relationships between realizing indicators and education. Useful work has already been done in this area in
relation to LA21, but it needs to be taken further. Meanwhile, the take-up of
EFS concepts, ideas and practices in education might be monitored through
indicators based on a schema such as that above (see also Ali Khan, 1995),
or on social learning indicators that attempt to evaluate the degree of
involvement, collaboration and personal and collective transformation
(Finger and Kilcoyne, 1995).

Conclusion

If real sustainability is to become increasingly meaningful and mainstream,
rather than devalued and marginalized, education in all forms and in all
sectors has a vital role to play. But this requires fundamental change in
education. We need an expanded, revitalized and purposive view of education as a whole, where, in Meadows's words (Meadows et al, 1992), every
person acts as 'learning leader' at some level and capacity. Kosko's (1994)
line neatly summarizes the holistic reality and dual challenge for education
and for society: 'You cannot learn without changing, or change without
learning.' What this means in practice in a range of sectors is the subject of
the following chapters.

References

Agyeman, J (1994) 'Next Step: Education for Participatory Democracy?', *Annual
    Review of Environmental Education*, 6, CEE, Reading

Ali Khan, S (1995) *The Environmental Agenda: Taking Responsibility*, Pluto Press, London

Ball, S (1990) *Politics and Policy Making in Education*, Routledge, London

Barber, M (1995) 'Ignore the Rabs at the Planet's Peril', *Times Educational Supplement*, 27 January

Berman, M (1981) *The Reenchantment of the World*, Cornell University Press, Ithaca, NY

Bowe, R, S Ball and A Gold (1992) *Reforming Education and Changing Schools*, Routledge, London

Brown, L (1990) 'Picturing a Sustainable Society', in L Brown et al, *State of the World*, Unwin Hyman, London

Callenbach, E et al (1993) *Ecomanagement: The Elmwood Guide to Ecological Auditing and Sustainable Business*, Elmwood Institute/Group West, Berkeley, CA

Deelstra, T (1995) 'The European Sustainability Index Project', in T Trzyna (ed) *A Sustainable World: Defining and Measuring Sustainable Development*, IUCN, ICEP, Sacramento

Downs, E (1992) 'DE: A Typology', unpublished thesis, Department of Environmental Management, University of Central Lancashire

— (1994) 'Education for Sustainability: Is the Whole More or Less than the Sum of its Parts?', *The Development Education Journal*, 1 (2), pp5–8

Ekins, P (1993) 'Making Development Sustainable', in W Sachs (ed) *Global Ecology: A New Arena of Political Conflict*, Zed Books, London

Elliott, J (1991) *Action Research for Educational Change*, Open University Press, Buckingham

Fien, J (ed) (1993) *Environmental Education: A Pathway to Sustainability*, Deakin University, Geelong

Finger, M and J Kilcoyne (1995) 'Learning Our Way Out: Indicators of Social Learning', in T Trzyna (ed) *A Sustainable World: Defining and Measuring Sustainable Development*, IUCN, ICEP, Sacramento

Fox, W (1992) 'New Philosophical Directions in Environmental Decision-Making', in R Eckersley and R Hay (eds) *Ecopolitical Theory: Essays from Australia*, Occasional Paper 24, Centre for Environmental Studies, University of Tasmania, Hobart

Giddens, A (1992) 'Socialism, Modernity and Utopianism', in S Hall et al (eds) *Modernity and its Futures*, Polity Press/Open University, Cambridge

Gough, N (1987) 'Learning with Environments: Towards an Ecological Paradigm for Education', in I Robottom, *Environmental Education: Practice and Possibility*, Deakin University, Geelong

Henderson, H (1993) *Paradigms in Progress: Life Beyond Economics*, Adamantine Press, London

Huckle, J (1993) 'Environmental Education and Sustainability: A View from Critical Theory', in J Fien (ed) *Environmental Education: A Pathway to Sustainability*, Deakin University, Geelong

IUCN, UNEP and WWF (1991) *Caring for the Earth, A Strategy for Sustainable Living*, IUCN/Earthscan Publications Ltd, Gland

Kemmis, S, P Cole and D Suggett (1983) *Orientations to Curriculum and Transition: Towards the Socially Critical School*, Victorian Institute of Secondary Education, Melbourne

King, A and B Schneider (1991) *The First Global Revolution*, Simon & Schuster, London

Kosko, B (1994) *Fuzzy Thinking*, Flamingo, London

Lucas, A (1991) 'Environmental Education: What Is It, For Whom, For What Purpose, and How?', in S Keiny and U Zoller (eds) *Conceptual Issues in Environmental Education*, Peter Lang, New York

MacGillivray, A and S Zadek (1995) *Accounting for Change: The Role of Sustainable Development Indicators*, Global Environmental Change Programme, ESRC, Wye

Macleod, H (1992) *Teaching for Ecologically Sustainable Development*, Department of Education, Queensland

Macnaghten, P et al (1995) *Public Perceptions and Sustainability in Lancashire: Indicators, Institutions, Participation*, Lancaster University/Lancashire County Council, Lancaster

Macpherson, N (1995) 'Assessing Progress toward Sustainability: A New Approach', in T Trzyna (ed) *A Sustainable World: Defining and Measuring Sustainable Development*, IUCN/ICEP, Sacramento

Macy, J (1991) *World as Lover, World as Self*, Parallax Press, Berkeley, CA

Meadows, D, D Meadows and J Randers (1992) *Beyond the Limits: Global Collapse or a Sustainable Future*, Earthscan Publications, London

Merchant, C (1994) *Ecology: Key Concepts in Critical Theory*, Humanities Press, New Jersey

Milbrath, L (1989) *Envisioning a Sustainable Society: Learning Our Way Out*, SUNY Press, Albany

— (1992) quotation in G Smith, *Education and the Environment: Learning to Live within Limits*, SUNY Press, Albany

Orr, D (1992) *Ecological Literacy: Education and the Transition to a Post Modern World*, SUNY Press, Albany

Pike, G and D Selby (1988) *Global Teacher, Global Learner*, Hodder & Stoughton, London

Reid, L A (1986) *Ways of Understanding and Education*, Heinemann Educational Books, London

Rifkin, J (1992) *Biosphere Politics: A New Consciousness for a New Century*, Harper-Collins, London

Robottom, I and P Hart (1993) *Research in Environmental Education: Engaging the Debate*, Deakin University, Geelong

Sachs, W (ed) (1993) *Global Ecology: A New Arena of Political Conflict*, Zed Books, London

Smith, G (1992) *Education and the Environment: Learning to Live within Limits*, SUNY Press, Albany

Smyth, J (1995) 'Environment and Education: A View of a Changing Scene', *Environmental Education Research*, 1 (1)

Sterling, S (1992) *Coming of Age: A Short History of Environmental Education (to 1989)*, NAEE, Walsall

Sterling, S and EDET (1992) *Good Earth-Keeping: Education, Training and Awareness for a Sustainable Future*, UNEP–UK, London

Tilbury, D (1995) 'Environmental Education for Sustainability: Defining the New Focus of Environmental Education in the 1990s', *Environmental Education Research*, vol 1 (2), Carfax, Abingdon

UNCED (1992) 'Promoting Education, Public Awareness and Training', Chapter 36, *Agenda 21*, Regency Press, London

van der Gaag, N (1993) 'Back to the Drawing Board', *New Internationalist*, October

Waldrop, M (1992) *Complexity: The Emerging Science at the Edge of Order and Chaos*, Penguin Books, Harmondsworth

WCED (1987) *Our Common Future*, Oxford University Press, Oxford

Chapter 3

A WWF VIEW of EDUCATION and the ROLE of NGOs
Peter Martin

The World Conservation Strategy (WCS) (IUCN, 1980) documented growing recognition that traditional methods of promoting environmental conservation — including public awareness of the problematic issues, the development and growth of conservation organizations, legislation and land set aside and protected — were insufficient to counter the detrimental impact of human activity on the planet. It strengthened and legitimized the growing notion that sound environmental management must be integrated into the continuing process of human, social and economic development. However, it also identified that the current dominant models of socio-economics were flawed by inappropriate attitudes and values towards the environment. The WCS called for changes in these attitudes and values, and advocated 'education' as the means by which these should be achieved. This analysis and exhortation has been repeated ever since, notably in Agenda 21 and the revised version of the WCS, *Caring for the Earth* (IUCN, 1991), and picked up by the environmental NGOs (non-governmental organizations) as their main educational *raison d'être*.

Unfortunately, the educationists had been handed a poisoned chalice, which, in their eagerness to obtain legitimacy and importance, they grasped. Yet, given the low status of education in the environmental NGOs and the limited resources available, the adopted aims were at best ambitious and at worst ideologically flawed and unrealistic. However, here were goals that non-educationists could understand, that provided a level of importance for education they could relate to — goals they were prepared to support by sanctioning the commitment of time and money through education.

Fragmentation and Unrealized Goals

Attitudes and values are the product of the generalities of upbringing and social interaction rather than specific parts of education. Unless environmental educators can influence all the key social and intellectual contacts and the direct or subliminal experiences that influence and inform an individual's world view and professional and personal behaviour, then transforming social values and attitudes as a whole is impossible. And even influencing individual parts of the whole educational spectrum is problematic.

Individually, NGOs are extremely small in person power, financial capacity and social influence and, in particular, have very little influence on education. Therefore, if the NGO is to be effective, these limited resources need to be extremely well targeted to achieve any form of fundamental change within the systems that do have person power, financial capacity and a social mandate to influence society. Thus, the only possible and practical solution is to target key aspects of the educational framework in an attempt to influence their specific role in the total educational process. Most NGOs have not done this, but have instead concentrated their resources on providing their own alternatives or additions to the education system. To a large degree, they have developed a subculture outside the mainstream, which has limited potential to influence education systems. The reasons for this strategy lie in the very nature of the NGO movement.

NGOs have grown out of specific concern about the condition of the world and the inability of available structures or social mind sets to resolve that concern. Some new organizations tend to appear when problems become horribly apparent and require instant, often short-term, remedial action. Whatever their genesis, fairly narrowly defined organizations have emerged, focusing on such things as elements of human welfare, human rights, specific aspects of environmental concern including such things as birds, endangered species and wetlands, heritage, the condition of the built environment, poverty, social development, gender and animal rights.

This focus is not only a product of specific concern, but also of clarity of purpose for promotional and marketing purposes — niche identification and niche marketing are seen as crucial to the identity of the NGOs, their visibility, and ability to increase numbers of supporters both as a numerically powerful lobbying weapon or as a source of funds. If we add to this the need of organizations to promote their individual excellence in order to raise the funds necessary to operate, we have a recipe for maintained separateness and competition — except in times of extreme need such as the Ethiopian crisis, or when forced to cooperate by outside influences such as major media or governmental initiatives. Even then, the organizations' press officers will be fighting for the TV and press cameras and column inches.

There is also another fairly fundamental factor that stands in the way of coherence and coordination. Even though there may be a general acceptance among NGOs that their different concerns may be a product of the same general social condition, the analysis of that condition and its remedies are steered by a wide range of political perspectives. In very broad terms, some of the larger traditional environmental agencies are broadly 'conservative Conservative', while some of the newer environmental and certainly most of the development agencies are 'radical socialist'. Thus the idea of the non-governmental agencies as a broad church of socially concerned organizations all pulling together to make the world a better place is somewhat far-fetched.

As far as education is concerned this has led to an array of 'adjectival educations' — development, peace, global, human rights, conservation — which have all been aimed at the education system either directly from the NGOs or from 'minority' groups supported by them. These differing political and interest leanings explain why the various umbrella organizations, such as the Council for Environmental Education (CEE), Scottish Environmental Education Council, and Development Education Association, which have been set up to try to coordinate activities, have such a difficult job and why the desirable linkages between development education and environmental education have also been difficult to make.

These issues, of differing interests and limited effectiveness, result in a mismatch between the demands and expectations set for education by such documents as the WCS and the realities. While the 'world changing' task is achievable only through the overall educational experience, it is being addressed by NGOs only through limited parts of that experience. Yet educators within the NGOs cling to world changing rhetoric to give credibility to their limited actions.

Let us take for example the most obvious and approachable systems and educational structures — schools, colleges and universities. Here, NGOs have undoubtedly played a significant role in the development of adjectival educations, which in turn have impacted on teaching method and content. They have also played an important role in financing radical and innovative approaches to new topics and contemporary issues in education at times when government, publishers and even academia have all been disinclined to support action research and resource publication (see Chapter 6 of Greig et al, 1989). And yet a number of factors limit the real effectiveness of such work.

While no formal education provision is value-free, there is throughout societies a consensus about what education is allowed to do. Educational institutions are not perceived by the educationists in them or by the governments and managers who control them, or in general the parents who send their young people to them, as places to be used by pressure groups for social manipulation — no matter how well meant. As far as formal education structures are concerned, therefore, the WCS exhortation of prescriptive attitudinal and value change is misguided.

A further issue concerns ideology, ie which attitudes and values the WCS is promoting. It seems clear that it criticizes attitudes and values related to the environment, rather than attitudes and values that underpin and motivate the main socio-economic model and its resultant impact on the environment. Even if not intended, this is certainly the interpretation that the environmental NGOs have taken up. Given their significant role in the development of environmental education, this interpretation has had considerable influence on the focus and content of environmental education.

NGOs tend to imply that education should change people's attitudes and values towards the environment, so they will then influence the socio-economic model, and that the environment will then be better looked after. This logic is clearly evident in the often quoted adage that school-focused environmental education should take place *in* the environment, be *about* the environment and be *for* the environment. It indicates that environmental education is out of the classroom, is to do with the structure of the environment or environmental issues and that it leads to some benefit to the environment. While not explicit, the logic tends to assume that the environment is something without people, the 'natural world'; and in the main the 'things' that benefit are natural systems and other non-human creatures that inhabit the world. Given the history of the environmental NGOs and their missions, this approach seems understandable, reasonable and logical. The power of the logic can be very simply illustrated.

Nature Experience is One Thing ...

One October afternoon I was walking around a gravel pit just off junction 12 of the M4 motorway about 40 miles west of London. It was one of those days when early morning promise had disappeared behind grey clouds gathering on a chill northern wind. On the surrounding trees, the leaves had not yet succumbed to the onset of autumn and what drab end of summer colours there were had been drained away by the steadily increasing gloom. It was turning into a monochrome day. The beginnings of wintering flocks of duck, pochard with a scattering of widgeon, gadwall, shoveller and one or two pairs of great crested grebes still feeding striped-necked young, were becoming dark but distinctive silhouettes on the wind ruffled water. Coots that pattered noisily across the surface and a solitary heron that flapped heavily from the flooded sallows added animation.

As the greyness spread, a small dark shape swept out from the base of the taller sallows that fringed the far bank. It sped low across the water and once more up into the cover of the overhanging branches. It was not something that you could say you saw but something that you were aware of. Yet, in the mind's eye, this small dark distant shape was a mixture of green blue, deep blue and luminous pale blue; it was chestnut, gold, orange and white. It was a concentration of all the memories of kingfishers I have seen.

For me, that momentary dark shape had a meaning and significance that was far greater than the reality of the occasion — just as the limp, rapidly browning vegetation signified the butterflies and scented flowers of summertime. This depth of meaning is related to the sense of loss I would feel should this gravel pit disappear. For me, the place is not what it is at any one time, but a mass of recollections of past pleasure and expectations of new pleasures next week, next spring, round the next bend, hidden by the sallows in the corner. For someone who does not perceive colours in distant dark shapes; for someone who does not in their mind's eye see coloured wings on strong-scented water mint — that loss would not be there.

. . . But Environmental Education is Another

Education as perceived by most within the environmental movement would, if possible, develop such meaning, a process of initiation where people would see the world as the environmentalist or conservationist would have them see it. And, as well as the central importance of introducing people to first-hand experiences, such education would also be augmented by a more fundamental, rational approach to the environment, using, in the main, ecology and the natural sciences to help demonstrate the scientific validity of the arguments for better environmental management. These conventions are related a lot both to the influence of the NGOs on environmental education and to the nature study, field study and rural study basis on which it grew.

This NGO influence has a lot to do with the hegemony of the powerful. The biggest environmental agencies are those that focus on a popular concern — they flourish because they also can afford to promote themselves and all they do. They are therefore able to influence public perceptions of whole areas of concern. The environment has thus become closely identified with the interests of the biggest conservation bodies, in the main those concerned about the popular aspects of the natural world, and likewise environmental education is synonymous with conservation education.

In the main, each NGO has focused on providing a methodology and content designed to create an awareness of the organization's concerns, whether it be birds, flowers, wetlands or woodlands, an understanding of what is wrong and what needs to be done to put it right, an understanding of the world view and values that underpin those perspectives and also a full promotion of why that point of view is right. There is nothing seriously wrong with this as educators on the receiving end can filter out anything they feel to be too unprincipled, and most of the environmental and developmental NGOs are involved in what most people consider to be good causes. In particular, the nature focus part of the environmental movement is seen to be particularly benign.

However, except to a few committed educators, this view positions much NGO educational activity as of little importance other than as a useful diversion, or as providing additional material for project work. At worst, it is totally confusing to many teachers, is seen as a mass of extra work in which, as is often the case, very specific teaching methods such as teaching outdoors are promoted, and is potentially alienating.

For most people and most educators, outdoor experience of the natural world, an understanding of ecology and an awareness of environmental issues represent the basics of environmental education. But this approach to education is severely limited.

Challenges and Constraints

Encouraging first-hand appreciation of the world we live in is without doubt an important aspect of any person's education. However, if this is viewed as a process of initiation into a particular set of world views, or even particular interests, then problems arise. All forms of initiation are selective, attracting in the main only the susceptible and potentially alienating the rest. They are also of dubious educational merit; it is far better if ways can be found for young people to explore freely and develop their own relationships with a variety of environments without prejudice.

In addition, the very specialized knowledge necessary to interpret the specifics of the natural environment — naming the parts — is daunting to most teachers and often difficult in terms of practical arrangements. The exploration of the environment using basic investigative skills *should* be within the ambit of most teachers. However, the hegemony of the specialist ecologist or naturalist maintains the mystique of environmental interpretation, which remains exclusive rather than inclusive.

More fundamentally, environmental or developmental concerns occur within and are a product of a particular social context. Accidents of history, social attitudes and values, economic, industrial and commercial development all enmesh to create the conditions from which the problems are an outcome. In the main, environmental problems are symptoms of entrenched social systems. Therefore, understanding requires critical social, economic and values investigation rather than environmental investigation. Unless the educational experience enables people to explore and analyse the fullness of the human–environment relationship, it is not possible to understand either the cause of the outcomes of human environmental management or any resolution to perceived problems.

However, if we do accept a more socially analytical approach to environmental education, this has its own problems within the formal education system. The overt or covert critical stance to social values and ways of life can create concerns about motivations, objectivity and sometimes relevance to what most teachers think they ought to be doing. Using education to challenge, even alter, social attitudes and values and thereby socio-economic systems and move them towards an alternative set of attitudes and systems — particularly if these are preconceived — poses enormous issues of acceptability from teachers, school managers, parents and the local and central government.

WWF–UK's Approach

Since January 1981, WWF–UK (World Wide Fund for Nature–UK) has been trying to struggle with these contradictions and to develop a rationale for environmental education that is not synonymous with a nature focus, is not prescriptive and not outside the mainstream. It has centred on the notion that unless environmental education can be rationalized as something more fundamental to the education process, then the likelihood of it achieving anything of importance is slight. Its work has been based on an alternative interpretation of the WCS statement about attitudes and values and also on an alternative — and we hope a realistic — view of education. Its main tenets are as follows.

Wherever we live and whatever we do, we all make decisions and take actions that directly impact on the structure and quality of the world we inhabit. Therefore, it is not unreasonable to propose that one of the key responsibilities of being human is to ensure we are fully aware of the complexities of our relationship with the world we inhabit and to gain a full understanding of the impact of that relationship.

It is also not unreasonable to propose that, given the undeniable impact of the quality and structure of the environment on the quality of life, every individual has a right to the opportunity and the appropriate understanding, insight and skills that will enable them to participate in the moulding of the world that they currently and will inhabit — competencies that will give them the power to intervene in the inevitable process of change.

If education, as indicated by a fairly universally held definition, should prepare people for their roles and responsibilities of life, it is a *sine qua non* that education must prepare them for their role as environmental decision-makers. The development of the environmentally literate citizen should therefore be a function of the education provision in any society.

The focus here is the development of the well-informed environmental decision-maker. It is not the development of a set of preconceived attitudes and values about the environment and it certainly is not about promoting certain institutional ideologies about the environment. Rather, it is about promoting a certain set of ideologies about an educational entitlement.

At the core of the WWF educational philosophy is a definition that focuses on helping people to understand and interpret the physical and social structures and processes that determine the quality and structure of the environment — whether that be the school they are taught in, the road they live in, the forest they read about, or the town or countryside they visit. It focuses on ways in which education helps people to explore the forces that define human activity in relationship to the environment — the social, cultural, economic, political and civil forces that determine the way people behave. It proposes that it is impossible, for example, to understand environmental problems in the United Kingdom without understanding how a capitalist economy motivated by competitive materialism affects the way we utilize environmental resources.

Broader influences such as conflict, human rights and gender also have a direct impact on environmental issues. It is impossible, for example, to understand environmental problems in the horn of Africa without understanding something about inter- and intra-national conflict. It is impossible to understand environmental problems in South America without addressing the human rights of indigenous peoples, and it is impossible to assess many environmental issues in the developing world without considering the role of women in society. Without understanding how a wide range of influences affect our behaviour in relationship to the environment, it is impossible to understand any problems and to determine realistic ways in which they might be solved. The WWF approach is also about people clarifying their stance to this understanding and analysis as well as their own relationship to the quality and structure of the world they inhabit.

As with the kingfisher, it is not the image alone that matters or the understanding of the image, but what that image means to the person. It is not what you see but how you see it. For example, if we see the images of hardship or poverty either directly or on TV screens, what do they mean to us? To all the viewers the picture is the same. But what do these experiences generate in the mind's eye? Do they generate pain, hurt, a sense of injustice, horror, bitterness or outrage? What do these distant dark shapes that flash across the consciousness of our daily lives mean to us — what personal significance do they have?

Challenge and Security

Environmental education cannot limit itself merely to an awareness of the issues. Neither is it sufficient for it to develop understanding and a merely utilitarian response, for sustainable environmental management without social justice and human care and concern would be fatally flawed. Therefore the environmental education experience should — and some say must — provide the potential for an emotional response to the educational experience. If not, we will be forced to share the concern expressed in the opening paragraphs of Ben Okri's (1991) book, *The Famished Road*: 'We feared the heartlessness of human beings, all of whom are born blind, few of whom ever learn to see.' Also, sustainable environmental management without concern about the impact of its quality and structure on the mental and emotional wellbeing of those who live in it is also untenable, certainly morally but probably also practically.

Does this therefore mean moving back towards the initiation approach where we educate towards a set of defined attitudes, values and perceptions? I think not; it is more an education that includes a set of experiences from which the child can extract and develop their own meaning from the world around them.

Their art can bring with it the sensitivity to light and colour and the ability to look with discernment; their creative writing can bring with it the development of their own voice to express their own feelings; their music can bring with it an ability to explore and communicate intangible feelings, emotions and sensations; their drama can bring with it the sensitivity to and empathy with other people — to joys and sorrows, the pain of injustice and the consequences of selfishness and cruelty. However, if we do make young people vulnerable to these feelings we also have a duty to the child.

If we are providing an education that can potentially engender a level of care and concern, it also requires the presence of a security from within which this care and concern can be felt and expressed. We cannot cry for others safely without the security of our own comfort. This is the gamble we take as parents and teachers. Do we expose people to the possibility of recognizing, experiencing and expressing feelings in a world where these securities are not inevitable? And do we try to create care where the potential for exposure to suffering is greater than ever before?

We also now have the additional problem in the UK of trying to create the possibility to care in a world where it is seen as detrimental to personal success. To be successful in the aggressively competitive world of consumerism, care is a counterproductive quality. Are we doing the child a disservice in our attempts to save the world, or are they more resilient than we perhaps imagine? If we choose to expose young people to this vulnerability, we cannot just leave them to cope empty-handed. We must offer them security for their caring, and the opportunity and support to express their care positively. They need to know that their care can be exhibited in their schools and in their lives and that, by proxy, it is expressed for them in places of hardship beyond their reach.

An Entitlement Curriculum

We all have a duty to create a social climate that enables people to live lives that are realistically directed towards solving the problems they care about. Thus, it is crucial that activity within the formal education system extends into the realm of professional and occupational education. This brings with it the need for other partners. Once again, this throws into clear relief one of the great failings of the environmental NGO movement. Essentially, partnerships have been seen as being between members of the NGO movement and directed at some other part of society, either as carriers of messages or as groups to be lobbied. WWF–UK has consistently identified its educational partners as being within the education system and, as far as professional and occupational education is concerned, partners from the world of industry and commerce.

Without doubt, public pressure, self-interest and, I believe, concern from within have created statutory and self-imposed regulation on the environmental performance of industry and commerce. Ensuring that young people receive an education that enables them to participate in the delivery of these requirements and move industry and commerce from within towards another incremental step in the direction of sustainable resource management and social and environmental justice, is another legitimate objective of environmental education.

This has as much to do with ideals about preparing people to participate effectively in the democratic process as it does with the condition of the environment. This would seem to be a far more telling and powerful argument to encourage the educational establishment to absorb the need for development of environmental literacy as a function of mainstream education provision than the very partial views of environmental quality or the prognostications of gloom and doom from environmental agencies.

WWF believes in 'an entitlement curriculum' that everyone has a right to receive throughout their lives consisting of the following elements:

- an entitlement to educational experiences and access to information that will enable the individual to understand, analyse and respond to the various environmental situations and issues they meet in their day-to-day living;
- an entitlement to educational experiences that empower the individual to have a well-informed and therefore confident and effective voice in the decisions that will determine the quality of the places where they live and work; and
- an entitlement that provides new or revived skills that enable the individual to participate in and benefit from the implementation of these decisions.

In total, an entitlement that enables participation through understanding and insight, and that encourages committed participation through personal care, relevance and benefit.

The following case study gives some idea of what might it look like in practice.

BOX 3.1 CORK AND TALK: AN EXAMPLE FROM SPAIN

The Extremadura region of southern Spain is an area of low population and extensive Dehasa woodland. This is the product of soil, climate and human interaction. The shallow soils suffer summer drought and a short cold period in winter. Cork and holm oaks are both drought and frost resistant and predominate in a human-introduced shrub growth and flower-rich herbaceous layer. The economy of the Dehasa includes cork and firewood production and pork production from acorn-eating free-range pigs. The environment also supports important populations of rare and endangered species, including European lynx, imperial eagle, black stork, black vulture and a huge wintering population of European cranes. The cranes arrive from their breeding areas of northern and eastern Europe in October to feed on the acorns from the cork oaks.

This area is in the process of change stimulated by a variety of forces, including EU farming subsidies and the inevitable rural drift as urban lifestyles are promoted and jobs, in particular those that enable people to achieve these dreams of urban excitement and fulfilment, are not available locally.

The traditional response from many environmental NGOs would be descriptive, explaining the ecological interactions that create this fascinating and exciting biological mix. It would also promote its importance and exhort what a loss to the world it would be if it disappeared. An alternative approach would start by investigating, with the local people, the unique socio-cultural and economic interactions that have created this landscape. Based on the above analysis it would explore alternative, but realistic, economic models for the region; models that utilize, but do not degrade, the social, cultural and environmental currency. It would work with the people of the area to explore these alternatives, provide them with the skills to participate in decisions about their region and to participate in and benefit from their implementation.

Conclusion

Since 1981, WWF–UK has chosen to work in conjunction with what we believe to be some of the best and most creative thinkers in the education system and, more recently, from within industry and commerce. Its ambition is to encourage, assist and facilitate those within the formal education system who are interested in exploring a more fundamental function for education in society. WWF has attempted to finance, promote and create an enthusiasm for these creative ideas that have been generated from the system. This not only ensures their suitability and credibility but also provides an enthusiasm in the system itself that generates and encourages others to take part. Crucially, this approach has the potential to influence the social momentum from within, unlike some elements of the environmental movement who fire off salvos from the outside in the hope that the momentum might be deflected.

The above rationale defines a broad approach to education, which we believe helps educationists to make some collective sense of the wide variety of adjectival educations (global, development, environmental, peace and human rights). In the case of the UK, it also makes some collective sense of the cross-curricular themes of careers, health, economic and industrial understanding, citizenship and environment. However, what is 'it' exactly? Is it a new definition for environmental education, is it EFS, or is it a new rationale for the role of education within society?

I believe that, having become institutionalized, environmental education is a lost cause and should be phased out as soon as possible. Its history and conventional wisdoms stand in the way of its morphosis into anything that can possibly achieve goals remotely akin to those set by the WCS.

Education for sustainability is a concept that can happily house all the necessary elements to be effective. However, I do believe that the ultimate challenge is to remove all the adjectival adjuncts (for that is how they are perceived) to education and develop the conventional notion that the education system must, as a key function, prepare all people for their role as well-informed, skilled and experienced participators in determining the quality and structure of the world we all inhabit.

An 'unpoisoned' chalice would be one that identifies that function for education. An achievable goal for the NGOs is to ensure that this entitlement is in place.

References

Greig, S, G Pike and D Selby (1989) 'Change from Without: External Agencies', *Greenprints for Changing Schools*, WWF–UK/Kogan Page, London
IUCN (1980) *World Conservation Strategy*, IUCN/UNEP/ WWF, Gland
— (1991) *Caring for the Earth*, Earthscan Publications Ltd, London
Okri, B (1991) *The Famished Road*, Jonathon Cape Ltd, London

Part II

The Formal Sector

Sustainability and Stewardship (one of three sets of key ideas central to environmental education): humans are necessarily consumers of the Earth's resources but they carry a major responsibility for maintaining the well being of the planet and all its inhabitants, human and non-human.

('Environmental Education: A Framework for the Development of a Cross-Curricular Theme in Wales', *Advisory Paper*, 17, Curriculum Council for Wales, Cardiff, 1992)

... provided the statutory requirements are met, it will remain for individual schools to decide how they wish to educate children about environmental matters and the priority they wish to give to this aspect of their pupils' education.

(Department for Education in a letter to WWF, 22 February 1994)

Coming here today, I have no hidden agenda. I am fighting for my future. ... At school you teach us to behave in the world. You teach us not to fight with others, to work things out, to respect others, to clean up our mess, not to hurt other creatures, to share and not be greedy. Then why do you go out and do those things that you teach us not to do?

(Severn Cullis-Suzuki, aged 12, to the Rio Earth Summit, quoted in Bayer et al (eds) *Rescue Mission Planet Earth: A Children's Edition of Agenda 21*, Kingfisher, London, 1994)

What is education for sustainability? It is the creation of a sense and a practice of global citizenship in all humanity.

(Timothy O'Riordan, *Annual Review of Environmental Education*, CEE, Reading, 1993)

We ought to encourage our students to find their calling in good and necessary work. The best and most necessary work for our age involves in a thousand ways the recalibration of humanity's values, institutions and behaviours with those of the Earth. This is the task of education in our time.

(David Orr, 'Greening of Education', *Resurgence*, 170, September/October, 1993)

Educational institutions need to be reoriented towards helping students learn systemic thinking, futures thinking, integrative thinking, probabilistic thinking, creative thinking, values analysis and moral reasoning.

(Lester Milbrath, *Envisioning a Sustainable Society: Learning Our Way Out*, SUNY Press, Albany, 1989)

As schools move into the postmodern age, something is going to have to give. It might be the quality of classroom learning, as teachers and their curriculum are spread increasingly thinly to accommodate more and more demands. It might be the health, lives and stamina of teachers themselves as they crumple under the pressures of multiple mandated change. Or it can be the basic structures and cultures of schooling, reinvented for and realigned with the postmodern purposes and pressures they must now address. These are the stark choices we now face. The rules of the world are changing. It is time for the rules of teaching and teacher's work to change with them.

(Andy Hargreaves, *Changing Teachers, Changing Times*, Cassell, London, 1994)

Chapter 4

THE PRIMARY YEARS
Gillian Symons

To begin this chapter I place education for sustainability (EFS) within the spectrum of environmental and social studies approaches that have influenced primary schools. I suggest there is a need to combine approaches that develop an affinity with nature and an understanding of ecological processes and interconnections with other approaches that develop understanding of such concepts as equity and social change. Ways of exploring complex issues of sustainability with young children are suggested, together with references to appropriate teaching materials. The rationale for involving young children in the types of local decision-making and action encouraged by Local Agenda 21 (LA21) is explored, and the potential for EFS within and beyond the national curriculum is examined. Finally, reassurance is given about the educational validity of working with complexity and uncertainty.

Two strands in the Development of Environmental Education

Nature Studies There is a long tradition of teaching and learning about the natural environment in primary schools. Every class has had its nature table where children could experience the excitement of watching frog spawn metamorphose and sticky buds explode into life. This focus is one which most primary teachers still espouse, building upon the enthusiasm and curiosity young children have for the 'magic' of nature and introducing them to positive and hopeful aspects of life. Steve Van Matre (1990), among others, has found innovative ways to help children to develop empathy and solidarity with non-human nature.

The sense of responsibility for nature which grows from this is often extended by teachers into practical activities such as looking after classroom animals, tree planting and litter picks. In recent years this approach has been supported by a range of environmental competitions and other outside initiatives, for example the Shell Better Britain Campaign or BT's National Environment Week, where the focus is mainly on clearing up eyesores created by humans and creating beautiful 'natural' environments.

While it is valuable for children to make a real contribution to their environment, there is a danger that they can end up by seeing everything natural — trees, plants, animals, birds — as good, and all human activity as bad and polluting. Nature comes to be seen not as something we are part of but as something that has to be protected from people. This approach is reflected in the school ecological area, which is fenced off from the rest of the playground and into which the children are allowed only for an occasional, carefully supervised lesson. On a global scale, it can be seen in the preservationist practice of excluding human activity from large areas of wilderness at the expense of the indigenous populations who may have had a sustainable relationship with non-human nature. An approach that seeks to preserve wildlife without addressing the growing social problems that will inevitably impact on it seems doomed to failure.

Social Studies An alternative tradition has focused on developing understanding of the urban and social aspects of the environment. In this tradition, teaching and learning processes became as important as content. The following are among the key players in the evolution of this approach.

Tony Gibson, working at Nottingham University in the 1960s, developed resources to encourage pupils to set and solve their own problems in order to convince them that 'the environment is theirs to change' (Gibson and Bean, 1980).

The Town & Country Planning Association's (TCPA) education department and its publication, the *Bulletin of Environmental Education* (*BEE*), were influential in the spread of urban studies in the early 1970s. The urban environment was chosen as the focus because the TCPA considered that there were many existing services and resources for teachers concerned with nature and the countryside, while there was a relative neglect of the town. Urban studies encouraged a multidisciplinary approach, starting with the pupils' own experience and reality. The movement is now coordinated by Places for People and its publication *Streetwise*.

Social studies, based around concepts such as distribution of power, division of labour, conflict, interdependence and change, was given formal recognition as an appropriate study for the primary school by the Inner London Education Authority in 1980.

Social studies is about people and their relationships in society. It is concerned with how children learn about society rather than what they learn. This concern with the processes of learning and thinking is characteristic of the approach of social studies teaching.

Social studies is concerned to develop children's critical awareness and understanding. It does this by using their everyday experiences of social life as a starting point and then, through discussion and techniques of contrast and comparison, the understandings that children have of their immediate world are explored and extended in wider studies.

(Brand et al, 1980)

The World Studies 8–13 project of the early 1980s grew out of the Schools Council curriculum development project Place, Time & Society, which focused on exploring concepts through active teaching methods such as games and simulations. World Studies 8–13 stresses responsible citizenship and interdependence and the importance of providing opportunities to explore children's own feelings and opinions.

The Global Futures project, culminating in *Educating for the Future* (Hicks, 1994) starts with the premise that interdependence exists not only spatially but across time, so children should be given opportunities to develop skills of forward thinking and to explore what sort of future they want for themselves and for society.

The Case for Education for Sustainability in the Primary School

EFS provides an integrating framework for social and environmental education together with human rights, development and peace education (Greig, Pike and Selby, 1987). The development of empathy with non-human nature is important if it is not to be valued solely as a resource for human use. A knowledge of natural systems helps children understand the interconnections between all life and the way human actions affect these systems. It should be linked with a critical knowledge of the social systems that shape our lives. Only this combination provides an adequate basis for understanding causes, exploring alternative solutions, making decisions and taking responsible action.

Is It Too Difficult? A common response to issues concerning sustainability is that they are too problematic for young children. However, children face difficult issues in their daily lives from which we cannot always protect them (see Box 4.1 for an example). If we do not provide opportunities in school to address these issues, children can become 'prisoners of fairyland' (Stevens, 1982), forced to collude with the silence around anything that may be painful, or that does not have clear answers.

At Key Stage 1 (5–7 years) there should be an emphasis on strengthening feelings of self-worth and developing skills of communication and cooperation. Research has shown that children with a high self-regard are likely to be more altruistic, generous and sharing. They will have more positive attitudes towards other people if they can express their own thoughts and feelings clearly and listen carefully to others (Borba and Borba, 1978). They can begin to explore options and to make choices based on available evidence. Grieg et al (1987) suggest that conflicts can, at this age, be used as opportunities to learn the process of generating alternative solutions (an essential skill in EFS) rather than relying on those provided by authority figures.

Joy Palmer (1995) found that many six year olds have considerable knowledge and understanding of the management of waste materials, but that 'school-based learning added to children's misconceptions and confusions, rather than developing accurate scientific concepts'. Palmer suggests this is because teaching had focused on encouraging children not to litter, to use bins and to recycle. 'Scant attention seems to have been paid to reasons why recycling is important, to details of the process, and to various methods of dealing with waste materials'. She concludes that well-designed courses could extend levels of conceptual understanding.

There is evidence from research that Key Stage 2 (7–11 years) children exhibit greatest openness towards the world (Torney, 1972). They are curious and open and do not yet hold too strongly the fundamental attitudes and stereotypes that later limit receptiveness to new ideas. However, their cognitive development is sufficiently advanced to accept a variety of viewpoints. This, therefore, is a vital age at which to encourage children to develop a questioning attitude to received wisdom.

The emphasis placed by EFS on equity, social justice and empowerment moves environmental education into a more controversial arena, but 'no lifestyle or education system is value free' (Prescott-Allen, 1991). By avoiding controversial issues, we reinforce the predominant values and perceptions currently held by our society, which are not leading to a sustainable future and may be perpetuating inequality and injustice. 'Controversy is part of everyday life; children are faced with issues inside and outside of the classroom. Learning to respond thoughtfully to issues is an important part of growing up and needs to be part of the school curriculum' (McFarlane, 1991).

Whether or not issues are appropriate for young children seems to depend on the teaching approaches used.

After observing pupils in several schools, one of the evaluators for the World Studies 8–13 Project remarked that the teachers were handling 'unteachable' ideas in their classrooms. Quite young pupils were, to his surprise, exploring world issues confidently and competently, with a remarkable level of sophistication. The fact that they were able to do so was due in large part to the style, approach and skill of their teachers, underpinned, crucially, by a high expectation of what the children might achieve.

(Fisher and Hicks, 1985)

Concrete examples of practical activities which explore complex issues are given in Boxes 4.1 and 4.2.

Box 4.1

Given that 1 in 15 children can expect to be injured in a road accident before their sixteenth birthday, teachers used the Global Futures framework to enable primary children to explore this issue in a positive way.

The children thought about what their environment is like now, considered probable and preferable future scenarios and clarified what action would bring them about. They were provided with information and resources, helped to develop skills and given experiences to support them in this process. For example, they compared the official number of reported accidents to cyclists in Sheffield in one year (47) with the statistics at the local children's hospital (300 head injuries in 60 days caused by falling from bicycles). Areas of risk and possible solutions were identified, public opinion was researched, and information gathered by the children was used by the city's road safety engineers.

'By considering the issues involved, pupils are made more aware of the political and economic factors that inhibit or promote change. ... The pupils are not only being given an insight into the ways in which change is brought about but are increasingly involved in those processes' (Margaret Noble, 1991).

Box 4.2

Sowing and Harvesting (Versfeld, 1989) an Oxfam activity about cash crops and food crops, has among its aims:

■ *'To show how the growing of cash crops can lead to a lack of food for the producers.'*
■ *'To show how market forces work by putting children in the role of farmers who have to cope with these forces.'*

The activity is run for three 15-minute periods, each representing a farming year, during which the children 'grow crops' (cutting around templates) and trade, with a debriefing after each 'year'. Additional complications, gradually introduced, include rises and falls in the prices of crop and tools and inputs of food aid.

It was trialled by year 3 teachers who were sceptical about whether such issues could be explained to children so young. After debriefing the activity, they found that it had helped to counteract commonly held mis-conceptions about causes of Third World poverty (for themselves as well as their pupils) and that their seven and eight year-olds showed an understanding of the unsustainable practices brought about by over dependence on market forces greater than that of many adults.

Critical Enquiry For real EFS to take place, opportunities for critical enquiry must be built into the mainly descriptive and practical nature of much current environmental education as suggested in Box 4.3.

Box 4.3 THREE PERSPECTIVES ON ENVIRONMENTAL EDUCATION

Knowledge bias
A concern for knowing about the physical, chemical and biological processes which sustain the environment. Examples include the hydrological cycle, nitrogen cycle, food webs, climate and vegetation, the mechanism of ozone depletion, acid rain and the greenhouse effect. It often describes human/environment interaction.
Key words: scientific, rational, abstract

Needs of society/capability bias
This is an element of active citizenship. Examples include recycling schemes, tree planting, green consumerism, tidying and enhancing school and community spaces, posters and litter campaigns. Often confused with education for the environment in an uncritical sense.
Key words: Practical citizenship, involvement, commitment

Critical enquiry bias
This is a process and context bias. It is less focused on the content and its application than in developing critical awareness. Its concern is the teaching and learning process and how issues which arise are dealt with.

> *There is particular concern with critically examining alternative solutions to environmental issues.*
> Key words: Values clarification, enquiry-based
> *(Webster, 1994)*

All three perspectives are necessary for education for sustainable development. Alternative solutions cannot be explored unless the children have an understanding of the basic processes involved and it is important that opportunities for practical action are provided. However, in much primary education the critical enquiry dimension is neglected. Particularly when the emphasis is on practical contributions the children can make, environmental education can tackle symptoms and avoid looking at causes within the wider society. Even teachers who encourage investigations of current issues often start with questions that fail to challenge the status quo. For example, 'Which would be the most environmentally friendly transport system for our town?' Such questions rarely prompt considerations of why people move around, which can be more to do with investment and planning decisions than straightforward transportation choices. Figure 4.1 suggests alternative questions which may be asked.

A useful framework of key questions that can be applied to any environment or place and which includes the major elements which need to be considered for sustainable development, is provided by the Development Compass Rose.

Active Participation Sustainable development is dependent on the informed participation of all sectors of society and it is essential that experience of democratic processes and thoughtful participation in decision-making and action should start early, as it is a skill that needs practice.

Research funded jointly by Learning Through Landscapes and WWF–UK found the hidden curriculum of the school to be as influential as the overt curriculum, with both the style of personal relationships and the management of the immediate environment having profound effects on the learning of pupils. Children became confused when what they were taught was not mirrored in the immediate environment of the school, leading 'some of them to question the integrity of what they were being taught and of those who were teaching it' (Titman, 1994). To prevent this mismatch, it is important that the school environment is cared for and that resources and habitats are managed as sustainably as possible. Learning Through Landscapes is a source of advice, resources and funding ideas to assist this process and *Eco-School* (Poulton and Symons, 1990) suggests ways of exploring the issues with pupils.

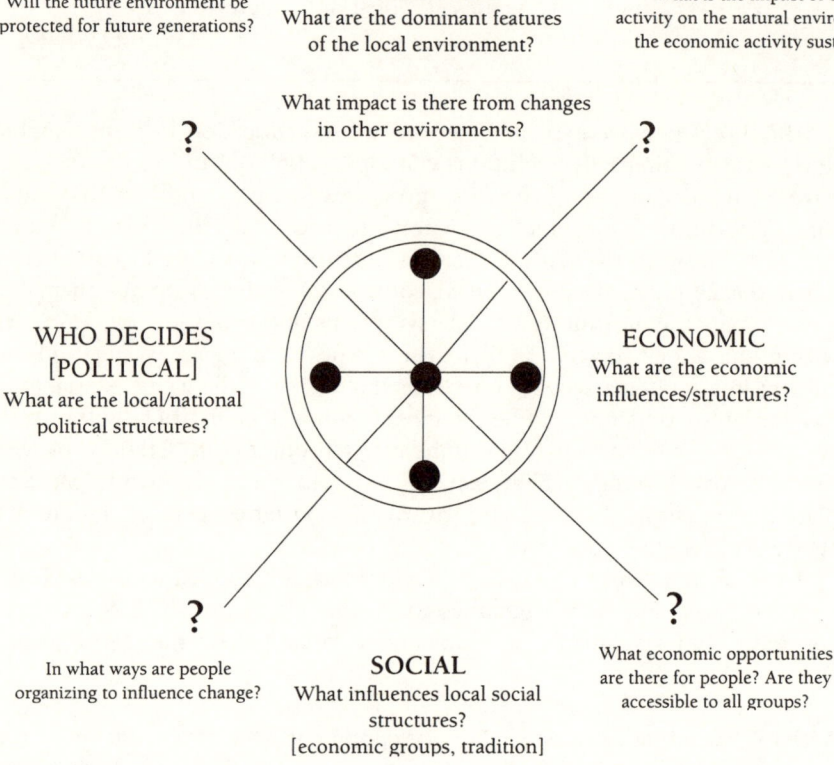

Source: Belk et al (1992)

Figure 4.1 Development Compass Rose

Titman's research findings stress the importance of participatory approaches but suggest that children are critical of tokenism. This is a danger to beware of once participation is asked for. Designs that children have spent much time and effort on are sometimes unthinkingly changed without explanation, though the children are still expected to look after the environment created. However, as a Manchester school found, plants that had been put in by the landscaping contractors were rapidly trampled, while those grown from seed by the children were protected and cared for. Such events suggest levels of participation towards the bottom of Hart's (1987) hierarchy shown in Box 4.4.

Box 4.4 *HART'S LADDER OF PARTICIPATION*

8 Child initiated, shared decisions with adults
7 Child initiated and directed
6 Adult initiated, shared decisions with children
5 Consulted and informed
4 Assigned but informed
3 Tokenism
2 Decoration
1 Manipulation

Hart suggests that in genuine participation the programme or product is more appropriate to the user; those involved develop confidence and competencies; and the organization's structure and function is improved. This has been borne out by the experiences of many schools which have developed mechanisms for participation (see Box 4.5 for examples). All stress that time must be allowed for the children to develop the skills to participate effectively and responsibly. They consider such time to be worthwhile because it brings a sense of ownership, greater motivation and self-discipline, and improved learning.

Box 4.5

In a Thameside school pupils evaluate their own project work and identify areas in which they need to develop greater skills. Looking back over the four years the system has been in operation, the teachers are able to see development in the sophistication of the evaluations, which help the teachers to plan work appropriate for each child.

A London primary school headteacher who introduced a school council found that at first the worst fears of the sceptics were realized as the children came up with unrealistic and inappropriate ideas. However, because their suggestions were all discussed with respect and trialled where possible, they developed their action research skills, devising short-, medium- and long-term plans, taking responsibility for implementation, monitoring the effectiveness of their proposals and developing strategies to deal with any difficulties that arose.

Do Children have the Power to Change Things? The ability to participate involves understanding that the systems we live in are social constructs that are not inevitable. It demands recognition that decisions are made within particular economic, political and cultural circumstances over which individuals may have little control and which can sometimes only be influenced by collective action. An exclusive concentration on personal responsibility can engender in children a sense of guilt and helplessness. Box 4.6 suggests three resources that begin to explore the context in which our lives take place.

Box 4.6

In People and Their Communities, *Poulton and Symons (1993) suggest activities through which children can begin to understand the building blocks of social organization; the range of needs and rights within any group of people; and their own place within communities of different scales. For example, most children when asked who makes the decisions in their school will believe it to be the head teacher. Investigating the responsibilities of all members of the school community introduces the complex web of power and decision-making in one small institution and can lead to an understanding of broader issues and of ways that individuals can make their voice heard.*

The Green Detective Series (Hirst) looks at the processes behind provision of our everyday needs (such as clothing, food and water treatment), exploring issues about the resources used, the conditions of workers and alternative, less damaging approaches. The series raises awareness of the global impact of our lifestyles while suggesting positive action children can take.

Why on Earth? An Approach to Science with a Global Dimension at Key Stage 2 (Barnfield et al, 1991) is concerned to dispel the myth that science is objective, culture free and neutral and to explore the social, political and economic impact of scientific experiments. For example, a section on soil begins with standard experiments on soil samples but moves on to investigate the effects on the soil of different farming machinery and practices, leading to solutions that people in different parts of the world have used to preserve soil.

Why on Earth?'s use of positive case studies avoids any danger of engendering a sense of hopelessness that may be caused by increased awareness of environmental problems. Other examples of positive change brought about by public action might include successful local campaigns for a new pedestrian crossing, to save a valued library threatened with closure, or a park that would have been built on but for public protest in Victorian times. Such local examples can be supplemented with global case studies such as the Chipko tree huggers or Chico Mendes's fight to save the Brazilian rainforest (Mendes, 1989).

LA21 emphasizes the importance of consulting with all groups in society, including young people. It therefore provides an excellent opportunity for primary pupils to begin to understand democratic processes and genuinely to participate in local decision-making, as well as providing a motivating context for the development of basic skills (see Box 4.7). *Rescue Mission Planet Earth: A Children's Edition of Agenda 21* (Bayer et al, 1994), which is written by children from around the world, is an accessible introduction to Agenda 21. Schools, with their broad base of pupils, teachers, support staff, parents, governors and local business contacts are in a strong position to raise awareness of Agenda 21 within the wider community.

Box 4.7

A Year 6 class was invited through Hammersmith Urban Studies Centre to contribute an exhibition to an LA21 launch for the borough. After exploring the context and content of Agenda 21, the pupils took photographs of 'the good and the bad' in the local environment, thinking about different viewpoints, long-term and global implications and who has the power to change or maintain the situation. Discussion took place about things that contribute to quality of life that cannot be photographed, including feelings of safety and problems created by prejudice.

Some of the people identified as having power and responsibility to make decisions affecting the local environment were invited to the school. They were interviewed about the possibilities and limitations of their role, what they thought needed to be done and what attempts they were making to widen participation.

Information gathered was presented by the children at the LA21 launch. The class plans to contribute to the establishing of indicators to measure local environmental change, which they can monitor.

Enrichment of the Curriculum After the 1995 review of the national curriculum, with less content and more opportunity to consolidate and innovate, many schools are feeling ready to return from planning the curriculum around attainment targets to what good primary teachers have always recognized as the real purposes of education. Education for sustainability offers an opportunity for primary schools to fulfil the national curriculum in a relevant context through good educational practices —

using active learning approaches to develop critical thinking; linking curriculum content with real life; developing forward thinking and involving children in planning, monitoring and evaluation.

Education for sustainability can enrich many subject areas. It draws on scientific knowledge and understanding and the processes of making predictions and obtaining and evaluating evidence. While it is an excellent vehicle for spoken and written language work, it also uses mathematical data and geographical skills and knowledge. It promotes historical understanding and can provide a stimulating and relevant context for work in almost every other area of the curriculum. Relevant sections of the geography and science documents are given in Boxes 4.8 and 4.9.

Box 4.8 *GEOGRAPHY IN THE NATIONAL CURRICULUM*

Key Stage 1 Programme of Study
In investigating the quality of an environment in a locality, pupils should be taught:

- *to express their likes and dislikes about the environment concerned;*
- *about changes in that environment;*
- *about ways of sustaining and improving the environment's quality.*

Key Stage 2 Programme of Study
Enquiry questions should be largely of the 'What/where is it?', 'What is it like?', 'How did it get like this?' type.

In studying how physical and human processes give places their character and distinctiveness, pupils should be taught:

- *about the environmental issues in the localities;*
- *about the relationships between the features of the localities and human activities; and*
- *about recent or proposed changes in the localities*

In investigating how the environment can be managed and protected, pupils should be taught:

- *that human activities affect the environment;*
- *ways in which people manage their environment;*
- *to consider whether some types of environment need special protection.*
  (*Geography in the National Curriculum*, Department
  for Education, HMSO, London, 1995)

Box 4.9 SCIENCE IN THE NATIONAL CURRICULUM

Key Stage 1 Programme of Study
Pupils should develop their skills, knowledge and understanding of science through focused exploration and investigation of living things, materials, phenomena and processes within their everyday experience.

Pupils should be encouraged to ask questions such as 'How?', 'Why?', 'What will happen if . . . ?'

Pupils should be helped, through the use of a variety of domestic and environmental contexts, to develop an awareness of the importance of science in everyday life and its relevance to their personal health. They should understand that living things and the environment need to be treated with care and sensitivity.

Key Stage 2 Programme of Study
Pupils should continue to be given opportunities to develop their skills, knowledge and understanding of science through focused exploration and investigation in familiar contexts. These activities should continue to involve first hand experience.

Pupils should continue to be encouraged to ask questions.

Pupils should continue to develop their awareness of the relevance of science to their personal health and their local environment. They should understand that living things and the environment need to be treated with care and sensitivity.

Pupils should begin to obtain evidence to test ideas in a range of contexts.

(Science in the National Curriculum,
Department for Education, HMSO, London, 1995)

The 20 per cent of time which has been 'freed up' following the review of the national curriculum provides scope for work outside the strict confines of the national curriculum. OFSTED inspectors must give due weight to success in reaching targets for achievement that have been set by the school itself. Recent educational reforms have tended to deprofessionalize teachers, removing their responsibility for what they teach and making the content of education a political decision. But the national curriculum provides a framework within which teachers can still make choices about how to teach the required knowledge and skills. The opportunities are there for teachers who choose to use them, but it is necessary to contextualize the knowledge, skills and attitudes written into the curriculum and to make explicit the connections with sustainable development for EFS to take place.

Although the cross-curricular themes have received little attention since Dearing, they are still in place and EFS encompasses all of them, particularly citizenship, economic and industrial understanding and environmental education. As with all the national curriculum documents, those for the cross-curricular themes are open to wide interpretation. It is interesting to compare statements from the English environmental education document with those from its Welsh counterpart (Box 4.10).

Box 4.10

Environmental Education aims to:

■ *provide opportunities to acquire the knowledge, values, attitudes, commitment and skills needed to protect and improve the environment;*
■ *encourage students to examine and interpret the environment from a variety of perspectives — physical, geographical, biological, sociological, economic, political, technological, historical, aesthetic, ethical and spiritual;*
■ *arouse pupils' awareness and curiosity about the environment and encourage active participation in resolving environmental problems.*

(Curriculum Guidance 7: Environmental
Education, *NCC, York, 1990*)

The Curriculum Council for Wales regards the goals of environmental education as being:

■ *to foster clear awareness of, and concerns about, economic, social, political and ecological interdependence;*
■ *to provide every young person with opportunities to develop knowledge, values, attitudes commitment and skills needed to protect and improve the environment and achieve more sustainable forms of human development;*
■ *to encourage the emergence of responsible patterns of behaviour towards the environment by individuals and communities.*

('Environmental Education: A Framework for the Development of a
Cross-Curricular Theme in Wales', Advisory Paper 17,
CCW, Cardiff, 1992)

Support for Teachers Wishing to Educate for Sustainability

Teachers, like everyone else, are products of the society in which they have grown up. They may themselves not question systems which, although they may be based on the available technology and dominant world view of the last century, are the only ones of which they have experience. Although teachers do not need to know all the answers (see below), there is a danger that primary teaching can be so absorbing and time consuming that practitioners find little time in which to expand their own knowledge and understanding of the world. This does not place them in a strong position to 'prepare pupils for the opportunities, responsibilities and experience of adult life' (Education Reform Act, 1988). For teachers wishing to learn more about issues concerning sustainable development, the environment pages of the *Guardian* are a good starting point. More systematic analysis of the issues can be found in the magazines *New Internationalist*, *Resurgence* and *New Economics* and through practical and readable books such as *Blueprint for a Green Planet* (Girardet and Seymour, 1987) and *Wealth Beyond Measure* (Ekins et al, 1992). Radio 4 programmes like *Costing the Earth* are a mine of information, as are a number of television documentaries.

Schools will need to maintain a resource bank of up-to-date information, pictures and statistics (many of which can be found in the media) to underpin their work. Teaching resources mentioned in the text (and many others) offer ways into educating for sustainability, but as with all resources it is the way they are used, including the teaching/learning approaches and explicit links that are made with sustainable development, that will determine their efficacy in practice.

The environment affects everyone and, as such, will gain the interest and support of many parents. A Northumberland nursery school surveyed parents about their concerns and interests in the environment and was surprised to find how high it came on their list of priorities. The parents felt their children, even at that age, were confronting environmental issues that they did not feel they had the knowledge and understanding to explain to them and welcomed the school's help both in educating their children and in increasing their own understanding.

Teachers are often afraid that they do not know the answers to all the questions that may arise, but defining the questions and thinking of strategies to find possible answers is a vital part of the education process. Environmental education has, in the words of Tim Brighouse (1989), 'the potential not of problem solving but of problem finding — in short to enter territory uncharted and through which teacher and learner together may find many routes to different but not absolutely right solutions.'

Reassurance about the validity of this approach comes from several quarters:

Empowerment is the recognition of the thousands of contradictions that govern our civil and personal lives. We may not be able to resolve all these inconsistencies but we should constantly be aware of them and ready, always ready, to recognize why they exist and are maintained in the economic and political structures that govern us.

(O'Riordan, 1994)

It is not only newspapers that make possibilities into certainties: some experts do so too — and that includes environmental education experts. It is not only better science to keep question marks present; it is better pedagogy too. A lesson with a question is much more likely to get pupils thinking actively than a lesson which states what is going to happen.

(David Wright, 1990/1)

References

Barnfield, M et al (1991) *Why on Earth? An Approach to Science with a Global Dimension at Key Stage 2*, Development Education Centre, Birmingham

Bayer, J L et al (eds) (1994) *Rescue Mission Planet Earth: A Children's Edition of Agenda 21*, Kingfisher, London

Belk, J et al (1992) *It's Our World Too: A Local-Global Approach to Environmental Education*, Development Education Centres, Birmingham/South Yorkshire

Borba, M and C Borba (1978) *Self-Esteem: A Classroom Affair*, Harper & Row, San Francisco

Brand, J, M Casey and S Mahon (eds) (1980) *Social Studies in the Primary School*, Inner London Education Authority, London

Brighouse, T (1989) 'Presidential Inaugural Speech to Council for Environmental Education AGM', *Annual Review of Environmental Education*, CEE, Reading

Ekins, P et al (1992) *Wealth Beyond Measure*, Gaia Books, London

(1992) *Environmental Education: A Framework for the Development of a Cross-Curricular Theme in Wales*, Advisory Paper, 17, CCW, Cardiff

Fisher, S and D Hicks (1985) *World Studies 8–13: A Teacher's Handbook*, Oliver & Boyd, Edinburgh

Gibson, T and J Bean (1980) 'Planning for Real and Neighbourhood Change', *Bulletin of Environmental Education*, 109, May

Girardet, H and J Seymour (1987) *Blueprint for a Green Planet*, Dorling Kindersley, London

(1995) *Geography in the National Curriculum*, Department for Education, HMSO, London

Greig, S, G Pike and D Selby (1987) *Earthrights: Education as if the Planet Really Mattered*, WWF–UK, Godalming

Hart, R (1987) 'Children's Participation in Planning and Design: Theory, Research and Practice', in C S Weinstein and T G David (eds) *Spaces for Children*, Plenum Press

Hicks, D (1994) *Educating for the Future: A Practical Classroom Guide*, WWF–UK, Godalming

Hirst, M (ed) (nd) *The Green Detective Series*, Wayland, Hove, UK

McFarlane, C (ed) (1991) *Theme Work: A Global Perspective in the Primary Curriculum in the 90s*, Development Education Centre, Birmingham

Matre, S Van (1990) *Earth Education: A New Beginning*, Institute for Earth Education, Martinsville

Mendes, C (1989) *Fight for the Forest: Chico Mendes in His Own Words*, Latin American Bureau, London

Noble, M (1991) *A Safer World, My World, Exploring the Future*, WWF/Scholastic Publications, Leamington Spa

O'Riordan, T (1994) *Annual Review of Environmental Education*, CEE, Reading

Palmer, J (1995) 'Environmental Thinking in the Early Years: Understanding and Misunderstanding of Concepts Related to Waste Management', *Environmental Education Research*, 1 (1) 35–45

Poulton, P and G Symons (1990) *Eco-School*, WWF–UK, Godalming

— (1993) *People and Their Communities*, WWF–UK, Godalming

Prescott-Allen, R (1991) *Caring for the Earth: A Strategy for Sustainable Living*, IUCN/UNEP/WWF, Gland

Stevens, O (1982) *Children Talking Politics*, Martin Robertson, Oxford

Titman, W (1994) *Special Places; Special People: The Hidden Curriculum of the School Grounds*, WWF–UK, Godalming

Torney, J V (1972) *Middle Childhood and International Education*, Intercom, Centre for War/Peace Studies

Versfeld, R (1989) *Sowing and Harvesting*, Oxfam, Oxford

Webster, K (1989) *Let's Reach Out (Secondary)*, WWF–UK, Godalming

Wright, D (1990/1) *Teaching about the Greenhouse Effect, Annual Review of Environmental Education*, CEE, Reading

Chapter 5 | THE SECONDARY YEARS
Ken Webster

'The difficulty lies, not in the new ideas, but in escaping the old ones, which ramify, for those brought up as most of us have been, into every corner of our minds' (John Maynard Keynes). What Newton started only lately hath the planet undone.

When humankind first saw the planet from space much as the falling apple might have looked at Isaac we knew, unlike the apple, that profound change was under way. A change as profound as any that Isaac could have imagined. We saw the earth whole and dynamic — a system of systems. Newton recognized a machinery of parts. All change at this level is that of perception and meaning first; our intentions and rationalization follow. This much we know from the history of science and Thomas Kuhn (1970) in particular. This much we know from physicists like David Bohm (Bohm and Peat, 1989). Or rather that is the meaning and system we are attracted to in this part of the century. And here within the question of meanings and order lies the root of all our discussions in schools and among colleagues.

Earlier chapters have charted the rise and fall of the modern experiment, yet it has fallen away only partially and everywhere the consequences of a mechanistic, linear, reductionist world view inhabit us, society and our actions. We do not choose our actions, according to Bohm (1995), rather they reflect what the whole thing means to us. In the postmodern world much of it means very little. We are half attached to the idea of material progress, individualism, free choice, getting and spending, a liberal rational thoroughly humanistic scheme, but as we have seen this railway line from the Enlightenment brought us Fordism, the division of labour and product, the substitution of capital for labour, conformism, specialization and global trade. The line broke up leaving behind the struggling engine and, marooned in a carriage of Victorian making, its passengers gasping for air, besieged and increasingly abandoned by the very people it was meant to serve — the school, the secondary school. A modern institution in a post-modern world.

It really is that serious. All the hallmarks of modernism are there in the school: the hierarchy, the fragmentation of function, the standardization of ethos, product, process and outcome. In a modern world of full employment, do-as-I-say jobs and Metroland it sort of worked. Now, with post-modernism's rush and scatter, simultaneous information overload and redundancy, the terminal decline in faith in the modern world and all its institutions isolates the school as some sort of irritant, or as a symbol of what has passed. The desperate traditionalist, sit-up-straight-lad-and-listen revival is evidence of how greatly misunderstood are schools and the forces at work in society today. We have nothing left to offer you, they seem to say, but our myths.

The question then arises what is to be done? Given, and there are always givens, that we look like being obliged to work in such institutions for the interval before truly postmodern educational arrangements emerge into the daylight, we must do something to educate for participation in a post-modern world, and a world faced with achieving ecological and social sustainability (see Chapter 1). Most teachers, or educators, are practical people doing the best they can in often appalling circumstances. Some colleagues, however, do not appear to have escaped the 1950s (tell-us-what-to-teach-and-we'll-teach-it). They take the public service to their heart as the last refuge of the poor in spirit. But, safe or sad to say, they will not be reading this book. God, like the editors of this book, loves a trier.

What is to be done first is to see just how far the secondary curriculum in practice is riddled with modernism and mechanism; the ideas, values, examinations and ethos are all to a greater or lesser extent affected. Once its limitations are recognized an outline of what is new or different or desirable is then possible. From here on the new enters a dialogue with the old, at first extending the vision of the old and eventually superseding it. At this point, or at some time previous to this, it hits a brick wall because the implementation of a radical, essentially postmodern curriculum innovation in a modern institution will only succeed in so far as the institution is not threatened by it; which of course it is, eventually. Witness the fate of many of the Schools Council projects, the 'adjectival' educations of the 1960s and 1970s, initiatives like the Technical and Vocational Education Initiative (TVEI), and the 1988 cross-curricular themes in England and Wales.

It would be too much to say that all these many curriculum developments, spanning a quarter of a century, were similar enough to deal with as a category, but they all appeared to share some features pertinent to the argument. The cross-curricular themes, to take the most recent first, traded on their 'relevance' to a student's life, the importance of exploring values with students and the breaking down of the artificial boundaries of the subject disciplines. They were intended to be process led. Looking again at this mix reveals something of our dynamic world view. First there is a concern for the meanings and connections between things rather than the things themselves. This is the heart of the 'relevance' argument — in translation, 'between me and the world there are a number of meanings. Things matter because they fit a greater or larger pattern which involves me.' The breaking down of the subject boundaries is part of seeing things more holistically and of following those leads from 'me to the world'. Because these features demand participation from students and an enquiry-based approach, knowledge fits in as part of that process of understanding and does not substitute for it.

This is a heady mix and it is little wonder that the guidance the National Curriculum Council published on cross-curricular themes looked confused: stressing process and enquiry but looking like a series of guides to mini subjects, stuffed with content, as though it were trying to please everyone. But in any form cross-curricular themes ran counter to a mainstream tradition where what is learned (the parts) matters most, for it confers status on those who guard this knowledge in the professional elite. This is especially true if the knowledge is the subject of external assessment. As soon as the parts come first we are back in the modern world's mechanistic world view. All of it is reinforced by the fragmentation of the timetable and the school day. Marginalization was the inevitable fate of the themes; if not marginalized they were simply knocked out of court.

Looking back over other initiatives, key criteria like 'relevance', 'process-led', 'enquiry-based', 'values clarification', 'active learning', 'participatory', 'critical awareness', 'cross curricularity' occur time and again. (They are key elements in coping with a 'loose fit' postmodern world.) Cynically, the more of these elements that occurred at one time in an initiative, the less chance it seemed there was of the initiative even scraping along.

But is this fair? Certainly it is not the whole story and many teachers and schools applauded the initiatives, claimed to get on board and indeed there was much good work while the impetus (and the money) was there. But schools as institutions tend to take what they want from the initiative and what they want, it seems, are the unchallenging bits, for example the active learning without the critical awareness and the triumphs of style over content and context. The real initiative goes skidding to the far field.

Whoops, bang! Lost ball. It is because they claimed to put the child first, explore values, meanings and process and, in claiming this, they all implied professional change and ultimately institutional change. In short, they were skewed towards education not schooling. Schools after all school: they are conservative institutions reflecting a vague sense of what society wants. Cross-curricular themes, like other initiatives, were emasculated by the way things are. This may sound trite but 'the way things are' is not a static but a dynamic interplay of vested interest. Change never comes because someone thinks it is rational, but only because the old system is falling apart. 'Every revolution,' as J K Galbraith remarked, 'is the kicking in of a rotten door.' The door is not yet rotten.

This need not mean giving up on an initiative like education for sustainability (EFS). As we have learned in other chapters there are strong and weak sustainability models. The distinction is quite important — one is more 'institution friendly' than the other. The weak sustainability thread is open for emasculation and absorption into the remains of the modern experiment because it accepts the world as it is but in need of fine tuning.

Education for sustainability at its best, however, is not an accommodating quasi-adjectival education but a Janissary education, running up to the ramparts of the Anglo-Saxon, Protestant work ethic walls of modernism because, well, it matters and because those wall are undermined and, er . . . we all deserve something better. Don't we? Education for sustainability in this strong guise comprehensively engages in the emerging new world view. In its weak guise it is suitable for everyday use, even if it sometimes causes indigestion in creaking modern institutions.

The moral is clear and laid out before the story is told. Remember that the theory determines what we observe. To attempt EFS in the secondary curriculum can be a difficult or suicidal task, depending on the circumstances, but as the fault lines of the old order are intellectually clear and getting clearer by the year, time and change are on our side. Our pedagogical 'sacrifice' could make a difference.

What can be done most usefully springs from internalizing the assumptions of a new world view and using these insights to look afresh, quite literally to 'review' our activities. Our activities cover curriculum development, professional development and institutional development. Change in our newly recognized non-linear and chaotic world can and does enter at any and all of these levels and spins off into all the other levels. This is a warning as well as a sign of opportunity, remembering that the inertia of the institution and its modernist outlook will marginalize or constrain radicalism for as long as possible. As a result, what is attempted needs to be as effective as possible.

The most important interfaces in schools and colleges are arguably those between teacher and student and between student and student. The proposal that follows is that for most of us in these years the seeds of an enlightened EFS are best sown at these interfaces. Immediately below is an example of this approach in practice, looking first at the way old ideas are embedded and secondly at how a comprehensive reworking of everyday activities can exemplify an EFS. Of necessity these examples are detailed because, as Keynes noted, the problem is in escaping our old ideas, and it is in the detail of everyday work that the old ideas ramify most.

Into the Secondary Sector: Economics and Business Education

There has been a retreat from pre-16 economics in the face of national curriculum pressures (in England and Wales) and of the growth in a perception that business education is somehow more relevant. This is rather disturbing. Economics is an investigative process, a series of questions about the best use of resources. Used imaginatively it can engage in philosophical deliberation about the purpose of an economic system, about its stakeholders, rewards and values. Business education is a subset of economics; it is economics with the values taken as given and the focus on how a business operates and survives. It is an example of the reductionist, utilitarian, modernist ethos carried to its limits. 'Never mind the values, how do I work this!?' To be fair, until recently, much of the economics taught pre- and post-16 was dry, theoretical, unreflective and pretty conformist. Business education at least dealt with case studies, problem solving and real life (if only based on a narrow vision).

Since business education's ethos is the equivalent of individualism, merely replacing the person with the company, it will come as no surprise to see a diagram like this in a text for business, this time at GNVQ (General National Vocational Qualification).

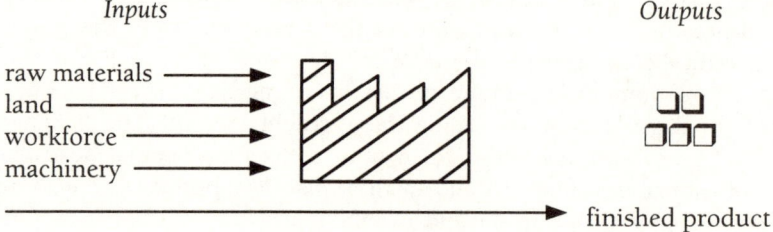

Figure 5.1 The Production Process

This diagram purporting to show the inputs and outputs of a firm was produced in 1994 for a new, supposedly enlightened qualification. What is missing?

The context. Just the whole context!

The book *Functions of Nature* (de Groot, 1992) lists the regulatory functions of the natural environment (Table 5.1). Some of these might apply to the firm perhaps?

There is the social side of the firm to consider as well. Customers, people living locally to the firm, employees and citizenry generally have a stake in any business which is a truly responsible business.

Table 5.1 Functions of the Natural Environment

Regulatory functions

---

protection against harmful cosmic influences
regulation of the local and global energy balance
regulation of the chemical composition of the atmosphere
regulation of the chemical composition of the oceans
regulation of the local and global climate (including water cycle)
regulation of run-off and flood prevention
water catchment and groundwater recharge
prevention of soil erosion and sediment control
formation of topsoil and maintenance of soil fertility
fixation of solar energy and biomass production
storing and recycling of organic matter
storing and recycling of nutrients
storing and recycling of human waste
regulation of biological control mechanisms
maintenance of migration and nursery habitats
maintenance of biological and genetic diversity

The premises of sustainability in its strong mode include the idea that decision-making has to include the social, ethical, environmental and economic for sustainability to have a chance. In terms of economics the 'new economics' has 'two central objectives in its thinking about allocation and distribution: the elimination of poverty and the maintenance of the economy at its optimal ecological size' (Ekins, 1992, pp40–1).

In sustainability's weak mode there is just the 'greening' of business. The same textbook that described the inputs and outputs of the firm (Figure 5.1) also included an assignment to promote and sell a green product!

More businesses are greening themselves. Typical examples are reducing energy and raw materials usage, recycling packaging and industrial wastes or reducing wastes, developing and selling products from sustainable sources.

Most people will applaud firms attempting this change of culture, but the change is effectively one of preserving the existing regimen, based on maximizing production and consumption while allaying fears that this will crack the ecosystem (and continue to contribute to a global trade system that guarantees poverty for the majority). The weak sustainability mode is being embedded in economics and business education, as is environmental education generally appearing in some guise throughout secondary school-ing. In economics its calling cards are phrases such as 'greening business', 'environmental responsibility', 'environmental valuation', 'environmental economics' and 'the environment industry'.

How limited this perspective might be when measured against the demands of a changing world view can be deduced from a worked classroom example, given here in summary but with sufficient detail for the practitioner to understand the development of the learning situation. An adaptation of the famous trade game points up the general preconceptions of economics or business students and the sorts of questions and reflections necessary to penetrate beyond the conventional wisdom.

Box 5.1 *AN EXAMPLE OF DECONSTRUCTING A SCIENCE ACTIVITY IN SEARCH OF 'EFS' OPPORTUNITIES*

Introduction

This is a highly modified production exercise, based on the famous trade game produced by Christian Aid. It has many similarities with production games used in business education. In this context the game is run first to illustrate some of the conventional wisdom of economics: that trade, the division of labour and competition all increase production; that money as a medium of exchange and store of value has a role in this process; that resource-rich and technologically advanced groups tend to dominate a trading system; and that organizational and entrepreneurial skills can affect the outcome or success of the individual or group. In the succeeding stages the game is run to reflect the existence of an ecological base and encourages students to reflect on the difference between needs and wants as well as aspects of social justice.

Classroom Organization

There are up to six groups supplied with resources as below. Each group represents a trading nation. The intention of such groupings is to suggest a system in which resources are unevenly provided. The resources for each group are placed in a large envelope so that the uneven distribution of resources is not apparent when students enter the room. The rules of the game are read out. The instruction is 'make shapes'. The rules indicate that production shapes can be sold to the World Bank (representing worldwide demand). A student is usually assigned the job of World Bank.

Resources

Two sets of each of the following to make enough for six groups:

A	B
1 pair of scissors	*8 sheets of red card*
2 rulers	*2 sheets of green card*
1 compass	*2 'pound notes'*
1 set square	*2 pencils*
1 protractor	*2 sheets of cardboard*
1 sheet of green card	
6 'pound notes'	*C*
4 pencils	*2 sheets of green card*
	4 sheets of red card
	2 'pound notes'

The uneven distribution of resources prompts trading activity.

The game ends after an allotted time. Students are asked to rejoin their group and consider:

■ *whether they thought they were a successful group;*
■ *how they would allocate accumulated cash and resources between themselves; and*
■ *how they would improve their performance if the game were rerun.*

Debriefing

The debriefing has two phases.

■ *Groups say how they felt. The teacher could use questions such as 'How did you get on?' 'How do you feel about what happened?' 'What did you think about the 'x' group?' 'How did you get on with the World Bank?'*
■ *Drawing out some facts and features about the game. On a matrix the teacher asks for starting and finishing positions under the following headings: Cardboard, Green Card, Red Card, Tools, Cash, Part-Finished Shapes, Distribution of gains.*

It is at this point that the teacher begins to probe students' assumptions, intentions and criteria for success. First their criteria for success: the teacher asks groups to describe in what way they felt they were successful and in what way they felt they had failed.

Commonly occurring criteria for success — 'more production', 'more shapes', 'percentage increase in cash', 'getting the upper hand', 'Winning'.

Are there signs of convivial social criteria? Do groups, for example, comment that 'we worked well as a group', 'we told jokes while working', or perhaps 'we were not rushing around all the time', or 'we told jokes instead of working!'

The teacher will be looking for a range of criteria and particularly items that begin to suggest that groups had reflected critically on the game's instruction to 'make shapes'. To what extent had groups asked those most basic of questions: Why make shapes? and Why make so many?

Were groups subordinating themselves to the 'rules of the economy' (that is 'make shapes') or were they bending the economy to their needs? (How many shapes do we need? What are shapes for?) Did they think about this? Was there a momentum to the game? Did groups get drawn into what was clearly a competitive game? What did the shapes represent anyway? How much production was enough? Did groups behave fairly to each other? Was there more cooperation than competition?

Students are asked to consider the colour and the hitherto concealed meaning of the card and the returns to shapes made from each. Did students wonder why there were different colours? Why the cardboard was harder to work and gave fewer returns?

Would knowing that only the red card represented the sustainable product of the land have affected their production systems or trading activities? Would groups have proceeded to use the valuable green card (non-renewable resources) and finally the cardboard (vital environmental functions/environmental capital) even if they had known what this implied?

Would knowing this beforehand have affected a group's decision on trading and production activity? Would it affect the mix of what they made or how many? Why? Or does the cash matter more? Or just 'having more'?

What was the role of technology — the scissors and the protractor especially — did it speed up resource (card) use? Who benefited — and how? What was the effect on price of not having access to this technology. Was this fair? What did this low price encourage? Cheating? Disregard for card use — whatever the colour?

The discussion can move towards a consideration of whether the real world appears closer to the game, despite our knowledge of environmental, social and technological constraints and pressures, than an enlightened position. Attention could also be drawn to the inequitable distribution of wealth within nations, which contrasts (in most cases) with the distribution of income within and between the group at the end of the game. Most students tend to allocate rewards within the group equitably.

Extension

Students could be asked to run the game again. The rules are the same and the instruction is once more to make shapes, except that a minimum of six triangles and one circle shapes are required to maintain the health of the population. Groups have to decide how to trade in the light of what they now know and of recent discussions (for example will they adopt a World Council?).

Summary

And what has this to do with green economics or an economics for sustainability? It should be clear that it mirrors real life dilemmas. While economic success is measured in terms of production and consumption, and largely mediated in money, the system has a bias towards competitive consumption to the extent that the economy is divorced from the environment and social cohesion that sustain it.

Moderating the bias towards conventional economics in lesson structures and processes is a key element in EFS, bringing the social and environmental parts of the total economy back into play as a central part of the lesson.

A follow-up activity to illustrate efforts in this direction is to compare different indicators of wealth and to ask students to decide which indicators are a good measure of a country's development. This data can be gleaned from UN publications such as the Human Development Index, *as well as surveys by government and business publications such as* The Economist. *A sample of such figures is given below. Of course this prompts a number of supplementary questions such as 'What do we mean by being better off?'*

Indicator	Poland	Nepal	Niger	France	China	Brazil
Food intake (calories)	3298	2050	2347	3273	2628	2643
GDP per head ($)	1719	160	359	17004	330	2160
Energy consumption (kg/coal equivalent)	4810	23	53	3710	749	767
Output per agricultural worker	1957	222	283	24743	228	2932
Life expectancy at birth	71.8	52.2	45.5	76.4	70.1	65.6
Adult literacy (%)	96	25.6	28.4	99	73.3	81
Adjusted GDP per capita ($)	4237	920	645	5048	1990	4718
Human development index	0.83	0.17	0.08	0.97	0.56	0.73

Net primary enrolment for girls (%)	n/a	n/a	n/a	100	91	n/a
Access to safe drinking water (%)	98	37	59	100	85	96
Telephones per '000 population	150	n/a	n/a	608	5	84

Into the Secondary Sector: Science

Science, like economics, has been reformed through the promotion of investigative science and the contextualization of science. The contexts are often social, utilitarian concerns: health, science in everyday life, a nod to environment and industry. Content still dominates, as does experimentation. As in economics, the hidden values and assumptions about the way the world works remain largely unexplored.

In a typical topic on water purification and distribution a diagram shows the route from rainfall to reservoir to house and factory and finally the sewage treatment works. Students are asked to purify dirty water experimentally using a variety of filtration techniques and through the addition of aluminium sulphate as a flocculent.

Is there a problem? In a number of in-service sessions run by WWF–UK using this lesson sequence as a stimulus, questions arose among teachers about the science and its contexts, including the environmental. For the publication *Let's Reach Out* (Webster, 1995) some of these questions were translated into an imaginary dialogue between an environmental education coordinator seeking to open discussion about teaching and learning and the teacher using the sequence.

Talking about Water

A dialogue takes place between the practitioner (P) who uses a popular text for 12–13 year olds and the environmental education coordinator in school (EE). Let us imagine they talk plainly: it will save paper. The context is the lesson on water purification and distribution.

EE What is the issue behind the work on water filtration?
P   The answer is obvious — we need clean drinking water.
EE Does filtration clean water?
P   It removes the solids.
EE Does it remove nitrates, chlorinated phenols, heavy metals and so on?
P   No, but this is just a lesson for younger pupils; we do other aspects of water purification later.

EE Like chlorination?

P Yes.

EE What might pupils know as a result?

P That almost all the drinking water we use is cleaned by filtering and treatment to keep bacteria within limits.

EE So if they are asked where clean water comes from will they have images of pumps and filter beds and reservoirs and pipes and remember that a slight taste to the water was from this treatment?

P Well that is a reasonable summary about the UK system. It is how it is.

EE Where will children get the opportunity to ask other questions, such as is this the best way of providing clean water? Why is so much water needing treatment? Why do we use drinking water to throw down the toilet? Is the current system sustainable? Is this system effective? Is water quality good? How do we know? Is it cheap or expensive? What are the alternatives?

P But these are not my department. This is geography or technology or something; besides the national curriculum does not leave me time. The pupils are too young anyway for these questions. You ought to teach more, you would find out.

EE Do you think pupils are entitled to study these other issues?

P Yes, it is not science really, but yes.

EE Leaving aside the role of science here, who is going to do it? Is it your colleagues? Can we be sure that they will?

P Well, we cannot be sure; there isn't time to meet. Is not the NCC supposed to sort these links out? Geography does 'siting reservoirs', I think, and where the main water networks are.

EE Even if the NCC did this, with respect, this does not address any of the key questions about the choices, environmental costs and benefits and issues surrounding clean water.

P It is sad, but is this my problem? Look I am trying to do my job, trying to do the best for my pupils. I think we cover the idea that water needs to be clean.

EE OK. Have you thought that there may be a way of covering your science experiments and so forth and still make some of these connections? And have a good lesson?

P Like Science and Technology in Society (SATIS) units, we do some of those, have done for a few years, they are what I was going to mention. They are the contextualization of science and the pupils do enjoy them. We are all used to this approach.

EE Yes, the pupils often find these units useful and they are flexible in use but, forgive me, they are science with frills. In the energy material for example, asking whether oil or coal or nuclear is cheaper, and harping on the money side or comparing wind power with other forms of generating capacity, but not asking whether we really need more generating capacity anyway and, well, the whole sustainable development thing is buried. Is not the main issue with energy to do with what task we need to undertake and how this can be done with lowest energy use and maximum access to all people?

P   But isn't the reality that we must let pupils compare generating options given that demand for electricity is rising and we need to maintain a standard of living? And it is in the programmes of study.

EE   Fair enough, if you believe that the future can be like today, or at least similar (more and more of everything), and if you do not mind leaving the question of what it means to be better off to one side.

P   This is totally unfair. You seem to be undermining my whole syllabus. We have good lessons, excellent results, we meet the needs of the statutory orders and I have the full support of the school. We do what we can. We do not have to take up this extreme environmentalism.

Quite right! Although fictional and exaggerated to the extent that neither party was being particularly circumspect it is possible to have sympathy with both parties.

The Wider Context

Although the discussion in this chapter has focused on little more than one or two lessons in each of two subjects, the outlines of the EFS debate should, however, be clear. It is developing critical faculties and exploring alternatives in the context of all forms of resource use, systems and technologies encountered via the curriculum. It is a complex, subtle process. It is something all teachers can participate in at the secondary level.

Little has been said about a number of other entry points for change in schools and colleges through the institution, community pressure and curriculum design. There is a greater development of this potential in a number of sections in *Reaching Out* (Huckle et al, 1995) and in *Let's Reach Out* (Webster, 1995), but for much of the time discussion gets little further than a weak sustainability mode: greening the school and curriculum rather than considering that the institution itself is a major barrier to an enlightened EFS. Deep down the whole sustainability 'thing' has a strong grassroots feel and intention and is in the long term not an adjustment to the modern experiment but a superseding of it.

Devolution and empowerment seem to be buzz words. Behind the buzz is something useful. Trusting teachers (and students?) cooperatively to review their work and intentions, to provide them with time and space to reflect and experiment with sustainability is a very powerful strategy. Professional development needs to be allowed progressively to influence other areas.

Some chance? Even if, for the time being, the institution resists change, a truly sustainable education system must eventually emerge as part of a pluralistic, varied, dare I say, postmodern schooling and education mix. The best of it will derive from the commitment and creativity of enlightened teachers and students as the greater forces at work in the postmodern world — the information revolution, fragmentation of work and leisure, the decline of middle management and the tax base which supports the formal welfare state — erode the *raison d'être* and the financial underpinning of the hierarchical, inefficient nine-to-four secondary institution. What shape this will take is not at all clear, but it will happen.

Perhaps it is time to attempt a summary. An attempt to come to terms positively with the rise of postmodernism brings new assumptions and modes of working. No clear sense of the future is emerging.

Education for sustainability shares some of the rather amorphous collection of 'green' ideas that could become the basis of a new world view. In its weak mode it is environmental education one stage on — looking at largely technological adjustments to how society works. In its strong mode it not only encourages student participation, as part of a democratic devolved decision-making ethos, it promotes critical awareness through enquiry processes and it questions the assumptions of the modern interpretation as revealed in subject disciplines (and schools) before offering, tentatively, some new models. It differs from other progressive educational offerings in making the link with new philosophical and economic models. It also has implications for schools as institutions and may contribute to the thinking behind new forms of educational arrangement that are more in tune with ecological principles and that are devolved, pluralistic and open.

References

Bohm, D (1980) *Wholeness and the Implicate Order*, Routledge & Kegan Paul, London

Bohm, D and Peat, F D (1989) *Science, Order and Creativity*, Ark, London

Ekins, P (1992) *Wealth Beyond Measure*, Gaia Books, London

Groof, R S de (1992) *Functions of Nature*, Wolters-Noordhoff, Groningen

Huckle, J, E Allen, P Edwards, G Symons and K Webster (1995) *Reaching Out: Education for Sustainability*, WWF Education Department, Godalming

Kuhn, T S (1994) *Theory of Scientific Revolutions*, University of Chicago Press, Chicago

Webster, K (1995) *Let's Reach Out: A Survivor's Guide for Coordinators of Environmental Education in Secondary Schools*, WWF Education Department, Godalming

Chapter 6 | GREENING the UNIVERSITY
Tony Alabaster &
Derek Blair

In this chapter we seek to encourage a further productive phase of 'greening' in UK institutions of further and higher education (FHE) as they approach the next millennium — an environmental landmark, which has perhaps been given extravagant expectations through Agenda 21. The need to galvanize and mobilize FHE is argued because the early waves and momentum of greening are threatened by the increasingly competitive and resource-constrained climate in which institutions are operating. Paradoxically, this has occurred at a time when individual and collective achievements have created the opportunity for environmental good practice to yield substantial benefits.

The term greening is commonly used to describe the integration of environmental perspectives into the corporate work of the FHE sector. It is essentially a phenomenon of the 1990s, for although its roots can be traced back into the 1960s, it was the publication of national statements between 1990 and 1993 that promoted the potential of corporate responses and individual responsibilities. Surprisingly, the FHE sector's response on greening postdate those in some other sectors (for example industry) and throw into question how far FHE has provided leadership in this trend as their advocates would presumably prefer. The ultimate aim of greening, to inculcate a natural 'culture' of environmental responsibility in FHE institutions, is still for the future, but tremendous progress has been made in the last ten years.

An early harbinger of greening in the FHE sector was the 1991 Scottish Enterprise/Scottish Environmental Education Council/WWF–UK initiative which commissioned an investigation into, and report on:

- the requirements of commerce and industry for environmental competence from prospective graduate employees;
- the role of professional bodies in emphasizing an environmental focus in university education for professional entrants; and
- the extent to which FHE prospectuses declared the environmental elements of their courses.

A further stimulus was two reports commissioned by the Committee of Directors of Polytechnics (CDP), one of which addressed institutional practice (Ali-Khan, 1990) the second of which focused on the curriculum (Ali-Khan, 1991). Unfortunately, they were restricted to the then polytechnic sector. Although the binary divide was abolished in 1993, 'older' universities have remained under-represented in responses to the environmental agenda.

A more significant step was the government's creation of an expert committee on environmental education in FHE. This met for 18 months and published *Environmental Responsibility: An Agenda for Further and Higher Education* in 1993 (DfE, 1993). The Toyne Report, as it is commonly called, was an authoritative and thoroughly disseminated document that partially redressed the previous under-representation of older universities. It gave greening a wider base and more official credibility. Although the new universities have invested more energy and priority to this agenda of environmental responsibility some of the older universities are leaders.

In old or new universities, however, greening was often heavily dependent on the role of individual champions. In some institutions these were ordinary academic staff associated with environmental courses who were becoming more and more uneasy at the disparity between what they were teaching and what was being practised throughout their campuses. Elsewhere, they were academic staff from other disciplines (for example sociology, biology, history, architecture, philosophy, engineering, information technology (IT), economics, marine studies), responding to the need to address emerging environmental professions. In a few institutions, the champions were the senior managers. At Edinburgh University, for example, Sir David Smith the principal inspired their drive towards improved environmental responsibility by building on the foundations laid by C H Waddington, a member of the Club of Rome. Sir David argued for an integrated environmental initiative; a feature which was maintained by the late Professor Wilson, senior vice principal of the university, and reflected in subsequent management.

However, large parts of FHE remain untouched by national greening initiatives, and there is still no national system to monitor progress. That is why, in response to a parliamentary question (Hansard, 1995), the government has said a review of how far the Toyne Report recommendations have been implemented will be undertaken in 1995/6. This review will probably reveal endemic and major variations between and within institutions.

The most reliable national information to date (Willis, 1994) reveals that, of 58 out of 86 FHE institutions that responded to a questionnaire, 26 per cent had established a general environmental policy, 22 per cent a curriculum policy, but only 5 per cent employed individuals to work on environmental issues (see Table 6.1); though clearly these data must be viewed with care.

Table 6.1 Survey of Environmental Sustainability in
Higher Education Institutes

Question: Has your institution established or undertaken any of the following?	Number of Yes answers	(%) Total responses
1. An environmental working party or committee?	25	43
2. A person employed to work on environmental issues?	13	22
3. A general environmental policy or statement?	15	26
4. A curriculum policy, statement or progress towards a range of environmental courses?	3	5
5. A comprehensive recycling scheme?	30	52
6. Energy efficiency measures or policy?	35	60
7. An environmental awareness-raising scheme?	14	24
8. A transport policy	5	9
9. An environmental purchasing policy?	9	16
10. An environmental audit?	14	24

Source: Willis (1994).

Corporate Environmental Responsibility

Corporate environmental responsibility in the FHE sector can be characterized by a range of factors and pressures shown in Figure 6.1.

Legal Compliance For many institutions the most immediate stimulus (and potentially threatening factor) is related to the raft of environmental legislation and the need locally and nationally to be able to demonstrate compliance. Legal pressures will not diminish, for European-led environmental legislation is moving at least as fast as British legislation and the FHE sector will benefit from being proactive in that context.

However, few UK universities and colleges can be confident that they record, assess and monitor their risk liabilities in, for example, their chemical and toxic waste disposal, as required under the Environmental

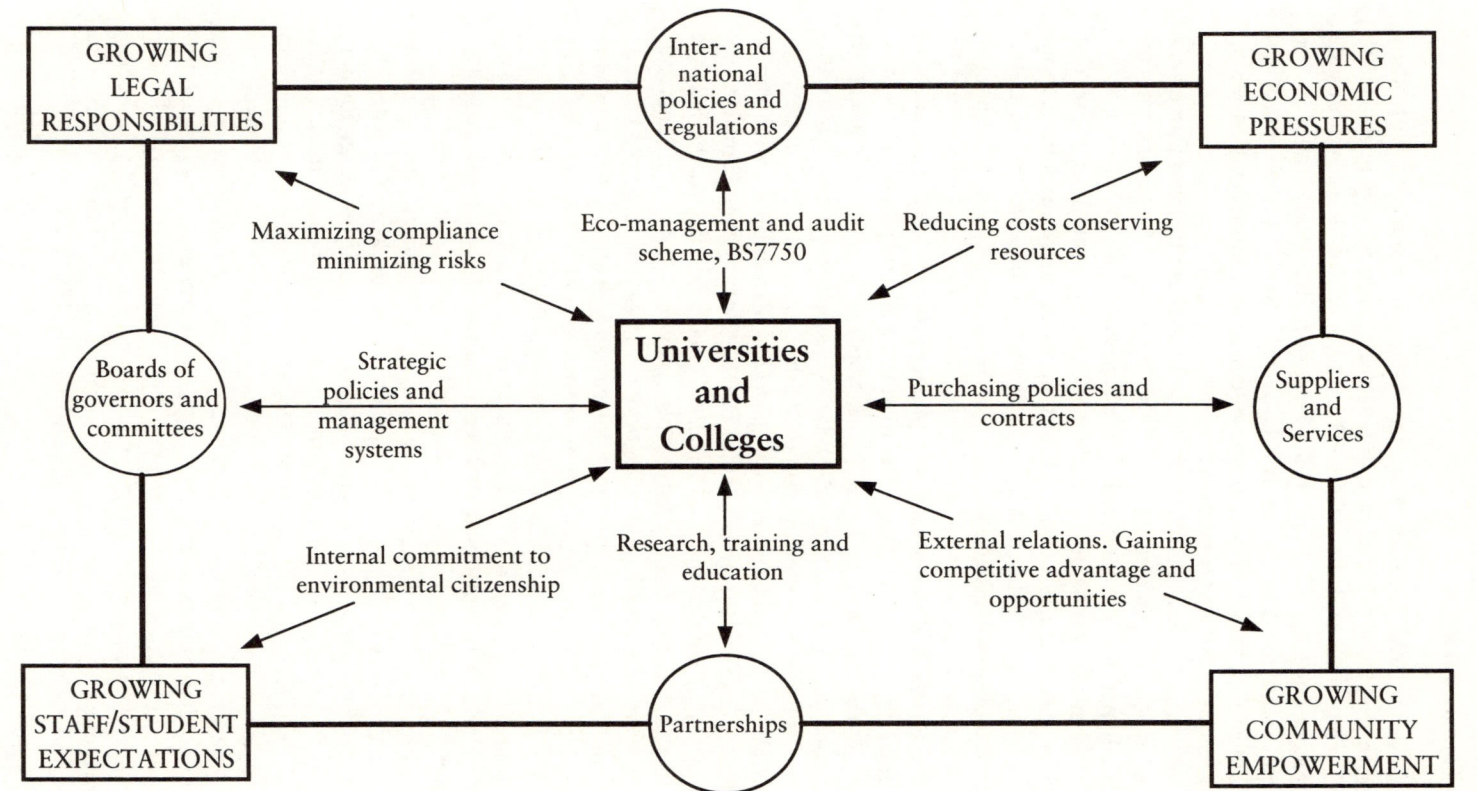

Figure 6.1 *Context of Corporate Environmental Responsibility within the Education Sector*

Protection Act (1990). Institutions may be more confident with their responses to the 1994 Control of Substances Hazardous to Human Health (COSHH) regulations and the 1974 Health and Safety at Work Act, despite the first recent court case in June 1995. However, they cannot afford to be complacent about the availability, reliability and quality of environmental information and data, all of which are essential to sound decision-taking and good environmental management.

The existence of a long-established national and institutional framework for health and safety explains why some university environmental policies have been aligned in that direction. The advantage of this approach is that the environmental agenda is officially and readily assimilated. The disadvantage is that it excludes wider components of environmental responsibility related to sustainable development, which, unlike health and safety, are not driven only by legislation.

Economic Savings Unlike the legal compliance issue which is a threat, here is a real opportunity. Many universities own large and disparate estates with buildings of obsolete and poor design. A massive £2 billion is spent on buildings each year (de la Cour, 1994). Even though only 1 per cent of this is on new buildings, there are some highly instructive and innovative architectural designs and approaches employed, for example Cheltenham & Gloucester College of Higher Education (CHE), Nottingham Trent University, University of Sunderland and Linacre College, Oxford. At the latter, a new residential block constructed to give environmental considerations priority at every phase will yield reductions of 35 per cent, 25 per cent, 31 per cent, and 36 per cent respectively for gas and electricity consumption, CO_2 emissions and water consumption compared with a standard building (Smythe, 1993). Department of the Environment (1993) guidelines exist to help FHE institutions to reduce an approximate 3 per cent of the total expenditure which is consumed in energy, producing an estimated three million tonnes of carbon dioxide per annum.

Universities that have systematically and seriously developed an energy conservation strategy claim persuasive levels of savings. York estimates efficiency gains of 40 per cent through changing the use of buildings to more efficient times, insulation, different boilers and electronic controls. Strathclyde believes it has achieved nearly 50 per cent savings on its investment in energy efficiency. Perhaps the university that has done most to pioneer and promote energy conservation is Edinburgh. Despite increases in its estate, growth in student numbers and boasting 160 buildings, energy consumption has actually fallen by 75 per cent, mostly in recent years with the establishment of a corporate energy management strategy led by an energy and environment group and a strong teaching and research tradition in buildings and architecture (Somerville and Talbot, 1991).

The scope for other substantial economic savings in other sectors of university management is considerable. Water costs increased by as much as a third in a typical university between 1993 and 1994. Paper consumption, partly through new teaching and learning methods, partly through bureaucracy, doubled in another university between 1991 and 1995. The technology exists to eliminate or reduce the need for memos and paper but the paper appetite of the FHE sector remains voracious. Few topics encapsulate as many environmental complexities and advantages as paper. Changing technology has produced confusion and conflict on the pros and cons of recycled paper, especially in relation to the apparent direct cost differentials between 'virgin' and 100 per cent chlorine-free recycled paper. Environmentally responsible institutions should be able to select the least damaging paper that meets operational requirements. The paper industry and related consultancies are fully capable of clearing up the confusion about the definition of recycled. No university subscribing to environmental responsibility can avoid using some sort of recycled paper if it wants to retain its credibility.

Savings in consumables and services bought into a university can be helped by tighter standards and controls on the purchasing and contractual criteria negotiated and applied to external suppliers and contractors. The University of Northumbria's approach is in accordance with the European Union Eco-label Award Scheme adopted in March 1992 to assess the environmental pedigree of products. At Manchester Metropolitan University a broad range of purchasing policy recommendations have been tabled to improve current and future performance. Leeds Metropolitan University has begun a dialogue with suppliers of personal computers based around a set of specific questions that interrogate the suppliers about their environmental standards and record. Green purchasing in the Leeds mode was pioneered outside FHE, especially in businesses and via local authorities under the aegis of the Association of Metropolitan Authorities (AMA). Universities can, for example, do worse than learn from Leeds and Sheffield City Councils, both of which are leaders in the greening of purchasing policies, and from some American universities.

'Social' Considerations The third encouragement for the FHE sector to green itself is a qualitative one compared to the legal and economic justifications. It should exhibit tangible signs that it is fulfilling its role as a sector with a deep and permanent sense of social responsibility to its own workforce, the local region in which it is situated and to the (inter)national community. So far, we have seen that the record of universities and colleges for leading the trend towards greater environmental responsibility is modest. Now that the philosophical basis of greening has been legitimized by the principles and practices of sustainable development, there is a greater acceptance to widen what was hitherto seen as a narrow interpretation of the environment to embrace issues of social justice and equity.

Universities now enjoy partnerships with local authorities, Technical and Educational Councils (TECs), enterprise agencies, statutory bodies and NGOs in exploring responses to the 1996 target date for Local Agenda 21 (LA21). In Nottingham, the universities are only two out of thirty partners tackling environmental issues through a city-wide partnership. In the Leeds Business Forum, partnerships are directed at small- and medium-sized enterprises (SMEs) and economic regeneration, and environmental responsibility is integrated.

Direct interuniversity links are rare. UK FHE institutions seem to have stronger affinities to work with overseas partners on research and educational projects than with their competing and competitive neighbours. However, new consortia are demonstrating the benefits of closer working relationships as in the Northern Environmental Network in northeast England. The Economic & Social Research Council (ESRC) interdisciplinary environmental research programme encourages universities to pool their resources and expertise in collaborative projects. The outputs of this £2 million funding have still to be evaluated, but progressively the research underpinnings for environmental responsibility are being strengthened.

Workforce Expectations The growing and increasingly informed expectations of staff and students in the FHE sector is a fourth key factor in environmental responsibility. As the portfolio of environmental courses expanded in the 1970s, new schools and faculties of environment, environmental studies and environmental management evolved. The disparity between what was taught in these curricula and what was practised in the institution became more obvious and questionable. The more perceptive and challenging students began to query the mismatch between theory and practice, as did individual pioneering green lecturers. But there was no overall and explicit culture of environmental responsibility. Through the 1980s environmental courses proliferated; public concern fanned by extensive and dramatic media coverage and political acceptance of the environment grew and university management, especially in the estates departments, was demonstrating massive savings through energy conservation. The publication of the CDP and Toyne reports in the 1990s marked the acceptance of environmental responsibility into mainstream senior management as sufficiently important to be allocated top-level responsibility. Was this merely a response to insure against compliance and to gain savings? Was it a cosmetic response to demonstrate a change in corporate image and responsibility? Is it the beginning of a culture change?

In truth, it does not matter which interpretation is correct. What began to be spawned were the now almost universal mission and environmental policy statements to reflect new environmental responsibilities and to satisfy the fashion of new management orthodoxies. While a survey of institutional environmental policy statements reveals variations in detail and depth, a lot of duplicative energy has been expended. Environmental policy officers, senior directorate and others have been busy rediscovering the same environmental wheel.

Nowadays, there are very few universities that do not claim some sort of corporate statement or policy advocating a commitment to improving institutional practices, continued development and promotion of environmental responsibility. Given the theoretical complexity, rarely is an institutional policy expressed explicitly in terms of sustainable development, even though the role of education in the transition to sustainability may be implied. However, many institutions have moved on to translating policy and word into everyday management practice. A few bold institutions, for example Strathclyde University (McDonach et al, 1994), are exploring and committing themselves to the formal British Standard (BS) 7750 environmental management system. Those who have committed themselves already to the quality standard BS5750 and total quality management may find the environmental standard justifiable. It will certainly produce a tight controlling and regulating mechanism in dealing with external suppliers and directly and proactively address the management processes embodied in Figure 6.1. But will the time spent be worth it?

FHE institutions are notoriously slow compared to industry to establish and pioneer formal management systems and related mechanisms. Environmental audits have been undertaken by a number of institutions, including Leeds Metropolitan, York, Liverpool John Moores, Sunderland and Central Lancashire (Merritt, 1993). In most cases these audits have been undertaken internally by staff and/or students and tend to focus on predictable sector areas, for example energy consumption, purchasing policy, waste minimization and the built environment. Over and over again the information returns from even fairly basic, small-scale environmental audits is extremely high in comparison with their expense.

But how are performance and progress measured and monitored? Voluntary environmental reporting is an emerging trend in industry and again the FHE sector lags. It is no longer enough to be at the forefront merely with an environmental mission statement and/or policy or committee. An institution should be seen to be implementing effective environmental management systems, monitoring progress and making the information transparent and publicly available.

A pilot project to examine how environmental policies and activities perform in individual FHE institutions is currently under way. Funded by the WWF–UK and planned for completion in July 1995, the project uses four universities and colleges — Edinburgh, Liverpool John Moores, Sunderland and the Surrey Institute of Art & Design. The task is to collect and present environmental information on a CD-ROM database (ECCTIS 2000). The ECCTIS initiative contributes to the integrative model in Figure 6.2 as it can provide staff and students with 'real world' information, which helps to reinforce commitment to their own institution. It increases the potential for better environmental management and has the knock-on benefits of, for example, understanding processes better, reducing costs, and updating skills and resources. Furthermore, the University of Sunderland is also looking at the Internet in terms of the ideal global environmental information and communication system, adapting the format from ECCTIS 2000. The Internet has the added advantage of rapid feedback, including relevant E-mail addresses to contact. In this way the report is not only informative but can easily be updated, is available to a larger number of people and helps to provide a good indication of the process and quality of management internally and externally.

The potential of students as part of the workforce contribution to the total future of environmental responsibility in an institution and nationally is still not fully realized. Apart from occasional important instances, environmental progress in FHE is dominantly centred on top-down management-led change. This needs to be complemented by a bottom-up student contribution. It is surprising that students have not been included as fully as might have been expected. The National Union of Students presented a significant contribution to the government's expert committee in 1992. Where students and senior management combine, a natural and powerful force for change is created. Also, to inculcate a sense of ownership and empowerment, students need to be engaged fully in the process of environmental change; otherwise policies and initiatives meet resistance and apathy and no culture change will result.

There are good and clear case examples of change led by students: Cheltenham & Gloucester CHE Student Community Action and the students' union, supported by Enterprise in Higher Education funds, produced a *Green Guide* to the campus. Bradford's union has done the same, covering aspects of recycling, banking, consumerism and energy use. Manchester University's union carried out an environmental audit as early as four years ago. The London School of Economics' students union is completing an environmental audit; its results will be known soon. Nottingham Trent's union recently gained recognition as the 'greenest' student union in a Cooperative Bank competition.

In 1993/4, the Cooperative Bank launched a competition for students' unions entitled 'How Green is Your Union?' Since then, with the launch of the Cooperative Bank's ethical and environmental policy and a student bank account package, the Lloyds and Midland Boycott (LAMB) campaign has gathered apace throughout the student community, with many student unions moving accounts. In March 1995, NUS Services Ltd (NUSSL), the trading arm of the NUS, moved to the Cooperative Bank in line with its ethical and environmental responsibilities. And NUSSL, through a sub-committee of its board, the Ethical & Environmental Committee, has promoted greener products to union shops and bars throughout the country.

In May 1995, University of East Anglia students organized a full-day conference for staff, students and local people on making their university a green institution. In July 1995, Community Environmental Education Developments (CEED) convened a national conference on 'Environmental Responsibility of Students in the UK' with the support of the NUS, WWF–UK and the Cooperative Bank. CEED is a student-run charity and has an impressive track record in developing environmental short courses, urban nature spaces, school projects, green radio plays and youth exchanges. The conference, aimed at students, student unions and societies, has produced a Student Environmental Declaration for a Sustainable Future to parallel the Talloires Declaration for Vice Chancellors and University Presidents.

The student declaration recognizes the alarming scale and rate of global environmental degradation and recognizes that students have a vital role to play in four key areas:

■ as learners, education enables all individuals to make informed decisions about their responsibilities toward their environment and community;
■ as consumers, students have significant purchasing power and as such can have a considerable influence on the behaviour of producers and suppliers of both products and of general and financial services;
■ as citizens, we will undertake to be proactive in coming together as a responsive global community through common environmental policy initiatives; and
■ as members of student organizations, we have power to effect change through our own activities and the activities of those with whom we interact.

The student declaration then sets out necessary steps through a plan of action involving staff and students to achieve such aims (copies of the full text are available from the CEED at the University of Sunderland, School of the Environment).

Greening the Curriculum The critical role of environmental education in producing environmentally responsible students and citizens in the work-place and elsewhere is acknowledged at all levels, and in both formal and non-formal education. The grand words and sentiments at Stockholm (1972), Tbilisi (1977), and Rio de Janeiro (1992) and scores of national conferences are all very similar, calling for interdisciplinary, life-long environmental learning and responsibility.

In the UK the white paper *This Common Inheritance* (DoE, 1990) calls for environmental concerns to be included in science, engineering and other courses. The Toyne Report is the most comprehensive statement on the importance of providing a wide range of courses to promote personal, social and occupational responsibility. A parallel national ten-year strategy of environmental education in Scotland entitled *Learning for Life* (Scottish Office, 1993, p101) has been widely acclaimed. *Sustainable Development: The UK Strategy* (DoE, 1994) includes a chapter (Chapter 32) specifically on FHE, as well as relating environmental education and training in others as and where appropriate. It is more difficult to find any specific initiatives that central government has developed to reflect its verbal exhortations. The first report of the British government's panel on sustainable development (DoE, 1995) finds the individual FHE institutional response to strategies for environmental education 'slow and patchy'.

The emergence of specialist and generalist environmental courses in response to growing public concern occurred in the late 1960s and early 1970s, both in the university sector (for example East Anglia) and in the then polytechnic sector (for example Plymouth). A parallel development took place in North America and in Europe (CERI, 1973). In this first wave of FHE courses in the UK, students applying (about 800) and enrolling (400) were small (Cousen and O'Sullivan, 1984) in contrast to those for traditional disciplines — a reflection of the fact that the new A level in environmental science was a minnow alongside long-established subjects like geography and biology.

Even by 1980 there were still fewer than ten universities and a similar number of polytechnics in England and Wales offering full interdisciplinary environmental degrees; and some of those were closely allied to subjects like geography and chemistry. Academics who called themselves environmentalists first, rather than subject specialists, were rare. The emerging environmental field experienced tensions between traditional departments, with promotion and resources weighted to the latter. Interdisciplinary environmental study was often inter-faculty and struggled with its distinctive identity. Questions were often raised about its core content (Clayton, 1976) and this issue is still not resolved. Before the coining of sustainable development, the philosophical and methodological underpinnings of environmentalism were not widely understood, although O'Riordan (1981, p409) and Pepper (1989, p246) did much to help rectify this gap.

The second wave of environmental courses in the 1980s confirmed that the environment was not a passing phase. Indeed, the recruitment potential helped to persuade management and reluctant academics that environmental courses could not be marginalized any longer. The acceptance of the environmental agenda in other sectors of society also helped to legitimize environmental education in FHE.

By 1990 student demand for environmental courses had risen to 11,000 applications, of which some 1600 enrolled in universities or, more usually, polytechnics. Indeed, while it is difficult to say exactly how many students are now on environmental courses in the UK, statistics for 1992/3 suggest around 12,000. As the Toyne Report notes, this was a period of growing diversity and confusion with a proliferation of environmental course titles (see Table 6.2).

Table 6.2 Growth in Numbers of Environmental Degree Courses, 1988–92

Course Title of First Degrees	Number of Institutions offering courses	
	1988	*1992*
Environmental Subjects	20	40
Environmental Health	5	9
Environmental Management Technology	2	22
Environmental Science(s)	13	26
Environmental Studies	8	9
Total	48	106

Source: Department for Education (1993, p36).

The doubling of degree courses meant that in one form or another environmental education was available at every FHE institution in the UK by about 1990. The similar emergence of environmental diplomas, certificates, Business and Technical Education Council (BTEC) qualifications in the FE sector, and the growing partnerships between and within FHE institutions completed the coverage.

A third wave emerged in the early 1990s when environmental educators began to assert the value and need for cross-curricular greening (Ali-Khan, 1991; DfE, 1993). The desirability of ensuring that all students should possess environmental education and training was advocated internationally (CONNECT, 1991). The Toyne Report made a similar plea for the UK observing that cross-curricular greening is poorly developed; which is not surprising given the controversy that has been fought in the national curriculum over the role of environmental education.

The Council for Environmental Education (CEE) has been consistent and active in its support of cross-curricular greening at all levels. Simultaneous with the government's Expert Committee on Environmental Responsibility it persuaded the DfE to sponsor 11 national seminars, mostly in the southern half of England and in new universities. In partnership with the WWF–UK these seminars have been published mainly for an academic audience (Richardson and Ali-Khan, 1995). While they are in places duplicative, and only modestly achieve their business aims under their title *Education and Training for Business and the Environment*, the booklets contain valuable theoretical and practical case studies. Some reveal the old conceptual and theoretical cul-de-sacs of 20 years ago and in places the debates reflect the narrow disciplinary paradigms and perspectives of the participants.

Academic staff are often ideologically resistant to curriculum changes that emanate from outside the bounds of their discipline. Greening is yet another initiative to accommodate in a workplace that has been flooded with others and is subject to major changes in terms of teaching and learning, structures and institutional reforms. Most academics were trained in disciplines before the interdisciplinary environmental agenda assumed such importance. Lack of staff confidence, time and training are real stumbling blocks to greening any curriculum. Perhaps the solutions to these problems can be derived from other initiatives, for example IT, targeted staff development, updating courses, time allocation, funding and the legitimizing of research in this field. Initiatives such as these are still relatively scarce for greening the curriculum, although the Greening of Higher Education Council's seminars incorporating areas such as history, biology, economics and education have brought together specialists who have greened their own curriculum to explain to others what they have done. In this respect the seminars are unique and deserve a wider audience.

If, as informed environmentalists believe, a more environmentally literate workforce and citizenry is urgently required (Boxer, 1995), then theoretical discussion of greening may delay the practical process. Does it matter if greening is *laissez-faire*, incremental and variable? Clearly some academic areas have varying propensities to 'green' and 'be greened'. There is no need to be prescriptive on grounds of political correctness. What is needed is a dilution of disciplinary elitism and autonomy and a continued move towards serving the real needs of society rather than arid theory.

So far greening of the curriculum across disciplines has been modest and, despite the liberalization of modular schemes, only a small number of students have benefited. Progress and coherence rest on the commitment and strategies of FHE institutions and their staff to build upon the good practices contained in the CEE series and elsewhere.

Cross-curricular greening is of course only part of the whole institutional response to environmental concerns. Developing an institution's curriculum is neither credible nor acceptable unless institutional practices subscribe to the basic ingredients of sustainability in other respects. If greening is not just an intellectual exercise but a real cultural change, it is important to know how to integrate these strands symbiotically.

Integrated, Interdependent Components of Environmental Responsibility: A Case Study

Key ingredients of the integrated approach are shown schematically in Figure 6.2 and include students, staff, the formal curriculum and the non-formal curriculum. Their interdependence can be illustrated using the University of Sunderland as a case study.

Students have been particularly prominent and active. Since 1990, students reading for a degree in environmental studies have filled top executive roles in the student union, thereby formally and informally influencing the evolution of corporate policies. The July 1995 national conference on the 'Environmental Role of Students' organized by the university's own student-based environmental organization CEED sought to share this experience and draw upon others. As in other universities, student audits have contributed to the efforts of estate managers, the directorate and academic staff in creating and refining internal environmental policies and practices.

Since 1993/4 an explicit element of the University Staff Development Programme has addressed environmental responsibility issues in the way the Toyne Report recommended. Personnel attended the innovative Tufts Environmental Literacy Institute (TELI) courses and adapted the best elements of this American model to local needs. Furthermore, the programme was extended in 1994/5 to include specialist sessions for senior managers, technicians, academics and all new staff. Representatives of the university's workforce meet on a monthly basis to address systematically the institution's environmental policy and agenda. Appropriately termed the Environmental Practices Group, as with Edinburgh, its emphasis is on initiating university-wide improvements in environmental performance.

Teaching and research are important formal curriculum elements of the institutional response to environmental responsibility. The environmental studies degree, one of the oldest and largest interdisciplinary degrees in the country, is now further supported by a more recently expanded portfolio of environmental programmes within the School of the Environment, which includes, at undergraduate level, environmental technology, environmental engineering, environmental geology and environmental biology and, at postgraduate level, wastes management and environmental management. Over 1000 students study environmental programmes and modules, mostly but not entirely led by the School of the Environment.

In the research arena, the university through its environmental policy

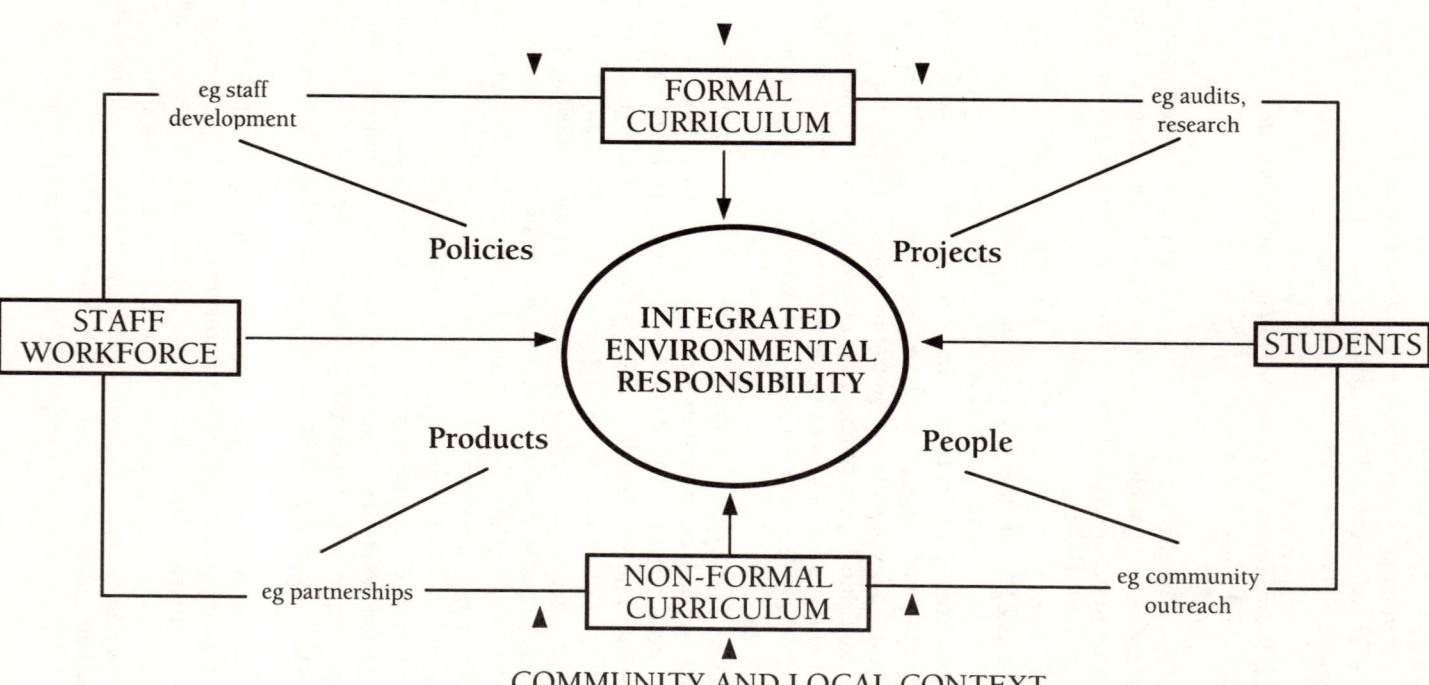

Figure 6.2 *University of Sunderland Integrated Model of Environmental Responsibility*

statement is committed to 'multidisciplinary and interdisciplinary environmental research projects' and actively supports a multiplicity of research studentships and consultancies complemented by local and regional partnerships.

The non-formal or outreach component of Figure 6.2 is increasingly becoming an important element at the University of Sunderland. Perhaps one of the most innovative and successful projects was a 1994 pilot programme of environmental education and vocational training for unemployed people on Wearside, funded by the European Social Fund and delivered by the University of Sunderland and CEED members. CEED subsequently gained accreditation from the Tyneside Open College Federation and unconditional approval as a National Vocational Qualification (NVQ) assessment centre and has now linked the delivery and development of its programmes to the portfolios of local FE colleges. This has created what is probably a unique student-based, nationally accredited community outreach programme in environmental citizenship. The relevance of this student experience to other countries is being piloted under a Trans-European Mobility Programme for University Studies (TEMPUS) youth project in Poland.

Learning from International Experience

The famous environmental slogan 'think globally, act locally' is apt for universities that internationally share similar challenges and opportunities (CONNECT, 1991). COPERNICUS (Cooperation Programme in Europe for Research on Nature and Industry through Coordinated University Studies), established in 1993 with a secretariat in Switzerland, claims 300 signatories on its charter on sustainable development. The Talloires Declaration is an American (Tufts University, Boston) originated charter with a similar number of signatories but dispersed globally. Paragraph 24 of the *British Government Panel on Sustainable Development, First Report* (DoE, 1995) recommends that UK universities subscribe to the Talloires Declaration in moving towards an environmentally sustainable future. By 1995, three universities had signed, Sunderland, Liverpool John Moores and Lancaster, plus the WWF-UK, the Royal Society of Arts (RSA) and Monkwearmouth FE College. In signing the Talloires Declaration, chief executives, principals or their nominees commit their institutions to ten key principles. The success of this top-down pledge depends on how it is translated into institutional policy and practice. For that, green champions are essential so that the ideal of a culture of environmental responsibility is nurtured.

The declaration is also consistent with, but can only complement, other specific but environmentally related networks such as UETP-EEE (University Enterprise Training Partnership in Environmental Engineering

Education) and the AUDES (Association of University Departments of Environmental Science). Furthermore, the support of the environmental agenda in the European Union continues. The Council and Ministers of Education's resolution (88/C/177/03) and conclusions (92/C/151/02) prove that the cooperation of FHE with partners across the European Union to address environmental citizenship, environmental education and networking is funded until at least 1996 (Schoof, 1993). There is much to be done in generating a university-wide response to environmental responsibility issues in the average European university.

The Way Forward

FHE institutions should be centres of innovation and leadership in how to improve environmental responsibility. Many are still struggling to green themselves and to establish a natural culture of environmental responsibility, especially in the current economic climate when expansion, innovation and proactive stances are more problematic.

Greening is not, however, self-indulgent. It is based on the assertion that FHE — its staff, students and activities — contribute towards environmental problems locally and globally. Cynics and sceptics struggle with this grandiose issue and are reluctant to accept unquestionably any agenda that smacks of political correctness.

On the contrary, environmental responsibility in FHE seeks to encourage flexible and cooperative initiatives harnessing all the ingredients noted in Figure 6.2 and the experiences that have accumulated over the last 25 years. The ultimate goal is a culture of environmental responsibility, naturally embedded in institutional policies and practices and through the workforce. Only then will greening be self-sustaining. As such, greening invokes value systems. Each institution recognizes that its own internal conflict involves senior management attempting both to respond to the manipulative sticks and carrots of targeted government funding and to accept the academic and social responsibilities drawn from different value systems. In most cases the former is dominant. Accordingly, the prevailing mode of greening in universities and colleges remains essentially reformist. Single issues can be dealt with more effectively than whole value systems and cultural change. Incremental organic change is more comfortable and less threatening. That is how greening has progressed.

Alternative and innovative change, appealing in theory, is more radical and difficult to construct and implement. Universities are conservative, bureaucratic and traditional institutions. Change tends to be implemented by top-down decrees, formal structures and line management systems. Bottom-up experiments and creative innovations are possible but are over-dependent on individual and voluntary enthusiasm. The strength of the integrated model (Figure 6.2) is to harness both. Environmental responsibility is neither a top-down nor a bottom-up issue. It is a shared responsibility for each individual member of that institution.

No FHE institution has yet had the confidence to promote itself specifically on the grounds of good environmental practice, or even to publicize, as fully as it might, its plans for improved environmental responsibility. Universities like Edinburgh, Northumbria and Nottingham Trent, which employ full-time environmental officers with varying budgets, may be in a better position to compete for students, staff and resources than those that try to succeed with volunteers and reduced priorities.

There is a long way to go before the ideal of a culture of environmental responsibility prevails in the FHE sector in the UK, but the achievements of greening over the last five years suggest guarded optimism as the twenty-first century beckons. There is at least an acceptance that greening has the capacity of contribute positively to other corporate objectives such as increasing market share. Its holistic philosophy can help to overcome wasteful inefficiency, inequity and individualism. The next phase of greening will be a creative and important one and will test the degree to which these changes herald that all-important change of culture.

References

Ali-Khan, S (1990) *Greening Polytechnics*, CDP, London
— (1991) *Greening the Curriculum*, CDP, London
Boxer, R (1995) 'Another Green Light for Higher Level Skills Development', *Higher Level Skills Bulletin*, 4, pp7–9
CERI (1973) *Environmental Education at University Level: Trends and Data*, OECD, Paris
Clayton, K (1976) 'Environmental Science/Studies: A Decade of Attempts to Discover a Curriculum', *Area*, 8, pp98–101
CONNECT (1991) 'Environmental Education for University Students', *UNESCO/UNEP Newsletter*, 16 (3)
Cousen, S M and P E O'Sullivan (1984) 'Environmental Sciences: Boom or Bust', *Proceedings of the Institute of Environmental Sciences*, 2, pp90–7
de la Cour, P (1994) 'Declaration of Independence from a Tyranny of Waste', *Times Higher Educational Supplement*, 24 June, p vii
DfE (1993) *Environmental Responsibility: An Agenda for Further and Higher Education*, HMSO, London
DoE (1990) *This Common Inheritance*, HMSO, London
— (1993) *Energy Efficiency in Building: Further and Higher Education Buildings*, Energy Efficiency Office, HMSO, London
— (1994) *Sustainable Development: The UK Strategy*, HMSO, London
— (1995) British Government Panel on Sustainable Development, First Report, HMSO, London
Hansard Reports Parliamentary Questions (1995) no 252, 16 January, from W Griffiths MP

McDonach, K, P P Yoneske and S V Emslie (1994) 'FHE and BS7750 Environmental Management Systems', in *Greening the Campus: Environmental Management in Higher Education*, Regents College, 7 March, Conference Report, pp1–11

Merritt, J Q (1993) *Environmental Audit Project, Final Report*, University of Central Lancashire, Preston

O'Riordan, T (1981) *Environmentalism*, Pion Ltd, London

Pepper, D (1989) *The Roots of Modern Environmentalism*, Routledge, London

Richardson, S and S Ali-Khan (eds) (1995) *The Environmental Agenda: Taking Responsibility (Promoting Sustainable Practice through Higher Education Curricula)*, Pluto Press, London

Schoof, D (1993) 'Environmental Higher Education in The Netherlands', Netherlands Workshop, Zandvoort, 23/24 March

Scottish Office (1993) *Learning for Life: A National Strategy for Environmental Education in Scotland*, HMSO, London

Smythe, J C (1993) 'Four Firsts for Eco-Design at Oxford', *Greening Universities*, 1 (1), p11

Somerville, D and R Talbot (1991) *Educated Energy Management*, Edinburgh University, Edinburgh

Willis, K (1994). 'A Survey', *Environmental Project*, University of Manchester, Manchester

Chapter 7

TEACHER EDUCATION
John Huckle

The rise of disorganized capitalism outlined in Chapter 1 has brought uncertain and changing times for teachers. They are being required to make schooling more responsive to new technologies and work processes, to restore national culture and traditional values against the threats of globalization and moral relativism, and to do more with reduced resources as the state seeks to reduce its spending on education in real terms. The introduction of a national curriculum and assessment, local management of schools, regular inspections and new forms of teacher education mean that teachers' work is being reorganized and redefined. There are ongoing debates about whether such changes amount to a new professionalism or to deskilling and proletarianization and about whether the restructuring of state schooling provides space for the kinds of education for sustainability (EFS) explored in Chapters 4 and 5. Top-down, bureaucratic reform threatens to reinforce the irrelevance of schools as 'modern institutions in a postmodern world', but there are opportunities to exploit the paradoxes of postmodernity and to develop new kinds of schools, teaching and teachers (Hargreaves, 1994).

Here I argue that a new phase of modernization holds both threats and promises for teachers. Though suffering from reduced status, autonomy and reward, they retain their role as potential bearers of critical knowledge and as experts in pedagogy who can help people construct alternative futures (Harris, 1994). Postmodernity offers new technologies for learning and teaching, more flexible and relevant ways of handling the curriculum content, new kinds of theoretical knowledge on which to base their practice, new forms of collaboration and professional development and new ways of remaining responsive in fast-changing times. It offers new structures and cultures of teaching, which lead in empowering and democratic directions and are essential if education for sustainability is to take root and grow.

Teachers as Transformative Intellectuals

Giroux and McClaren (1986) remind us that schooling is part of an ongoing struggle for democracy and strong sustainability (see Chapter 1). Teacher education should therefore develop transformative intellectuals who have acquired a language of critique and possibility and are capable of guiding a school's staff towards more effective forms of EFS. Such teachers will use critical pedagogy (Box 7.1) to work democratically with pupils, colleagues and the local community, and will encourage everyone to see the school as a democratic site where students develop the knowledge, skills and values needed to live more sustainably. This means regarding the classroom as a contested cultural terrain where interests and practices collide and knowledge is socially constructed in more or less democratic ways. Education for sustainability has to question dominant forms of knowledge and values, rediscover lost histories, knowledge and values, and encourage pupils to envision and realize desirable futures. Above all, it has to deconstruct and reconstruct culture (the particular ways in which a social group lives out and makes sense of its given circumstances and conditions of life) since cultural issues are the starting point for understanding the issue of who has power and how it is reproduced and manifested in the social relations of everyday life.

Box 7.1

Socially critical pedagogy has the following characteristics:

- *learning is active and experiential;*
- *classroom dialogue introduces elements of critical theory and encourages pupils to think critically;*
- *pupils begin to see themselves, their histories and futures in new ways. They develop a sense of their own power to shape their lives;*
- *'values' education develops comprehension of the sources of beliefs and values, how they are transmitted and the interests they support;*
- *pupils reflect on the structural and ideological forces that influence and restrict their lives and on democratic alternatives; and*
- *pupils are taught how to act democratically with others to build a new social order.*

A consideration of Giroux and McClaren's description of transformative intellectuals helps us to consider the sources of their authority.

> By the term 'transformative intellectual' we refer to one who exercises
> forms of intellectual and pedagogical practice which attempt to insert
> teaching and learning directly into the political sphere by arguing that
> schooling represents both a struggle for meaning and a struggle over
> power relations. We are also referring to one whose intellectual practices
> are necessarily grounded in forms of moral and ethical discourse exhibit-
> ing a preferential concern for the suffering and struggles of the disad-
> vantaged and oppressed. Here we extend the traditional view of the
> intellectual as someone who is able to analyse various interests and con-
> tradictions within society to someone capable of articulating emancipatory
> possibilities and working towards their realization. Teachers who assume
> the role of transformative intellectuals treat students as critical agents,
> question how knowledge is produced and distributed, utilize dialogue, and
> make knowledge meaningful, critical and ultimately emancipatory. . . . In
> effect, we want to define teachers as active community participants whose
> function is to establish public spheres where students can debate,
> appropriate and learn the knowledge and skills necessary to live in a
> critical democracy.
>
> (Giroux and McClaren, 1986, p215)

The authority of transformative intellectuals and of those who seek to
develop them through courses of teacher education rests on the assumption
that state schooling should promote social justice and a critical democracy.
Such authority is currently under attack from the right, which seeks a
tighter correspondence between schooling and the needs of disorganized
capitalism, and from postmodernists who suggest that the concept of the
transformative intellectual is no longer tenable since all knowledge is
contextual and all claims to authority in the realms of discourse and
representation are relative rather than total. Postmodernism questions
notions of authority grounded in universal rationality, knowledge and
values but can support an authority linked to the production of socially useful and emancipatory knowledge through participatory community development or critical action research. In this chapter I examine the theory and
practice through which radical teacher education for sustainability has
sought authority in recent years. I outline the developments based on the
critical theories of Jürgen Habermas before suggesting how these should be
revised to take account of a new era of reflexive modernization.

The Critical Theory of Jürgen Habermas

In the 1980s when socialism had lost much of its authority, some teacher
educators who saw their work as developing and supporting transformative
intellectuals turned their attention to the critical theory of Jürgen Habermas

(Layder, 1994; Craib, 1992; White, 1989). This draws on both Marx and Weber and shifts its focus from labour and the social relations of production to social interaction and the nature of language and morals. Habermas's principal claim is that interaction has become distorted by the rise of instrumental reason, which promotes science as universal and value-free knowledge and so fosters a distorted and incomplete understanding of our relations with one another and the rest of nature. His critical theories seek to reveal this distorted or incomplete rationality and empower people to think and act in genuinely rational and autonomous ways. They deal with legitimation crises, knowledge constitutive interests, communicative action and the colonization of the lifeworld, and can all be applied in developing critical teacher education for sustainability.

Habermas sees ecological problems as compounding a larger crisis as advanced capitalism's economic difficulties result in further uncertainties first in the political and then in the socio-cultural sphere. In trying to regulate political economy the state is unable to respond rationally to all demands. Its inability simultaneously to maintain capital accumulation, full employment, social welfare and a safe and healthy environment contributes to a legitimation and motivational crisis as people lose faith in state institutions and liberal democracy. The state then develops new forms of regulation and consultation such as sustainable development and Agenda 21 in an attempt to restore legitimacy and motivation, but opposition parties and movements within civil society may use such innovations to reveal the limits of technocracy and the continuing need for decision-making governed by genuine rationality, democracy and moral principles (Drysak, 1992). Teacher EFS should therefore introduce teachers to the political economy of the environment and education, and the roles that environmental education can play in either ameliorating or accentuating the legitimation crisis.

In criticizing reformist or weak notions of sustainability transformative intellectuals may be guided by Habermas's notion of knowledge constitutive interests. He suggests that human beings have three district categories of interests that shape their social construction of knowledge. While their technical interest in the control and management of their physical environment leads to empirical and positivist knowledge and forms of environmental education, which can be labelled education for environmental management and control, their practical interest in understanding and participating in society through communication with others leads to interpretive or hermeneutic knowledge and forms of environmental education, which can be labelled education for environmental awareness and interpretation. Both positivist and hermeneutic knowledge can, however, act as ideology, for positivism treats the social world as if it were part of the physical world, while hermeneutics recognizes the difference but is too inclined to accept the social world as it is. Both encourage people to over-look the true form of their relations with human and non-human nature, which can only be revealed through a grasp of critical theory.

Critical theory serves people's emancipatory interest in being free from the constraints of ideology or distorted communication and so enables them to become autonomous and self-determining. It recognizes the difference between the physical and social worlds but, unlike hermeneutics, it questions and seeks to improve the latter by, for instance, making it more egalitarian and sustainable. The emancipatory interest leads to EFS, which draws on the kinds of critical theory mentioned in Chapter 1 and employs a critical pedagogy that owes much to Habermas's theory of communicative action. Teacher EFS should develop empirical, hermeneutic and critical knowledge in the teacher's chosen subject specialisms and should explore how this can be combined with knowledge from other specialisms and with pupils' everyday knowledge to produce socially useful and empowering curricula.

The theory of communicative action maintains that the ideal of undis-torted communication or reasonable discourse is implicit in any use of language. All speech presumes an ideal speech situation in which partici-pants are required to sustain and defend four kinds of validity claim; only the force of better argument decides the issue. What they say should be meaningful, true, justified and sincere and, in a truly democratic society, it will be possible to redeem all such claims and so arrive at consensus in ways free from distortion, manipulation and domination. The process of actively constructing and reconstructing theory and practice through rational dis-cussion and democratic politics leads to communicative action based on shared understanding rather than strategic action based on instrumental reason. It leads to universal knowledge and values, serves to validate critical theory and may be described as praxis or participative action research. This provides EFS with a process for the development of pedagogy, curricula, teachers as transformative intellectuals and sustainable communities. All represent forms of democratic problem solving in which different kinds of practical and theoretical knowledge are combined to decide what people can, might and should do. It is through such research that the technical, cultural and moral/political principles and strategies of sustainable develop-ment and EFS emerge.

Teaching and teacher education for sustainability should be a process of communicative rather than strategic action. Teachers should learn through critical pedagogy in universities, school classrooms and the community and should thereby develop skills in planning and delivering a wide range of experiential and democratic teaching and learning activities of the type now used in moral, social, developmental and environmental education (Smith, 1991). They should learn how to collaborate with colleagues in creative ways; to negotiate curricula with learners and communities while remaining aware of wider perspectives and agendas; and to improve their work through critical reflection on theory and practice (Adler, 1991; Griffiths and Tann, 1992). Participation in the local Agenda 21 process provides an ideal setting to develop such skills.

Finally, in his discussion of the colonization of the lifeworld (that set of background assumptions that guides everyday conduct and allows communicative action) Habermas explains that money, political power and 'expert systems' have become the main steering mechanisms of late modern societies. Money and the market dispense with the need to bargain, negotiate and agree on the real value of such commodities as tropical hardwoods; political power cuts through the need to achieve understanding of such concepts as sustainable development by democratic debate; and 'experts' play an all pervasive role in deciding the form of social provision in such areas as environmental management and education. Power and decision-making are detached from popular control and transferred to social structures which then colonize our lifeworld. Radical environmentalists and environmental educators are among those who object to this colonization and who seek more self-management so that people can improve the quality of their lives. Habermas's ideas explain why some teachers resist the deskilling and deprofessionalization that accompanies current educational reforms and suggest that teacher education for sustainability should explore teachers' lifeworlds, develop their commitment to radical democracy and foster the political skills with which to resist further colonization (Zeichner, 1993; Hargreaves, 1994).

Having reviewed Habermas's critical theory and its relevance to teacher education for sustainability, we should note that he clings to the modern notion of a universal rationality, knowledge and values; can be seen to reduce politics solely to a matter of communication; and has been criticized as being too homocentric (Eckersley, 1992). His theory unites social system and lifeworld, structure and agency, but is essentially modernist in clinging to a single grand theory or narrative of emancipation, and is idealist in locating the causes and solutions to our current crisis in modes of discourse. He assumes that undistorted communication necessarily corresponds to universal needs and knowledge claims, gives too little attention to the power that sustains technocracy and instrumental reason, and puts too much faith in the new politics of social movements rather than the old politics of class. Situated knowledge and truth need to be acknowledged; the contradiction between immanent rationality and its arrested realization needs to be related to the political economy of global capitalism (Rustin, 1994); and teacher education for sustainability needs to acknowledge the related nature of conflict in the economic, political and cultural domains. We will examine some advances in social theory and critical pedagogy that address these weaknesses once we have reviewed some recent developments in critical teacher education for sustainability.

Habermas and a Critical Teacher Education for Sustainability

Following the application of Habermas's ideas to a critical theory of education (Carr and Kemmis, 1986; Gibson, 1986; Grundy, 1987; Young, 1989; Ewert, 1991), Australians took the lead in applying them to environmental education. Robottom (1987) suggested that professional development should be based on action research in order to close the gaps between what environmental educators think they are doing and what they are actually doing, and between what they would ideally do and what they are able to do in particular educational settings. Such research should take the form of collaborative and critical enquiry and practice and has far-reaching implications for teacher education. They are explored in The Deakin–Griffith Environmental Education Project, which resulted from collaboration between Deakin and Griffith universities. It consists of distance learning materials and course readers (for example Fien, 1993a, 1993b; Robottom and Hart, 1993) which support a masters' level course designed to assist the mid-career development of environmental educators working in school and elsewhere. Critical EFS is a central theme of the course and one of its principal authors has also coordinated a workshop-based environmental and development education project for teacher education entitled *Teaching for a Sustainable World* (Fien, 1995).

In the UK, meanwhile, the World Wide Fund for Nature's education department was reviewing its strategy. After a decade of producing educational materials, some of which encouraged more critical forms of teacher education (Huckle, 1988; Greig et al, 1989; Williams, 1989), the publication of a revised world conservation strategy and preparations for UNCED prompted a decision to focus more sharply on EFS and devote more resources to teacher education and support for innovative schools. A teacher education officer was appointed in 1991 and he invited a team of writers to prepare an in-service education programme *Reaching Out: Education for Sustainability* which was published in 1995 (Huckle et al, 1995). Like the course developments in Australia, it is strongly based on critical theory and action research.

Reaching Out consists of a set of workshop materials in three parts, which make up a comprehensive course in the theory and practice of EFS. It draws on existing WWF materials and is designed to support a wide range of courses from a one-hour in-service session in school to a 30-hour module that contributes to a certificate, diploma or higher degree. A common core of sessions in Parts 1 and 3 introduces EFS and its implementation in schools and the wider community, while different routes in Part 2 support primary school teachers or a range of secondary subject specialists (English, geography, science, and technology) carrying out action research projects. *Let's Reach Out (Primary)* (Symons, 1995) and *Let's Reach Out (Secondary)* (Webster, 1995) suggest how the materials can be adapted for use in shorter courses and conferences. Short *Reaching Out* courses have been run in association with many local authorities and a number of universities have expressed an interest in using *Reaching Out* as part of pre-service and higher degree courses for teachers. *Reaching Out* is supported by a network of tutors, a newsletter and pages on the Internet.

Teachers wishing to study EFS in depth, at diploma or masters level, have a growing number of options. Nottingham Trent University's environmental education through action enquiry integrates the three themes of environment, enquiry and education; includes a placement in education, the community or business; and involves a major research dissertation. Like the MSc/PgDip in environmental and development education at South Bank University in London, it is delivered mainly by distance learning and supported by study guides and readers. The South Bank course is the first masters level course in Britain to combine environment, development and education in one programme and expertise and materials from non-governmental organizations (NGOs) are used throughout. The aims of the course include analysing the role that education for sustainable development can play in social, political and economic change, and the course content includes modules on EFS, media literacy and applied research methodology.

Teacher educators should also be aware of other relevant developments. The Council for Environmental Education (CEE) has produced an in-service education package to promote environmental education in schools (Baines and Gayford, 1992) and WWF has published materials for tutors and students involved in pre-service education (Brand and Marlow, 1995; Inman and Champain, 1995). The Environment and School Initiatives (ENSI) project (Laine and Posch, 1991) has promoted environmental education through action research in schools throughout OECD countries, including Scotland (McAndrew, 1993) but not England (Elliott, 1992), and a working group of the Association for Teacher Education in Europe has examined the role of environmental education in initial teacher education (Brinkman and Scott, 1994). The UNESCO/UNEP International Environmental Education Programme continues to publish reports relating to teacher education (for example Hungerford et al, 1988), but to date these make little reference to EFS. All these publications can be usefully analysed by tutors and teachers to assess the extent to which they contain critical perspectives.

Reflexive Modernization

During the time that *Reaching Out* and the courses at Nottingham Trent and South Bank were being developed there were considerable advances in social theory, which the courses incorporate in different ways and to differing extents. Particularly significant was the theory of reflexive modernization developed by Beck (1992), Giddens (1991, 1994), Lash (1994) and Lash and Urry (1994). This suggests that the more societies are modernized the more people acquire the ability to reflect on social conditions and change them as a result. It holds out the possibility of a creative self-destruction of modern societies from which more sustainable alternatives could emerge. By establishing a position between modernism and postmodernism, integrating issues surrounding the social construction of nature and suggesting new approaches to critical pedagogy it also offers ways of overcoming some of the limitations of a critical teacher education for sustainability based on the theories of Habermas.

Lash and Urry link reflexive modernization to the decline of organized capitalism (simple modernity) and the rise of disorganized capitalism (reflexive modernity) or what others label postmodernity (see Chapter 1). Capital now circulates over longer routes at greater velocities and increasingly takes the form of post-industrial information goods with a cognitive content (for example a software programme) and postmodern goods with primarily aesthetic content (for example a pop video). They argue that in the emerging economies of signs and space, global information and communication structures are displacing the social structures of organized capitalism as the prime determinants of social life. This results in a loss of the previously existing meanings of objects and subjects and of the spatio-temporal contexts in which they are found, and prompts a growing number of people to take advantage of increased access to cultural competencies to create their own meanings, monitor and organize their own life narratives and attempt to shape society itself. The detraditionalization and individualization prompted by disorganized capitalism sets individuals free to be self-monitoring and reflexive and the resulting transfer of powers, from structure to agency, mirrors the self-monitoring workers and more reflexive processes of accumulation which characterize the post-Fordist economy.

The educational potential of reflexive modernization lies in its prompting more people to use judgement to monitor themselves in relation to their society and environment (cognitive reflexivity) and intuition to interpret themselves and their lifeworld (aesthetic reflexivity). Cognitive reflexivity carried out by individuals and institutions means that knowledge provided by the social sciences is fed back into society which itself becomes reflexive and self-constituting. Aesthetic reflexivity is a central feature of youth and consumer cultures and plays a key role in the creation of those meanings that sustain the new social movements. Cognitive reflexivity is based on structured flows of information and questions the particular (social conditions) by means of universals (reason or ethics), while aesthetic reflexivity is based on structured flows of expressive symbols and questions universals (for example modern notions of development) by means of the particular (for example popular or local culture). Both have been present within modernity from the outset and they coexist in creative tension within environmentalism and environmental education.

In an era of reflexive modernization much of people's insecurity is focused on the loss of nature and tradition. Images and news stories from around the world make them increasingly aware that nature has ceased to exist as environments and events independent of human actions and that manufactured uncertainty or risk now threatens their very survival. In these circumstances culture, in such forms as green consumerism, seeks to rescue nature by restoring it as an external and comforting reality, but such efforts are contradictory and may serve to heighten awareness of the social construction of nature and the need to construct it in more sustainable ways. Reflexive individuals are more prepared to question conventional science, technology and notions of progress, to express solidarity with people across space and time and to realize the need to establish new forms of political economy and global governance. Giddens (1994) echoes Beck in suggesting that ecological politics is a politics of the loss and recovery of nature. Nature and tradition have to be reconstructed by a new conservative radicalism which offers people security by stressing repair, conservation and care (Blackwell and Seabook, 1993). It should unite the politics of lifestyle with the politics of life chances while reviving civil society and should be guided by utopian realism. We need to be realistic about the structures and processes shaping the world yet recognize that, with increasing reflexivity, utopias can help constitute the future.

Before turning to the value of these ideas for teacher education, it is important to stress that the impact of reflexive modernization is spatially and socially variable. In Britain it is well established in some sectors of the economy and society and absent from others. New technologies promise heaven or hell (Harrison, 1995) and, for those living in environments bypassed by the leading sectors of disorganized capitalism, life is increasingly desperate. As the public sphere is increasingly superimposed on information and communication structures, through for example the Internet, the minority will be excluded from civil society and citizenship. While some become increasingly 'clever' and reflexive the rest will merely be entertained, confused or forgotten. Social and environmental inequalities will grow unless people turn new technologies in radically different directions.

Teacher Education and Reflexive Pedagogy

Reflexive modernization holds the promise of everyone becoming a transformative intellectual. It prompts self-awareness and a search for meaning and is fertile ground for a critical pedagogy that combines elements of modernism and postmodernism (Firth, 1995). Reflexive pedagogy should draw on modernity's concern for the enlightened subject and its insistence that we link memory, agency and reason to the construction of a democratic public sphere. This need not mean a commitment to master narratives or universal rationality, knowledge and values, but it does mean rejecting total relativism and accepting that it is possible to judge one validity claim against another in specific circumstances. Such pedagogy should incorporate postmodernism's emphasis on diversity, subjectivity and cultural pluralism, which can rid modernism of its excesses and exclusions, but should not abandon a utopian realism which gives shape and unity to collective struggles. Aronowitz and Giroux (1991) and Giroux (1992) use the adjectives 'border' and 'post-colonial' to describe such pedagogy. It brings in voices from the borders (including those of non-human nature) and seeks to de-centre Eurocentric, imperialist and racist discourse in an age of globalization and multiculturalism. It uses cultural politics to link abstract rights to everyday life and this allows a reconfiguration of citizenship to allow radical democracy.

Such pedagogy has been extensively developed by many of the new social movements, NGOs and the new green left. It is partly a response to a consumer capitalism in which seduction largely replaces repression and in which education's preoccupation with cultivating desire through experience partly replaces its preoccupation with cultivating reason and autonomy (Usher and Edwards, 1994). Experiential learning is therefore a central element of such pedagogy and a prime feature of progressive and radical forms of contemporary environmental and development education. Teacher education for sustainability should devote considerable attention to such curriculum frameworks as world studies (Hicks and Steiner, 1989; Hicks, 1995), global education (Pike and Selby, 1987) and what we consume (Huckle, 1988, 1992). These and other frameworks are attempts to develop curricula for an age of reflexive modernization at a time when appropriate critical theory is poorly developed. Tutors should now encourage an assessment of their strengths and weaknesses and consider how the new critical ideas and pedagogy surrounding reflexive modernization can inform an EFS that connects with youth culture and turns its hedonism and concern for identity politics towards more relaxed and sustainable ways of living. They are likely to decide that cultural studies should form a more significant element of such education and that they have considerable potential for educating student teachers in citizenship (Gilbert, 1995; Steiner, 1996).

The Prospects for Teacher Education for Sustainability

Having outlined an emerging theory and practice of teacher education for strong sustainability, it is necessary to conclude by reminding readers that courses based on the critically reflective practitioner model of the new left are rare. Most pre-service education is now based on the classroom competency or skills model of the radical right and 'hard centre', or the reflective practitioner model of the 'soft centre' and 'left in the centre' (Hill, 1991), while what in-service education remains is largely concerned with the pragmatics of delivering the national curriculum. Under the rhetoric of quality, standards, freedom and value for money, the right has taken new powers over course content and accreditation, attacked the theory and practice of professional teacher educators and required an increasing part of pre-service education to take place in schools. Its distaste for theory means that fewer young teachers get the opportunity to understand children's learning and to reflect on the social context of education. Teacher education risks becoming an apprenticeship rather than an induction into a professional culture that values diversity, autonomy and critical debate.

In this climate we find that environmental education is marginal to mainstream teacher education. The new emphasis on the 'efficient' delivery of specified subject knowledge in the classroom means that few students are exposed to the kinds of ideas and pedagogy outlined above. Tilbury's (1993) study of some courses provided for primary and middle school teachers points to tutors' limited perception of environmental education, their readiness to associate it solely with geography and science, their reluctance to acknowledge young children's readiness for social and political education and their failure to acknowledge the urgency of introducing environmental education into their courses. Few departments of education have responded to the challenge to 'green' their provision and students are often ahead of their tutors in acknowledging young people's interest in the environment and realizing the potential of environmental education in schools.

We should not, however, be too pessimistic. The paradoxes thrown up by reflexive modernization mean that it can facilitate an alternative restructuring of education and allow more teachers to claim the role of transformative intellectual. Some teachers, schools and university departments of education are beginning to recognize and develop the more empowering structures and cultures it allows and their attempts to create a new conservative radicalism in education are likely to be more appealing and successful in the long term that those of the new right. The pendulum in politics and education is set to swing back towards regulation, equality and democracy, and we should be ready with the kind of critical teacher education this chapter has explored.

References

Adler, S (1991) 'The Reflective Practitioner and the Curriculum of Teacher Education', *Journal of Education for Teaching*, 17 (2), pp139–50

Aronowitz, S and H Giroux (1991) *Postmodern Education: Politics, Culture and Social Criticism*, University of Minnesota Press, London

Baines, C and C Gayford (1992) *INSET for Environmental Education: 5–16*, CEE, Reading

Beck, U (1992) *Risk Society, Towards a New Modernity*, Sage, London

Blackwell, T and J Seabrook (1993) *The Revolt Against Change: Towards a Conserving Radicalism*, Vintage, London

Brand, J and C Marlow (1995) *Bright Sparks: An Introduction to Environmental Education for Trainee Teachers*, WWF Education Department, Godalming

Brinkman, F G and W A H Scott (eds) (1994) *Environmental Education into Initial Teacher Education in Europe*, ATEE

Carr, W and S Kemmis (1986) *Becoming Critical: Education, Knowledge and Action Research*, Falmer Press, Lewes

Craib, I (1992) *Modern Social Theory*, Harvester Wheatsheaf, London

Drysak, J (1992) 'Ecology and Discursive Democracy: Beyond Liberal Capitalism and the Administrative State', *Capitalism, Nature, Socialism*, 5 (2), pp18–42

Eckersley, R (1992) *Environmentalism and Political Theory*, UCL Press, London

Elliott, J (1992) 'The Political Response to the ENSI Project in the UK', paper presented to the Annual Conference of the American Educational Research Association, San Francisco

Ewert, G D (1991) 'Habermas and Education: A Comprehensive Overview of the Influence of Habermas in Educational Literature', *Review of Educational Research*, 61 (4), pp345–78

Fien, J (1993a) *Education for the Environment: Critical Curriculum Theorizing and Environmental Education*, Deakin University Press, Geelong

— (ed) (1993b) *Environmental Education: A Pathway to Sustainability*, Deakin University Press, Geelong

— (1995) 'Teaching for a Sustainable World: The Environmental and Development Education Project for Teacher Education', *Environmental Education Research*, 1 (1), pp21–34

Firth, R (1995) 'Postmodernity, Rationality and Teaching Environmental Education', *International Research in Geographical and Environmental Education*, 4 (2), pp44–64

Gibson, R (1986) *Critical Theory and Education*, Hodder & Stoughton, London

Giddens, A (1991) *Modernity and Self Identity: Self and Society in the Late Modern Age*, Polity, Cambridge

— (1994) *Beyond Left and Right: The Future of Radical Politics*, Polity, Cambridge

Gilbert, R (1995) 'Education for Citizenship and the Problem of Identity in Post-Modern Political Culture', in J Ahier and A Ross (eds) *The Social Subjects within the Curriculum*, Falmer, London

Giroux, H (1992) *Border Crossings: Cultural Workers and the Politics of Education*, Routledge, London

Giroux, H and P McClaren (1989) 'Teacher Education and the Politics of Engagement', *Harvard Educational Review*, 56 (3), pp213–38

Greig, S, G Pike and D Selby (1989) *Greenprints for Changing Schools*, WWF and Kogan Page, London

Griffiths, M and S Tann (1992) 'Using Reflective Practice to Link Personal and Public Theories', *Journal of Education for Teaching*, 18 (1), pp69–84

Grundy, S (1987) *Curriculum: Product or Praxis*, Falmer Press, Lewes

Hargreaves, A (1994) *Changing Teachers, Changing Times*, Cassell, London

Harris, K (1994) *Teachers Constructing the Future*, Falmer Press, Lewes

Harrison, M (1995) *Visions of Heaven and Hell*, Channel Four Television, London

Hicks, D (1995) *Educating for the Future: A Practical Classroom Guide*, WWF Education, Godalming

Hicks, D and M Steiner (eds) (1989) *Making Global Connections: A World Studies Workbook*, Oliver & Boyd, Edinburgh

Hill, D (1991) 'What's Left in Teacher Education: Teacher Education the Radical Left and Policy Proposals for the 1990s', in C Chitty (ed) *Changing the Future: Redprint for Education*, Tufnell Press, London

Huckle, J (1988) *What We Consume: Teachers Handbook*, WWF/Richmond Publishing, Richmond

— (1992) *Our Consumer Society (What We Consume, Unit 3)*, WWF/ Richmond Publishing, Richmond

Huckle, J, E Allen, P Edwards, G Symons and K Webster (1995) *Reaching Out: Education for Sustainability*, WWF Education Department, Godalming

Hungerford, H R, T L Volk, B G Dixon, T J Marcinkowski and P C Sia (1988) *An Environmental Education Approach to the Training of Elementary Teachers: A Teacher Education Programme*, Environmental Education Series 27, UNESCO–UNEP International Environmental Education Programme, Paris

Inman, S and P Champain (1995) *Thinking Futures: Making Space for Environmental Education in Initial Teacher Training*, WWF, Godalming

Laine, Kelly and P Posch (1991) *Environment, Schools and Active Learning*, OECD, Paris

Lash, S (1994) 'Reflexivity and its Double Structure, Aesthetics, Community', in U Beck, A Giddens and S Lash, *Reflexive Modernization: Politics, Tradition and Aesthetics in the Modern Social Order*, Polity, Cambridge

Lash, S and J Urry (1994) *Economies of Signs and Space*, Sage, London

Layder, D (1994) *Understanding Society Theory*, Sage, London

McAndrew, C (1993) *Environment and School Initiatives (ENSI) Project in Scotland: The National Report*, Scottish Consultative Council on the Curriculum, Dundee

Pike, G and D Selby (1987) *Global Teacher, Global Learner*, Hodder & Stoughton, London

Robottom, I (1987) 'Towards Inquiry-Based Professional Development in Environmental Education', in I Robottom (ed) *Environmental Education: Practice and Possibility*, Deakin University Press, Geelong

Robottom, I and P Hart (1993) *Research in Environmental Education*, Deakin University Press, Geelong

Rustin, M (1994) 'Incomplete Modernity: Ulrich Beck's Risk Society', *Radical Philosophy*, 67 (summer), pp3–12

Smith, D (1991) 'Educating the Reflective Practitioner in Curriculum', *Curriculum*, 12 (2), pp115–24

Steiner, M (ed) (1996) *Developing the Global Teacher: Theory to Practice in Teacher Education*, Trentham, Stoke on Trent

Symons, G (1995) *Let's Reach Out (Primary)*, WWF Education Department, Godalming

Tilbury, D (1993) 'A Grounded Theory of Curriculum Development and Change in Environmental Education at the Teacher Education Level' in J Fien (ed) *Final*

Report of Unesco Asia–Pacific Regional Experts' Meeting on Overcoming the Barriers to Environmental Education Through Teacher Education, Australian Association for Environmental Education, Brisbane

Usher, R and R Edwards (1994) *Postmodernism and Education*, Routledge, London

Webster, K (1995) *Let's Reach Out (Secondary)*, WWF Education Department, Godalming

Williams, R (1989) *One Earth, Many Worlds: Preparing Teachers for Environmental Education across the Curriculum*, WWF Education Department, Godalming

White, S K (1989) *The Recent Work of Jürgen Habermas*, Cambridge University Press, Cambridge

Young, R (1989) *A Critical Theory of Education*, Harvester Wheatsheaf, London

Zeichner, K M (1993) 'Connecting Genuine Teacher Development to the Struggle for Social Justice', *Journal of Education for Teaching*, 19 (1), pp5–20

Part III

The Informal Sector

Clearly environmental education far transcends the boundaries of formal education. Work in the field as well as in the classroom, bringing in local communities, is an essential part of the education process from nursery and primary schools upwards. The business, commercial and professional communities and the voluntary sector have vital roles in continuing environmental education and training. Sustainable development involves society as a whole.

(British Government Panel on Sustainable Development, *First Report*, HMSO, London, 1995)

The involvement of today's youth in environment and development decision-making and in the implementation of programmes is critical to the long-term success of Agenda 21.

(UNCED, 'Children and Youth in Sustainable Development', Chapter 25, *Agenda 21*, Regency Press, London, 1992)

Education as a social process and function has no meaning until we define that kind of society we have in mind.

(Dewey, J, *Democracy and Education*, Macmillan, New York, 1916)

Self-reliant participatory development is an educational and empowering process in which people, in partnership with each other and with those able to assist them, identify problems and needs, mobilize resources, and assume responsibility themselves to plan, manage, control and assess the individual and collective actions that they themselves decide upon.

(Ian Askew, quoted in Stan Burkey, *People First: A Guide to Self-Reliant, Participatory Rural Development*, Zed Books, London, 1993)

How far has the rise of the environment on the political agenda been brought about by the mass media? To what extent are the mass media an important or significant agent in the general political process? How far is mass media coverage of the environment structured by the economic context of the media, by the professional norms and practices of journalists, by news values, and by the strategies of information management adopted by the major actors on the environmental stage? Who gets to define what environmental issues are about? How do the mass media contribute to policing the boundaries of public debate about the environment? How do mediated images contribute to the formation of public opinion? In what ways do different publics draw on media representations for making sense of environmental images?

(Anders Hansen, *The Mass Media and Environmental Issues*, Leicester University Press, Leicester, 1993)

Capitalism's media triumph conceals the truth that it has never been more fragile, threatened, catastrophic. Something else has surpassed both the Marxism figure-headed by a totalitarian Soviet bloc and its liberal free market opponent. This 'something' is a set of hyperreality transformations in the spheres of science, technology and economics which put our traditional notions of democracy in grave doubt. The crux of postmodernity is that there are two 'presents'. One is a 'spectre' present, a Virtual Reality techno-media simulcrum that makes the other 'real' present appear borderline, fugitive, elusive.

(Richard Appingnanesi and Chris Garratt, *Postmodernism for Beginners*, Icon Books, Cambridge, 1995)

Chapter 8 | # WORKING with the YOUTH SERVICE
Lisbeth Grundy &
Bud Simpkin

The terminology 'education for sustainability' (EFS) may be new to many of those working with young people in non-formal settings; however, the concept itself is certainly not. The idea that young people should meet their current needs without compromising their ability to meet future needs is a foundation stone of the majority of youth work. Initiatives tackling crime, employment, homelessness, debt and health that exist within the youth work sector encourage young adults away from behaviour that only provides instant rewards in favour of action that may sustain their pleasures.

The purpose of this chapter is to consider whether the introduction of education for sustainability to youth work is simply a semantic exercise or if the philosophy brings a new dimension to those currently engaged in it. First, it is important to establish what we mean by youth work.

The Youth Service

The youth service is a generic term used in the UK to describe the collection of voluntary and local authority agencies that provide social, educational and recreational opportunities for young people. The age range varies from 7 through to 25 but focuses mostly on 12–18 year-olds.

As is true of nearly all social and educational movements, the beginnings of the youth service can be found in philanthropic initiatives started in the middle of the last century. Many organizations founded in the mid-1800s still survive today, although a number of them are struggling to retain the interest of the young people of the 1990s. However, long-established traditional uniformed organizations like the Scouts (700,000) and Guides (650,000) still attract large numbers of young people to their membership — a fact not to be disregarded.

The local authority sector of the youth service can be traced to the First World War. The Juvenile Organizations Committee was established in 1916 to combat the rise in delinquency thought to be a result of changing home circumstances with fathers away at the war and mothers working in factories. This state intervention in the youth service was once again activated at the start of the Second World War and resulted in the youth service being identified in the 1944 Education Act as part of further education (Leighton, 1975).

The wording of the 1944 Act brings into question the 'statutory' nature of the youth service. The youth service is statutory in that it is in the Act and local authorities are charged with the responsibility of providing an 'adequate' service for young people. But the term 'adequate' is not clarified in the Act and remains undefined to this day, offering no recommended minimum level of financial provision. This fragile base has inevitably resulted in underfunded provision and the economic stringencies of the mid-1990s have left local authority youth services very vulnerable to cuts in funding.

Nevertheless, youth service provision in some form or other does exist in more than 120 local authorities, usually under the aegis of the education department. The total net expenditure of all local authority youth and community services in 1992/3 was in excess of £256 million. The budgets of some of these local authority youth and community services are quite sizeable. For example in 1992/3 Derbyshire had a net expenditure of over £7 million, Lancashire was around £8 million and in London the net expenditure was £46 million (NYA, 1995). In addition, some £2.8 million was distributed by the Department for Education to national voluntary youth organizations in 1993/4. This government funding scheme was recently applauded by the Office for Standards in Education as being cost-effective (OFSTED, 1995).

A recent survey undertaken by the Office of Population Censuses and Surveys (OPCS) revealed that 59 per cent of young people aged between 11 and 25 had taken part in a youth service activity at some time — about 5.9 million young people (OPCS, 1994).

In the early 1990s the youth service was caught up in the great national curriculum debate. While the national curriculum for formal education was being established in schools, a series of ministerial conferences was held with the specific purpose of creating a core curriculum for the youth service. The conclusion reached, although never officially acknowledged, was that the rich range of work undertaken within the youth service made the task of establishing a common curriculum for voluntary and local authority sectors impossible. What did prove possible through the ministerial conferences and a consultation process with the youth service coordinated by the National Youth Agency was the creation of a statement of purpose for the youth service.

Box 8.1 *A STATEMENT OF PURPOSE FOR THE YOUTH SERVICE*

The purpose of youth work is to redress all forms of inequality and to ensure equality of opportunity for all young people to fulfil their potential as empowered individuals and members of groups and communities and to support young people during the transition to adulthood.

Youth work offers young people opportunities which are:

■ educative — *enabling young people to gain the skills, knowledge and attitudes needed to identify, advocate and pursue their rights and responsibilities as individuals and as members of groups and communities locally, nationally and internationally;*
■ designed to promote equality of opportunity — *through the challenging of oppressions such as racism and sexism and all those which spring from differences of culture, race, language, sexual identity, gender, disability, age, religion and class; and through the celebration of the diversity and strengths which arise from those differences;*
■ participative — *through a voluntary relationship with young people in which young people are partners in the learning process and decision-making structures which affect their own and other young people's lives and their environment;*
■ empowering — *supporting young people to understand and act on the personal, social and political issues which affect their lives, the lives of others and the communities of which they are a part.*

(NYB, 1991)

While the nature of the youth service makes it difficult to quantify endorsement, this statement of purpose has been virtually universally accepted as the foundation stone of youth work. While EFS is not explicit in the statement, it is reflected in it. It is therefore interesting to consider how far EFS is in practice demonstrated by those endorsing the statement.

We hope this section has established, especially for those not familiar with the youth service, a sense of the purpose and significance of what is often regarded as a fairly *ad hoc* collection of agencies. We now review the strength of youth work in relation to experiential learning which we believe to be central to EFS.

Experiential Learning

amidst all uncertainties there is one permanent frame of reference: namely the organic connection between education and personal experience.

(Dewey, 1932 in Bowen, 1990)

Integral to any educational process is the need to provide and impart information. Undoubtedly, the formal educator's didactic approach is a widely accepted and often effective method of raising awareness through the accumulation of knowledge. However, in relation to EFS it can be argued that the most effective indicator of success in the process would be an individual's change of behaviour and values.

It is questionable how successful an institution like a school can be in undertaking a process of education that seeks such change. The limitations of the average primary or secondary school are both logistical and philosophical — the former in that even the most able of teachers is unable to support the same degree of investigation among a class of 30 as the average youth worker can with a group of eight; the latter because the freedom of opportunity for experimentation and subsequent reflection is seldom available within the bounds of a national curriculum-led education establishment. Consequently, many schools find it impossible to change the balance from being an institution that teaches pupils to one where individuals can learn.

In contrast to formal education, the informal educational opportunities of the youth service lend themselves more readily to the principles of experiential learning. Yet it is vital for those involved in the youth service to remember that simply providing experiences for young people is not enough. For experiential education to be effective it has to be undertaken as part of a learning framework.

Education for sustainability could have the effect of collecting together a range of existing strategies, providing a collective purpose and making a stronger learning framework. At present, the youth service is actively involved in a wide range of social and personal development strategies; these include health, social justice, diversions from crime, and environmental and political education initiatives. Elements of sustainability are already in evidence. For example, in diversion from car crime projects, it is demonstrated to young people that they can enjoy motor sport permanently in contrast to any thrill they may derive from car theft, which is rarely sustainable. Similarly, a basic premise of most health education is linked to the sustainability of our first environment, our own body.

But there is a need to go further. In our view, EFS should not be just a semantic exercise but one that enables the youth service to review and revise its programme and provide it with a coherence and relevance that will take it into the next century.

Global-Local Aspects

So far we have considered working with youth groups from a UK-based perspective. The importance of structures like the youth service to global environment and development — and therefore to EFS globally — was highlighted in 1992 at the Rio Earth Summit.

Principle 21 of the Rio Declaration on Environment and Development states: 'The creativity, ideals and courage of the youth of the world should be mobilized to forge a global partnership in order to achieve sustainable development and ensure a better future for all' (UNCED, 1992).

Agenda 21, and particularly Chapter 25, calls for the participation of today's young people in environmental and development decision-making. It recognizes that their involvement is critical in moving towards more sustainable ways of life. Young people are recognized as stakeholders in the process — not only in the future but right now.

Although Agenda 21 is an international agreement, two thirds of its proposals can only be achieved through local action, and the setting up of 'Local Agenda 21s' is widely seen as an essential way of doing this (see Chapters 9 and 12 of this book).

Local Agenda 21s aim to:

■ promote consultation on sustainable development with the whole community — and that should include young people;
■ make sure that the different sectors in the community, for example industry, local council, voluntary organizations and youth, are talking to each other as part of the process; and
■ identify actions that people can take locally that actually make a difference.

The youth service, with its links with local councils, the voluntary sector and young people, is ideally situated to facilitate the participation of young people in LA21s. According to Agenda 21, national government should be supporting this process: 'Governments should ... give support to programmes, projects, networks, national organizations and youth non-governmental organizations to examine the integration of programmes in relation to their project requirements, encouraging the involvement of youth in project identification, design, implementation and follow-up' (UNCED, 1992).

The UK government response to Agenda 21, *Sustainable Development: The UK Strategy*, specifically identifies 'peer education' in the process of raising young people's awareness: 'Youth groups are particularly active in this field and in many cases "peer education" — young people passing on their skills and knowledge to other young people — is used to great effect' (HMG, 1994, paragraph 32.12).

The success of this peer education process internationally can clearly be identified in *Rescue Mission Planet Earth*, a children's edition of Agenda 21. This unique book is designed, written and illustrated by young people and aims to inspire young people all over the world into environmental action (Bayer, 1994).

Strategies for Youth Workers

In 1993, the Council for Environmental Education (CEE) completed a three-year national environmental youth work training programme which identified three basic approaches to environmental youth work: political education, outdoor activity and personal and social development (Rogers, 1994). These broad categories are in practice further broken down in the strategies adopted by workers.

CEE's research was based on examples of environmental education youth work taken from around England. We feel such work to be inextricably linked to EFS, and attempt to demonstrate this in the next section, by looking at sustainability within the three broad strategies.

Political Education Approach: Focus on Power and Decision-Making

Social justice It is widely accepted that sustainability can only be achieved by the eradication of poverty and inequality. The starting point for this could be taken from a young person's immediate experience. Simple observations made about the contrasts in housing conditions, income and quality of life both locally and then internationally will help to raise awareness about the difficulties encountered within some communities and by some individuals in trying to pursue a sustainable lifestyle.

Campaigning There is little doubt that young people are knowledgeable about human impacts on the environment and many have a good grasp of the concept of sustainability. The frustration they feel is in not being able to do anything to change things. While a key objective of youth work is the empowerment of young people, it is probably the most difficult aspect of the youth service curriculum to deliver. This is partly due to the criticism that a youth worker who encourages a young person to take action can invite. The youth worker could be perceived as using young people to deliver his or her own personal message.

This anxiety about accusations of indoctrination undoubtedly explains the absence of any significant youth service presence in the recent radical protests about animal rights and motorway construction that are often dominated by young people. It may also explain why campaigning environmental organizations like Greenpeace and Friends of the Earth make few concessions to the development of a youth section. Nevertheless, campaigning for some form of sustainable practice is a very powerful way to understand the political process and gather a sense of actually being able to do something.

Community action A natural extension of awareness and understanding of issues is the involvement of young people in a democratic way in the redesigning of their own living, playing and working spaces. The LA21 process is offering new opportunities for young people to participate in the local consultation processes (Agyeman, 1995).

Using the Outdoors: Environmental Perspectives in Outdoor Activity

Conservation Wildlife and conservation groups offer a wide range of opportunities to observe natural processes that have sustained themselves over long periods of time despite human intervention, and to observe degraded ecosystems and analyse and act on the causes and issues. Learning traditional sustainability skills such as hedge-laying and coppicing are also valuable.

Outdoor education While it is vitally important to maintain the fun and sporting element of outdoor education it also provides the opportunity to engage in sustainability issues in action. For example, unless it is undertaken with care, climbing on sandstone rock can have a deleterious effect on both the sport and the environment. In this case, lack of EFS would very quickly remove the climbing opportunity.

As well as allowing young people to assess the effects of continuous leisure use of the environment, outdoor education also presents the opportunity for young people to observe at first hand the impact of the built environment on the countryside. The young person learning to sail or canoe on a river is in a much better position to appreciate the importance of sewage treatment than he or she would be during a rather sterile geography field trip to a water treatment works.

Sensitization to nature Building a sense of affinity with nature extends young people's awareness. Activities such as those based on Earth Education emphasize the magic of nature and offer young people the opportunity to appreciate the strength and significance of nature. They can help young people understand the natural order of life and people's dependency on nature. From this, a sense of the need to develop a way of life based on a sustainable balance with nature may emerge.

Personal Action and Social Development: Exploring Issues and Action for Young People and Youth Groups

Consumerism This is an area with a very strong potential for youth participation. It is widely believed that the very successful awareness-raising campaign with children and young people was a major element in the eradication of CFCs from aerosol cans. (Parents who were foolish enough to purchase a non-ozone-friendly brand were treated to the sort of reception usually reserved for mass murderers!) This was a definite example of the information being clear and children and young people feeling they could take action; the result was revolutionary. That CFCs used in aerosols were probably only responsible for a tiny part of the overall problem was to some extent irrelevant. The point was it was an unnecessary and unsustainable use, which young people understood.

The problem generally is that the issues are rarely so uncomplicated. Getting further than such activities as 'refuse, repair, recycle' is difficult. For example, while the feel-good factor of a variety of fund-raising campaigns such as Comic Relief and Band Aid can bring tremendous responses, especially from the young, the movement towards fair trade is very slow and fraught with difficulty. Giving a little bit of surplus cash once every so often is sustainable at a personal level. But embarking on a fair-trade purchasing campaign that costs the young consumer more means that his or her current standard of life cannot be sustained. It is not until young consumers are convinced that not following a fair-trade policy will lead to an unsustainable way of life that they will change what they buy — and in this they do not differ from most adults.

The challenge to the EFS movement is to convince young consumers, not simply through their high street spending but also in their banking and pension plans, that they have tremendous power to make change by directing their resources towards fair and environmentally sustainable trade.

Creative expressive approach Drama, poster-making, T-shirt printing, writing and music are part of a whole range of methods for experiential learning. Not only can EFS be included in the design or end-product of the approach, it can be integral to the process.

Auditing and policy-making Young people can express and explore their views and gain social and personal education through investigation and participation in decision-making within their immediate environment. This might be their home, youth club, school or workplace. They can investigate a whole host of practices for their sustainability value and then take measures to change and improve them. Such an approach is exemplified in CEE's *EARTHworks* resource (Edbrooke et al, 1990).

Theory into Practice

These strategies hopefully provide a useful series of examples for developing a programme for young people of EFS in the informal setting of the youth service. However, they underplay the complex set of pressures that young people encounter in our Western industrial society:

- the contradiction of a young person who understands that an integrated transport system is a sustainable solution but cannot wait to get his or her first car;
- the dilemma of knowing that a pair of expensive trainers are the result of unfair exploitation of workers in a developing country while needing to preserve one's personal image; and
- understanding that a fast food restaurant is pursuing unsustainable practices to produce hamburgers but giving in to peer pressure because it is the place to eat.

In short, in the modern idiom, it is not 'cool' to be green. Conservationists, animal activists and vegetarians do not project role-models that the majority of young people want to follow. Education for sustainability can only succeed by creating an image with which the young can align themselves. Greener lifestyle choices will only engage young people if they are pursued in partnership with a strategy that empowers.

Youth Work in Practice

In 1994, CEE sought to support the further development of environmental youth work through the identification of good practice criteria, attempting to develop a framework for the planning, monitoring and evaluation of environmental work with young people. Acknowledging that the framework would be dynamic and should support the needs of both workers and young people, the following criteria were identified to be used alongside existing youth work criteria.

Good practice in environmental youth work should:

- illustrate the links between the local and the global environment;
- make connections between social issues and the environment;
- enable individuals to convert their environmental concern to action;

- develop skills in changing things at a political, social and practical level;
- enhance understanding of the ecological processes that sustain life and our own relationship to the environment (Rogers, 1995).

The list of criteria provides a framework for assessing a piece of work from an environmental point of view, complementing existing criteria for good youth work practice. The expectation is that individual projects or activities would focus on only one or two of the environmental criteria, within the context of a long-term programme or series of projects aiming to address all criteria.

The framework was tested during its development by groups of youth workers and young people who were asked to assess their experience against the criteria. Two of the groups are included below.

BOX 8.2 A GLIMPSE OF YOUTH WORK IN PRACTICE

Envirochange and the Three Rs: Birmingham *The Envirochange group started four years ago with a group of young people talking about the attractions of leaving their home area of Handsworth. Sangeeta Soni, their neighbourhood youth worker, encouraged them to talk about whether this was realistic — at least in the short term — and to ask themselves whether they could do anything to make their own neighbourhood more attractive.*

The group wanted to do something to change its own environment — hence the project name. It managed to attract funding and support for its plans to introduce litter bins and create hanging baskets for homes in three local streets. Another dimension was added when they began to work alongside adults with learning difficulties at the Hockley Adult Training Centre. Subsequent projects have included growing and planting herbs and perennials (not as attractive to thieves as the original hanging baskets!) and an 'adopt-a-garden' scheme.

Envirochange has increasingly used arts-based activities, which serve to get a message across to others while adding to the range of options for group members. The Streetwise drama group, now independent, started from an Envirochange play with an environmental message.

Sangeeta has also been involved in the development of the 3Rs group — the 3Rs being reduce, reuse and recycle. Like Envirochange, the 3Rs group meets once a week and was set up to attract an older age range, since Envirochange was beginning to drop below its initial 13–15 years.

The 3Rs group focuses on projects, often with an arts element, which draw attention to the environment. So far they have built a huge tomato to promote their can crushing for Comic Relief, worked on a mosaic, begun

---

compost-making and banner-making and composed a rap for a radio item. The group also has 'fun' sessions where the focus is on doing something together, rather than just working on environmental issues and projects.

Urban Specialist Team: Worksop *In Worksop, Nottinghamshire, Robin Packer, senior youth worker, has used his own commitment to the environment to enhance youth and community work in the area, a task which he thinks has been made easier through Nottinghamshire Youth Service's inclusion of environmental aims within its policy objectives.*

Robin's environmental youth work is all project-based. There is usually a major summer project — a week-long task or activity — and during the year this is supported by occasional one-day and weekend activities.

The work began three years ago with a tree-planting programme at the National Trust's Hardwick Hall. The county youth service works annually with the National Trust to organize a weekend for youth groups in the county. Around 200 young people are involved over the two days and Robin took around ten from the Worksop area.

Young people have taken on a number of major projects in recent years, for example path and pond clearing in areas near to Worksop. Recently, this involved a project nearer to home. The Worksop Boys' Club was in the process of changing to become the Teen Club, to reflect its mixed membership. As part of the change, the idea was taken on to make something of the waste ground outside the club building — an eyesore to the club's neighbours.

The project was carried out over one week and involved around 40 young people and other local residents. It was started after Robin overheard a conversation about the state of the club, its surroundings and its image among local people. A planning group was set up, which developed the design of the area, sought funding and liaised with local residents to seek practical help and general support.

With help and advice from the local Groundwork Trust, the group was able to attract some funding. The conditions of the grant provided an opportunity for more learning. The plants used were to be indigenous — native to this country, not imported. This ruled out conifers (preferred by the neighbours as they would soon hide the club from view).

A video has been shot of this project. It was done with a grant from the county youth service by two young people who now work for themselves, having developed some of their skills through involvement with the service. The result is a four-minute video with music which presents the achievements of the group in a dynamic way.

The Criteria and Success Factors

The combination of the already widely accepted criteria for effective youth work relating to participation, empowerment, education, equality of opportunity and enjoyment, together with the five environmental criteria, offers the youth service the basis of a planning and evaluation framework for EFS.

The feedback from the case study groups on the assessment of their experiences against the criteria revealed a range of 'success' factors significant to both youth work and EFS. For example, the enthusiasm and commitment to the environment of the workers was essential, and was far more important than a high level of environmental knowledge.

The building of alliances, of networking with others, was a part of the strategy of successful projects whether drawing on the skills of artists, funding bodies or environmental groups. There was a clear commitment to taking an environmental youth work approach, where participation and empowerment are central to the process, rather than merely involving young people in environmental projects. Perhaps unexpectedly, nearly all the successful pieces of work were project-based, asking for specific, time-limited and often practical commitment from young people, reflecting the environmental concern of many young people — 'what can we do about the environmental issues that concern us?'

Linked to this emphasis on practical involvement is the positive feedback associated with young people being actively involved in the community, potentially opening doors to greater involvement in community decision-making.

Looking back at the criteria, those involved agreed that the most difficult or neglected sphere related to ecological understanding, for a range of reasons, and this reflects one area that needs to be addressed in EFS.

Conclusion

We started with the purpose of investigating whether EFS within youth work is a regurgitation of old methodology or if it genuinely does introduce a new dimension. We have demonstrated that the underlying values of EFS did exist in youth work prior to the use of the phrase in an environmental perspective. However, we have firmly stated our belief that EFS is more than a semantic exercise and can serve a purpose within youth service of collecting together a wide range of youth work settings and methodologies under one coherent philosophy.

A central pillar of youth work is the promotion of personal and social education of young people. While this is a very useful general purpose phrase, it fails to provide the youth service with a pivotal focus for the broad selection of activities and organizations. The combining of a programme of personal and social education with the objectives of EFS not only provides a purpose for youth work but sets it within a contextual framework.

It is difficult to envisage a successful national strategy for EFS that ignores the youth service, but it is equally important for the youth service to recognize the significance of EFS as an underpinning element of its whole curriculum.

References

Agyeman, J (1995) 'Role Reversal and the Three Green Rs', *The Times Educational Supplement Extra — Environment*, 23 June, London

Bayer, J L (ed) (1994) *Rescue Mission Planet Earth*, Kingfisher Books, London

Bowen, P (1990) 'A Curriculum Model for Outdoor Education', unpublished manuscript, University of Sussex

Edbrooke, J, L Grundy and A Rogers (eds) (1990) *EARTHworks: Environmental Awareness Resource and Training Handbook*, CEE, Reading

HMG (1994) *Sustainable Development: The UK Strategy*, HMSO, London

Leighton, J P (1975) *The Principles and Practice of Youth Work*, Chester House Publications, London

NYA (1995) *Policy Update*, Issue 4, 1994–95, NYA, Leicester

NYB (1991) *Towards a Core Curriculum: The Next Step*, NYB, Leicester

OFSTED (1995) *Grants to National Voluntary Youth Organizations*, HMSO, London

OPCS (1994) *Survey of Youth Participation*, HMSO, London

Rogers, A (ed) (1994) *The Story So Far*, CEE, Reading

— (1995) *Good Practice: Criteria and Case Studies*, CEE, Reading

UNCED (1992) *Earth Summit '92*, Regency Press, London

| Chapter 9 | # COMMUNITY-BASED LEARNING
Geoff Fagan |

Agenda 21, the 'Earth Action Plan' that resulted from the Rio Earth Summit of 1992, recognized that any pretence at sustainability practice that failed to embrace local people and their aspirations, fears and needs for the future was doomed to failure. Local people were at the core of sustainability for the earth and its people: anything less could not be sustained. So it stressed the need to devolve decision-making and power to the very simplest and lowest community levels that could be identified. It would seek the help of local, indigenous people and recognize their particular and peculiar commitment to the locality and its role in their future. It emphasized the role of the family, of women and of traditional and socially learned knowledge. 'There is a need to increase public sensitivity to environment and development problems and involvement in their solutions and foster a sense of personal environmental responsibility and greater motivation and commitment towards sustainable development' (UNCED, 1992).

These are fine inexpensive words, but how do local people engage? How can they be supported? What education process places them at the core of their learning and engages them in the decision-making that is central to the principles of Agenda 21? How do informal educators bring local people back into the educational fold? This chapter seeks to provide some insights into such questions.

Education Beyond Schooling

Education appropriate to Agenda 21 is not neutral. It is steeped in the politics of justice and equality. It helps in the resolution of problems, the better understanding of issues and constructive thoughtful action. The purpose of education is engagement — democratic, negotiated and pragmatic. Action-based education confronts people with the reality of their locality, an assessment of what is truly happening in their home environment and helps them to demand change and take action. These are the educational processes needed for Agenda 21.

But this approach poses a problem for education. It asks educators to assume a role radically different to that of a teacher. It seeks a new contract with parents and young people; it insists on new definitions of knowledge and links knowledge to application. It accepts that local people, parents and young people are perfectly capable of enabling their own learning given help and support in doing so. It seeks a change in power between the learner and the learned and in the acceptance of what knowledge might be, how it is generated and how it is endorsed. It challenges the notion that knowledge belongs to the intellectually rich, that local people are wrong until proved right and that learning is the domain of an educational hierarchy.

This redefinition is at the core of Agenda 21. It is also the only way to bring the vast majority of adults and young people back to the educational fold and engage them effectively in a learning process that has meaning and purpose for them and contributes to an owned notion of sustainability. This is the 'reorientation' of education called for by Agenda 21.

Ownership, Empowerment and Action

Faced with the choice, most people seem more on the side of unfettered economic world development than environmental or species protection. Before making that choice, however, they should be confronted with alternatives. They should know the real cost of change and be allowed to make decisions on the basis of understanding and real term costs. 'Sustainability' appeals to basic values of justice, fairness and equality. These are not alien to Northern people: they are part of our common tradition. They are common core values that link all people in the Northern democratic states.

Common understandings are a central facet of a sustainable community. Shared beliefs, attitudes and values are reinforced by communication and dialogue. Tradition, culture and behaviour are part of the framework within which security is established and people grow and act. The mix of values, concerns, ability to act, learning and knowing are at the heart of sustainability. But what values, beliefs and attitudes are appropriate? 'What they must have in common to form a community or society are aims, beliefs, aspirations, knowledge — a common understanding' (Dewey, 1916).

There is nothing contentious here. It has long been known that cultural celebrations and traditions have formed very important boundaries to human behaviour in community organizations. Thus, it would seem logical to ask what structures need to be in place before eco-friendly core values become embedded in people's behaviour. Or is it behaviour that tends to inform and reassert core values? Change the behaviour and you change the value base. This is a very important debate.

Clearly, education has to address both behaviour and core values. It has to enhance future security. It has to be recognized as a process that helps alleviate community concerns. This means that education has to spring from local people: their values, aspirations and beliefs. It has to be both real and active. And it has to promote 'ownership' and 'empowerment'.

'Ownership' is the term that describes the place where attitudes, values and behaviour are defended. That personal territory where ideas become beliefs, where positions become owned — a place only exposed rarely and at considerable personal risk. It is to this place that education must seek access through dialogue.

What about empowerment? All people have some degree of power, so to speak of 'powerlessness' as a state of being is simply inaccurate. However, there are people with more power and people with less power. Usually, the people with more power are those who belong to the political and intellectual elite. Powerful people generally do not give away power: it has to be taken, fought for and won. The transfer of that power, the process of enabling one person to become more powerful by making another less powerful, is the practice of empowerment.

Key processes are tied into the notions of action and empowerment. If action is not to be anarchic, it has to be thought through, planned and coolly implemented. It must project out of core values, be of immediate concern, be collectively owned and thereby protected, and be performed by the local people for themselves. In doing so, a local group will be committed to its outcome and will protect this new position. They will own the outcome; they will be empowered by the process. This is in essence the idea of praxis, which is central to sustainability and Agenda 21.

Praxis: Action and Learning as One

It was Aristotle who first legitimized the split between education as an intellectual function or production, and education as a process or practice. This fragmentation has caused great difficulties over the years. In the abstract view, 'real' understanding could only come from theory — a thorough, scientific, 'objective' investigation. The notion of training professionals, or apprentices to a trade, has long been downgraded. Truly worthwhile knowledge was the territory of intellectuals only, the domain of academics and priests. Mix this with a male power elite, top-down institutions and political processes that discourage the engagement of local people — and it is easy to see how, through its institutions, education has failed vast numbers of its clients.

Praxis and liberational education address the issue of intellectual elitism and the intellectual assessment of what is worthwhile. Liberational education accepts and embraces the notion that education flows through the marriage of skills with intellectual and mechanical training. It accepts that learning must be for use, must stem from and reside in its clients' reality and must continue to make sense there. It must be designed with local people to meet their ends and objectives. It recognizes local people as the key players in the game. It uses their frame of reference and encourages them to generate knowledge; and it celebrates their view of the world, their learning and their own selves as researchers and activists.

Praxis means learning through simultaneous action and reflection, a rolling process in which action is informed by distillation and reflection followed by further action and reflection. It does not separate education into unnecessary hierarchical structures and sees education as being in one place. It is local, process embracing, pragmatic, intellectual and action led — no separation is necessary.

Education for Sustainability

What does this mean, for sustainability? Sustainability education must be linked to the reality of its clients; it must marry action to intellect; it cannot and must not allow any one section of education to invade and persuade local people that to think 'about' is a fair exchange for thinking about and taking action.

Education for sustainability involves a commitment to a framework of specific, global, ethical goals which speak for justice, equality and democracy. Above all, it needs to be designed and celebrated for its ability to embrace eco-sensitive action as its legitimate output. Nothing less is sustainable. Anything else fails to allow local communities to sustain themselves — and if local communities fail, global unsustainable behaviour spirals beyond control.

Gaining Entry to the Community

The problem of identifying what group to work with and gaining entry to it is relatively simple. Conservation and Development in Sparsely Populated Areas (CADISPA) (Fagan, 1992) advocates 'partnership contracts' with existing local groups on the basis that these are more sustainable because of the groups' prior identity. Other ways include using local networks, community radio, local institutions, the formal schooling network, community education, training and local enterprise councils, and community councils.

The purpose behind the intervention is critical. Entry into a community beyond a superficial level depends on the assumptions fieldworkers display in the very earliest encounters. Before that vital first encounter they must be clear about the key questions. Where are they coming from in terms of their expectations? What do they expect will happen? How clear are they about their role and commitment to power sharing? Do they have the skill to facilitate democratic learning rather than teach? For what purpose, outcome, process and cost are they seeking involvement?

CADISPA recommends a twin agenda approach with local community groups being actively supported while the same local groups are engaged in the process of research and re-presentation. Groups more used to discursive outcomes may be readier to see their end point as less definitive and active. Whatever approach is used, CADISPA has always maintained that EFS must have action at its core, a change in understanding and behaviour that can be tested by performance observation. Education and action, praxis in Freire's terms (Freire, 1972), is at the very core of understanding.

Education and Action

Action has always been a problem both for professional community development workers and educationists. Being drawn in to a local action might put workers in confrontation with their local authority, and raises acute questions of legitimacy and the morality of involvement. For educationists, action has always been something that is done somewhere else. Action and education have historically been kept separate. This view is limited and limiting, but the counter view, that they are intimately connected, presents a host of decisions which a worker must confront before engaging in the process. It is too simple to say that the choice is either to act with the group or abandon group work. It is perfectly possible — even essential — that the facilitator remain detached from any action in which a group may engage. There are good professional reasons for this, survival being one. However, the more important reason is to do with dominance, invasion and ownership.

The learning and action programme belongs to the local people. The facilitator rides alongside and within the group for a very short time with a clearly defined and limited role. He or she has a crucial part to play in helping the group think through strategy, preferred outcomes, processes and the result of action. At no time does the facilitator engage in action. The action belongs to the people alone.

Sensible practical support is necessary to prove the facilitator's worth to the group. It is an active not a passive role, and one that must continually prove to be helpful. This does not mean negotiating important issues for the group or carrying placards at demonstrations. It does mean gathering, supplying and accessing information, printing and publishing material, attending conferences and offering day-to-day counselling.

Critical Issues and Questions

Moving from Reaction to Proaction Do local people ever create the circumstances that enable them to make real decisions? This question lies at the heart of Local Agenda 21 (LA21). If sustainability is to mean anything and be nurtured by ordinary people, it must allow decision-making to be based on early and detailed involvement in information gathering, analysis and action.

It is a difficult process. We are immersed in top-down, prescriptive solutions that are inextricably linked to others' analyses of the problem. Though Agenda 21 education insists on both urban and rural local people demanding information and influencing legislation and implementation, there are often significant barriers to overcome.

Barriers to Proactive Behaviour Anxiety related to perceived low levels of skill and competence lies at the heart of non-engagement or poor performance. There is often anxiety caused by the incremental elements of a particular issue being too technical or complex; anxiety that participants' level of intelligence is too low, that they will be shown up, that they might fail, look foolish or make matters worse. There is anxiety that they might upset powerful people and be hurt or damaged in the process, or be smothered by overpowering professionals who delightfully destroy their embryonic self-reliance and reinforce the myth and language abyss.

People who have experienced many years of a life in which decisions are made slowly and are perhaps low-level, need support and time to handle painful or powerful information. They need to be constantly reminded of the sufficiency of their ability and competence. They need to be allowed to make real decisions and live with the excitement and anxiety of making them.

The starting point must be the territorial boundaries which all people establish. It is the extension beyond the familiar that allows 'reaction' to be transformed to 'proaction'.

Box 9.1 JENNY'S CARAVAN

Jenny Smith has a caravan which she lets out to provide a small second income. She prefers friends and friends of family to use it. She hardly

---

> *charges anything; cleans it excessively and is continually asking her clients if all is well. Last year, she returned two weeks' letting money because two of the gas mantles were inoperative.*
>
> *By bringing Jenny Smith and those other caravan owners in the same area together it has been possible to share experiences. She realizes and sees how others manage and operate. She has examples of marketing flyers used by others and has shared her own anxieties.*
>
> *For the first time this year she has advertised her van. The price has been raised to match others, targets have been set and materials typed for distribution.*
>
> *By starting where she was, it was made possible for Jenny to move at her own pace, set the direction in which she wanted to go, counter her anxiety and watch and learn from others. She moved from being reactive to being proactive. She moved the boundaries herself. She started with the familiar and dictated outcome, pace, direction and degree for herself. She was at the centre of the decision-making process.*
>
> *The worries that Jenny held (and still holds) of her level of competence, her self-perception, her understanding, her ability to control and her interactive performance were mitigated by allowing her to move by degrees from owned and protected territory to somewhere less familiar. A place slightly less protected and slightly more exposed. However, at no time were the decisions usurped from her and at no time was anything prescribed.*

Problems in Practice: The Facilitator Finding the right facilitator is the main problem for any group engaged on a community development experience. While not the only problem, it is the one which, if not resolved effectively, will destroy whatever work the group might achieve.

Speed and direction are common problems for facilitators. For some reason, facilitators need to control: both physically and psychologically. It seems to be an immensely difficult task for them to allow the group to move in its preferred direction while facilitating and supporting them towards that end. Facilitators must also address the issue of personal preferences, ideas and silent bias. If it is believed that clients bring understandings and preconceptions to the engagement, then facilitators too must shed, or better still declare, their preconceptions. This is a necessary step towards equity and power sharing.

Problems in Practice: The Group The group will find a multitude of reasons for not engaging: the issue is not important enough, it is too local, it is personal. They cannot find the time, it is just a simple problem — 'please do not create a fuss.' Any, or all of these might be used. Any, or all might also be legitimate. Gentle processing by the facilitator will test whether the group is ready or willing to engage further: if not, the group will fold or change its focus and it is right that this should happen.

Anxieties are also exposed and created as the work progresses. Feelings of inadequacy and competition between group members and pressures on time and on external relationships might grow rather than dissipate as the issue unfolds. The work of the facilitator at these moments is crucial both to the group's survival and to the experience being judged a success.

Success is the key to further work and must be experienced and celebrated. Experiencing success and growth can take many forms and there is no substitute for it — while failure brings problems of its own. Failure to achieve a particular outcome is the least damaging, but failures of personal understanding and of individuals to perform adequately within a team setting might have serious consequences for that group. Conflict and a breakdown in relations between group members might have long-lasting, deeply wounding consequences for individuals.

The facilitator's role is therefore central, critical and crucial to each individual's growth and to the group's performance. But the facilitator's role as educator, counsellor and group worker is also highly exposed. In asking ordinary people to risk their own exposure through group learning, facilitators must first understand their own motivation, skill level and commitment. This is the crucial first step, for once inside the issue, the process and the dynamics, it is too late for the facilitator to cry 'help'.

Creative Engagement People act because they are hurt, angry and emotional or because they wish to initiate or prevent change or mitigate circumstances. The first is reactive: the second proactive. Action itself holds no intrinsic credibility. Anarchic, emotive, irrational and blind action is also hurtful, energetic and wasteful. This has no place in community development and no place in EFS. Instead, action needs to be cool, rational, and based on a clear moral and ethical platform. There are two reasons for this.

First, for longevity, the changed circumstances which will follow the action will need continued commitment and support from those held within its grasp. Intense emotion of the degree that might have initiated an irrational action cannot be maintained over time.

Second, action must stem from a clear and calculated understanding of the issue, the process, the potential outcome and the potential critical circumstances the action may have caused. This necessarily dictates a process prior to and after the action that helps the actors think through and make decisions about final or staged outcomes. Many different kinds of action are possible. It takes a calculating, cool head to choose the one that matches the most appropriate outcome to the group's talents, experience, competence and commitment. This is calculated, creative engagement.

This educational action/reflection cycle is central to LA21. It stems minimally from emotion. It is clearly thought through and is enacted by the group on the basis of a process which has enabled them to see with more clarity the objectives and consequences of action. It takes local people centrally to their concerns, empowers them and supports them while they both consider and take action. It cocoons them in an informal, educational, learning experience, which, once experienced, can usefully be applied anywhere.

Towards the Popular Curriculum

As well as process, the other key ingredient in community education is curriculum. In his research, Groombridge (1983) identified three positions on a power continuum which involved differing contracts with local people: the prescriptive, the partnership and popular curriculum. The prescriptive curriculum in this context is of limited use, an uncomfortable place within action-based community learning programmes. The partnership curriculum is perhaps more appropriate where an open negotiation of learning content takes place between educator (as expert) and local people. This negotiated programme is then run for and with local people. Though this position still has uncomfortable 'top-down', 'power elite' elements within it, it is seen as one within which local people, many of whom are insecure, might feel more comfortable in the early stages of the programme.

By far the most appropriate model of a community-based learning curriculum described by Groombridge was the one he defined as 'popular'. This has significant implications for Agenda 21 education. A popular, local curriculum uses the local issues, fabric and resources in a programme delivered, researched, actioned and reflected upon by local people for themselves. This does not make the educator less important but it does give him or her a different and more difficult role. It is supportive, facilitative and securing: not teaching.

Fagan (1992) has taken the Groombridge notion of popular curriculum and secured it to a local environmental and issue-based framework. The work of the CADISPA project in Scotland and four other European countries is focused entirely on education as a local process within sustainable development.

The Role of Education in Sustainability Practice

Education is a prime ingredient in sustainability, both in challenging the present situation to enable it to become more eco-sensitive and in establishing new paradigms of thinking and behaviour which will stem from that. It is fraught with problems but does have within it the potentiality for lasting change. If people are to save and protect species, to be enabled to care deeply for cultural identity and to be able to make choices about crucial economic development issues, then local education has a key role to play. It will not frighten people into obedience and it will not buy particular behaviour. However, it will engage people in the prospect of their future by making them central to its design.

Turning Issue into Material

A multitude of processes are available to help the facilitator translate local experiences, issues and actions into learning programmes. These are a few of them:

Photo deconstruction The group records the issue by taking photographs. These are then enlarged and used by the facilitator to reflect the issue back to those people who own it. By progressively deconstructing the photographs and stepping back into the facets of the image, it is possible for the group to challenge assumptions, perceptions and romantic myths.

Open/closed scripts These are generated stories of the issue and reality of the group. The group can supply key words for the facilitator who then uses them to create a story line — or the stories generated are actual life experiences from the group. These are used by the facilitator as a means of illustrating issues and developing contextual understanding with the group.

Role-playing around the concern The group itself identifies the concern. The facilitator helps it record and illustrate the issues. This is then enacted and the performance itself, with its invited audience, is used as the vehicle for further discussion and action.

Investigation and presentation This is at the heart of the community-based learning programme. 'Investigation' means planned information gathering by the community for itself, with the facilitator's help. 'Presentation' means more than reporting. Presentation means that the subgroup engage the rest of the clients in working through the materials gathered. There is a critical role in this method for the facilitator.

Review of experience The personal experience of a particular event or action is reviewed in turn by individuals within the group. Each person shares his or her interpretations and feelings, and voices concerns and misunderstandings.

Co-counselling and co-investigating For people not used to the exposure of individualized research and performance, co-investigation, namely dual research, cooperative learning and sharing together along one theme, is very powerful.

Futuring This can be done in many ways, but it is essentially trying to imagine particular facets of the future, be they familial, environmental or commercial. The group may want to use an aerial photograph and discuss a whole variety of future possibilities. Personal futuring — next winter, next year, in five years' time — is a very creative group work method. The facilitator must be prepared for a personal and intimate encounter if this option is chosen.

Planning for real This is based on the work of Tony Gibson and involves local people choosing a variety of possibilities for the development of their particular territory.

RRA/PRA (Rapid Rural Assessment/Participatory Rural Assessment) Both of these involve gathering local people together to chart and better understand the demography and resource issues in their locality. These are very useful tools for community development and are published through the International Institute for Environment and Development (IIED).

Others There is a multitude of material available for group discussion and investigation. Care must be taken not to allow the programme to become prescriptive or the facilitator to become a teacher. The learning programme, its facilitation, content and processing must have local people central to it. The curriculum must stem out of and embrace local issues, perceptions and cultures.

If it is true that all people step into the future facing backwards, then this process of experience reconstruction seems vitally important.

Box 9.2

Andy is 12. He has had French, maths and chemistry this morning and goes back to double physical education (PE) and something else. He likes maths and hates PE. The rest is much of a nothingness. It is a beautiful, sunny June day and we planned our trip to Arran at lunchtime. He said he was going to think about the mountains while trying to do the high jump. He wants to know more about the Superquarry, drugs, relationships, money, God, the Brent Spar and how secure my marriage is. He gets home economics and German tomorrow, and PE.

Catherine is 30. She lives in a village with 41 other people, all older except five children who are educated 40 miles away: a journey of one and a half hours each morning and night. She did not do well at school and got married early. Her husband is a fisherman — and it is clearly obvious that times are difficult — what with the trawlers and all.

Five of the women have got together to think through what they might do to help. Tourists there are in excess. How to tap into that resource? How to find the cash without having any yourself? How to write a business plan? How to confront 20 years of being told how useless one is? How to solve, contribute, move forward? If she had listened at school would that have made a difference?

Conclusion

Education is a process not a place. The kind of education Andy and Catherine need is one that continually speaks to their 'real' needs. To help make sense of the world, to seek and engage in opportunity, risk and process. Education is about confrontation: external and internal. Stretching the boundaries of comfort, change and challenge. It is about embracing personal needs in a local context. It is about understanding the local to make sense of the global. It is about being informed, celebrating experiences and fitting that experience into a framework of understanding which includes an assessment of our impact on others.

Education is about confidence — about saying to Catherine, 'You are able and clever, you do understand, you are perfectly competent and able to engage.' Education is also about risk — about creating the conditions in which people can engage and learn without being castrated in the attempt. It is about the knowledge they own and share, the knowledge they generate and update, and the knowledge that has purpose, direction, meaning and location.

Education is about skill and practice for local people in seeing problems inside other problems and solving those bits that need solving. It is about seeing those solutions as problems in themselves. Education is about solving problems in a way that does not create problems for others. It is about doing what you would wish to do — being challenged, making a mark, passing on to the young people a better place than the one that now exists.

Education is also about research — finding out, application, more finding out, seeking understanding, application, action and reflection, analysis and application, application and reflection. Local education has at its core, negotiation, research, action and reflection.

It is impossible to think of a world in which sustainability is important if education itself does not adhere to those very principles which underpin it. This means that education has to prove its equality, its justice, its democracy — each and every time it engages with local people. Education in this context is vital, but it is also different. It is local, owned by local people, informal, action oriented, moving, exciting and risky. It is the education Andy wants and Catherine needs.

References

Dewey, J (1916) *Democracy and Education*, Macmillan, New York
Fagan, G (1992) *Cadispa: Community Education*, WWF–UK, London
Freire, P (1972) *Pedagogy of the Oppressed*, Penguin, London
Groombridge, B (1983) 'Adult Education and the Education of Adults', in M Tight, *Education for Adults*, vol. I, Croom Helm, London
UNCED (1992) *Earth Summit 1992*, Regency Press, London

Chapter 10 | TOWARDS a CRITICAL MEDIA
John Howson & Adrian Cleasby

The media, particularly television, have an important place in any transition to a more sustainable society. This raises fundamental questions about the role of the media in reflecting or shaping society's culture, about the potential role of a reflective media concerned with sustainability, and about the role of critical media education in evaluating 'sustainability' or 'non-sustainability' messages, whether intended or not.

John Howson
Critical Education Through and About Media

Few would deny that in industrialized nations the media play a significant role in the day-to-day lives of young people. Television provides them with an important window to the outside world at a time when they are still forming opinions and getting to grips with wider realities. In the UK, young people watch on average about three hours of television a day (Cullingford, 1992), but we still have a long way to go to understand the psychological, developmental and educational effects of this viewing.

The problem for those studying the relationship between media and society is that it is neither linear nor straightforward. For example, as Midwinter (1994) puts it, 'Images are not simple. The notion of representing implies an action performed by someone, a process that requires a perpetrator and an audience. It is, though, a process that we all experience and can understand.'

For a number of years, there has been a move away from seeing the media as a one-way information funnel. As Hastings (1990) points out, even in areas such as advertising, there is a trend towards seeing the consumer as an active participant in a broader process rather than the passive recipient of a media message. In discussing education for sustainability (EFS) therefore, it is important to come at the issue from 'both ends' — the media and wider society — and attempt to clarify the complex relationship between them.

What Are Critical Media? Let us ask first, the question of how far the media are aware of their own values and assumptions — how far they take a critical and reflective approach to their work. Much of the criticism of the media with regard to this issue has centred on news coverage. The Glasgow Media Education Group (1984) argues that:

> *It would be inappropriate to blame the mass media for failures of political imagination on the part of those who are responsible for the peace of the world. Clearly, too, journalists can be on the receiving end of censorship, disinformation and propaganda campaigns from powerful pressure groups. What this does point to, however, is the need for critical journalism, an approach which does not accept unquestioningly the official line or the press handout. Alternative sources of information can provide some check on the reliability of data and can affect the texture of a news story.*

Some writers such as the American radical Noam Chomsky (1991) have taken this argument much further, asserting that some sections of the media have become so good at sticking to official press releases that they have become little more than adjuncts to government. Chomsky argues that media institutions are answerable to no-one apart from the large organizations that control them. These, he says, are largely undemocratic in structure, with aims and objectives that rarely take into account the interest of the wider community. But it is arguable whether this line takes sufficient account of the power of the audience — an idea we return to later.

Beyond these political issues, a further key question concerns how far media institutions arise out of and are steeped in an unsustainable consumer culture and are therefore predisposed to be unsupportive of any change liable to undermine that culture. This view may have some credence when applied to sections of the press, which as Longman and Lacey (1994) point out, produced a hostile response to the 1992 Earth Summit. However, television coverage in the UK has often been sympathetic to environmental perspectives and it is probably not an exaggeration to say that television more than anything has been instrumental in raising awareness of environmental and development issues.

As Huckle (1995) points out:

> *The demands of reflective individuals for more sustainable kinds of development are often prompted by the information and images they see on television. . . . As the media production of ideology lessens in favour of the production of differences for difference's sake, television news broadcasts and documentaries are more likely to make people aware of the environmental costs of global industrialism.*

The degree to which this becomes the case, and whether it is possible to go beyond 'environment and development' issues to sustainability, will depend in part on the amount of coverage and credence given to these areas. In the short term, if the media regard sustainability as peripheral to mainstream concerns, the sustainability agenda may need to be carried by oppositional groups. Sullivan (1987) describes the role of separate groups such as ecology, labour, Third World solidarity and peace movements:

> *It would be foolish to intimate that mass media programming is totally devoid of oppositional currents. . . . However, in relation to all of commercial television programming these attempts are minuscule in relation to the total programming fare. . . . Rather than seeing these oppositional strains as resistance to the dominant myth, they are frequently characterized within the mass media as simply deviance from the accepted cultural norm (ie hegemony).*

However, from the media's point of view, striking the correct balance between programming that relates to the majority in a way that reflects their lives, interests and ambitions and programming that gives air to new and oppositional voices is neither straightforward nor simple. From the radical point of view, it is easy to say that the media are not being critical if they do not reflect the radical case, but an 'open door' policy could give air to voices that most people would find extremely disagreeable, such as extreme right wing views, racism or sexism.

Given the political and cultural contexts which influence media, we can now ask where the entry points are for those wishing to promote sustainability.

Gaining Ground The media are not monolithic. New technologies such as satellite, cable and digital communications make it increasingly possible for groups to give air to an amazing variety of views and perspectives. As Huckle (1994) points out, 'Electronic media can introduce a dizzying variety of images, cultures and voices.' Thus they can encourage subcultures including environmentalism.

However, it can be argued that it is necessary to raise the awareness of producers and editors. One problem is that issues that involve or bridge a range of divergent contexts are difficult to weave into a concise story line. Let us consider the following definition of news:

> *It has to be an event. It has to be something that has happened, rather than a long process that's been unfolding for over time. It has to have happened recently. It almost always involves elite figures. . . . It has to be an event that has some significance for the country as a whole. There are whole areas of the world . . . which are very sporadically covered in the news. The other criterion would be human interest: something like a disaster would be automatically news.*

> (Murdock, 1973)

Taking this definition, many of the complex issues related to sustainability such as Third World debt or the plight of native peoples would not be news, but by contrast issues such as an increase in child asthma due to pollution would be news, simply because of the local 'human interest' aspects. I would suggest that this is, in fact, largely the case, although further work would need to be done to confirm this pattern. Television magazines and documentaries are a little more flexible in terms of their content and have traditionally been the home of debate on environment and development (see second section of this chapter).

Environmental pressure groups have demonstrated that it is possible to work with and through the media and thus get their message across in a way that would have been impossible otherwise. Cases like this illustrate that the situation is far more complex than Sullivan would lead us to believe. Part of the reason why environmental pressure groups were so successful in the 1980s was that they made a proactive attempt to work with and to educate the media. While this did not have an immediate effect, when environmental news arose it meant that the media were far more sympathetic to the perspective of pressure groups than they would otherwise have been.

However, campaigning is not the same as providing EFS. If we value the media's public education role, it seems important that we not only debate what the news is or could be, but also which aspects of the sustainability debate are newsworthy. Further, we need to continue the debate about the role of media in a democracy. Vital to such a debate is media literacy through media education.

Media Education and the Critical Audience If the media have a vital role in helping young people get a balanced view of the world, then there is a strong educational argument for providing them with the tools necessary to deconstruct media messages. This issue has been tackled by many authors including Hart (1991), who develops the idea of a 'media-educated person'.

He outlines five principles that would be understood by a media-educated person. These are:

- the media do not simply reflect or replicate the world;
- selection, compression and elaboration occur at every point in the complex process of editing and presenting messages;
- audiences are not passive and predictable but active and variable in their responses;
- messages are not solely determined by producers' and editors' decisions — nor by governments, advertisers and media moguls; and
- the media contain a multiplicity of different forms shaped by different technologies, languages and capacities.

Hart argues that critical media education should include and go beyond these five principles to look at issues such as what constitutes campaigning and advertising.

If young people were media educated as well as educated for sustainability they would be able to interpret messages in the context of sustainability. How we set about achieving this is an area for future debate, but it seems that elements of media education need to come into EFS. Several authors, such as Midwinter, have examined that question from the point of view of the outlooks of developing nations, but now this work needs taking further to look at the broader sustainability debate.

The role of critical education should be to form what might be termed a 'critical audience'. At present, it could be argued that in choosing to view particular programmes, audiences bring about a type of 'viewer democracy'. In the UK, the audience is likely to become more important as new channels open up and competition for viewers increases. However, the degree to which media output is guided by audience choice seems to vary enormously. As Worcester (1993) points out, media coverage of environment and development issues declined at a time when audience interest was at its peak. With news programmes, viewers have no method of indicating which items they consider newsworthy (see Curran and Seaton, 1993).

A critical audience is, in my view, one step beyond a media-educated audience in that it would be willing to engage the media in proactive discussion about programme content and let programme makers know what their preferences were. Such an audience would be empowered consumers rather than discriminating consumers, working with the media in much the same way as pressure groups have done so successfully in the past.

While the current influence of the audience is to some extent unquantifiable, it seems certain that audiences could have an even greater influence on programme makers if they had sufficient understanding of the way the media agenda is set. As audiences develop more sophisticated forms of media awareness — as seems the current trend — it is not difficult to foresee a situation in which the audience's views become key to television output and even, in this way, instrumental in moving forward important debates such as sustainability. Meanwhile, two conditions need to be fulfilled if the critical audience is to be the norm: one, that media seek to empower audiences; and two that educators seek to increase critical media education at all levels of education.

Conclusion I have tried to flag up some of the issues for further debate in the area of EFS and the media, and to look at the concept of critical media. I have tried to emphasize that media coverage is not simply a one-way process and have introduced the concept of critical audiences working hand in hand with critical media. By twinning audience response with media content we can begin to overcome some of the pitfalls intrinsic in looking at media content in isolation. Raising awareness of sustainability issues in the population at large, goes hand in hand, I believe, with raising the media profile of these issues (see also Abrahams and Lacey, 1990).

As educators it is surely our job to tackle and debate questions relating to lifestyle and sustainability, and to help resolve the broader issues that arise from this debate. But can the media play a role in the process of change in society? I believe the answer to this is a firm yes.

Adrian Cleasby
Content, Constraints and Prospects

The rest of this chapter considers the extent to which critical media already exist and looks at some of the cultural and structural constraints inhibiting media from becoming more actively involved in EFS. It discusses the prospects for developing a critically autonomous, participative, tolerant and environmentally aware audience through mass media. While other mass media are implicit, our prime concern here is television as it is the predominant communication medium in most industrialized and developing countries. This pre-eminence means that the EFS movement can ill afford to treat television as a peripheral concern.

Understanding Television as Cultural Artefact Television is an audiovisual medium which integrates animated images with narrative structures to create what John Eldridge of the Glasgow University Media Group has called a 'semblance of reality' (Eldridge, 1993). The medium is stylistic and editorial conventions are often blatantly to the fore in drama programmes, openly encouraging the viewer to 'suspend disbelief' and interpret the representations of various social situations, historical events, futuristic whimsy and so on 'as if' what is depicted were real.

With many factual programmes like news, current affairs and documentaries, a similar suspension of disbelief occurs as the audience views what is depicted as if it were impartial, unfiltered truth. Acceptance of the stylistic and editorial conventions of factual programmes is often so widespread that the processes by which these 'truths' are represented in our living rooms appear to be as transparent as a pane of glass. Yet value-laden conventions and encrypted messages abound in factual programmes. News bulletins begin with images of swirling globes suggesting comprehensive world coverage; and news readers appear behind impressive consoles that exude executive authority. Nevertheless, as Fiske (1987) notes, this 'transparency fallacy' is so pervasive that it is often an assumption made as much by people working in television newsrooms as by the less media-literate members of the audience.

The complex technological feats and social discourse involved in manufacturing, packaging, marketing and transmitting television programmes, and the editorial and proprietorial decisions about what to show, how to show it and what to exclude generally remain hidden from public scrutiny. Nevertheless, they suggest that television programmes are highly selective, contrived and sophisticated cultural artefacts. As Masterman (1993) points out, we are often justified in accepting the authenticity of much media output. But as media assumptions and values exert formative and persuasive influences, we need to examine critically those assumptions to justify our acceptance.

Information and Influence The rapid growth in television set ownership and usage during the second half of the twentieth century is remarkable precisely because of the extraordinary influence visual images and narrative structures exert on audience perceptions. Researching for a report on the impact of images of Africa, van der Gaag and Nash (1987) found evidence to suggest that: 'The public's perceptions, though they were influenced by other factors like family, friends and school, were ultimately formed by the media. ... The visual images were dominant, and the images were remembered when even significant facts and figures had been forgotten.'

Television is used, not just as a source of trivial distraction and light entertainment, but as a primary source of information on world affairs by at least 70 per cent of the British population, according to the 1991 results of an annual survey carried out by the Independent Television Commission. The BBC's highly respected foreign affairs editor, John Simpson, in an interview published in *Crosslines Global Report* (Shuffell, 1995) has suggested that the narrative structure of news 'stories' can create a convincingly logical, simple, linear structure by which apparently chaotic events 'out there' can be comprehended and categorized by the audience at home.

There is good reason to suspect that the output of mainstream media is more influential on young people's perceptions and attitudes than classroom-based learning. For example, Masterman (1993) begins his account of the theory and practice of media education by relating that, 'In the 1970s it was estimated that children between the ages of five and 14 were spending 44 per cent more time watching television than they were in lessons in school.' Though such tendencies are often bemoaned, we would be wrong to assume that 'tuning in' to television equates to 'switching off' our critical faculties. Studies into viewing habits carried out by the Independent Television Commission (ITC, 1993) indicate that up to two thirds of the British public claim to watch television 'often' or 'occasionally' because they think they will learn something.

Education for sustainability must take serious account of the power and influence of television since so many of us look to learn through it and rely on it for information, and since our outlook can be so unwittingly yet so profoundly influenced by its implicit values and conventions. The implication perhaps is that the promulgation of critical autonomy, cultural pluralism and environmental sensitivity — central planks of EFS — must come *through* the media if they are to have any significant impact on majority attitudes and behaviour.

Cultural Constraints on Critical Media Competitive pressures to maximize audiences have led to a news culture that handles events in a particularly brisk fashion ('sound-bites', headlines and reports lasting an average of two and a half minutes on the mainstream bulletins, for instance) and rarely returns to an 'old story' since 'today's news wraps tomorrow's chips'. Cataclysmic events lend themselves to this kind of reporting; complex processes do not. What results, in the words of Anne Winter (1991) of UNICEF, Geneva is 'a peek-a-boo world where an event pops into view for a moment and then vanishes. It is a world of fragments, discontinuities, where the worth of information lies in its novelty and entertainment value rather than in its relevance to social and political decision-making and debate' (Benthall, 1993).

The view, described by Murdock and Phelps (1973), that a news story has to deal with an event rather than a long drawn out process seems to be borne out in newsroom practice according to research from the Third World and Environment Broadcasting Project (see Cleasby, 1993, 1995; Firebrace, 1990; Hardstaff, 1992, 1993). Between 1989/90 and 1993/4 this research showed that around two thirds of all mainstream UK television news reports from low and middle income countries focused on sensational events emanating from conflicts and disasters such as war, crime, civil unrest, famine, drought and pestilence.

This presents us with a central problem since, as Orr (1995) notes, in the move towards sustainable living, 'Education must equip students to think in systems and patterns . . . to comprehend how cause and effect work in complex systems.' While television is fixated with events which it handles curtly, with little regard to underlying context or longer-term ramifications, the processes of sustainability will not feature in the news agenda. As Smythe (1981) has noted, 'What is omitted will hardly shape the strategic level of policy determination for that society.'

Contextualization A main source of complementary, contextual programming has traditionally been the documentary film. 'Long-form' factual programmes have been used to address issues, environments and cultures, which news crews rarely cover and can only report superficially when they do. Documentaries can contextualize and draw out complex connections because of their longer duration and because they are often thematically serialized over a period of weeks. For example, BBC2 commissions ethnographic films and screens them in an eight-week series (*Under the Sun*) in which audiences can expect to view extended and precisely observed films about foreign cultures. When a news story erupts in or around one of these cultures, the audience has already encountered information, images and narratives of what everyday life can be like there. In the absence of first-hand experience, this background cultural context is crucial to the audience's ability to interpret news reports of isolated, exceptional events as part of wider dynamic systems.

However, audience research indicates that international topics generally attract fewer viewers than UK-based programmes. This, and the additional cost of such programmes, can make them difficult to justify in a commercial environment where decisions about what to commission and schedule depend more on such factors than on social or educational value. Research into levels of documentary output on international issues on British television carried out by the Third World and Environment Broadcasting Project (Cleasby, 1995) indicates a fairly dramatic decline in recent years. Between 1989 and 1994, broadcast hours of in-depth factual programmes about international topics on the four major channels fell by just over 40 per cent with a much more marked decline occurring on the 'mainstream' channels (BBC1 and ITV) in the peak-time schedules. This trend is unlikely to be reversed given that, for example, the BBC's recent programme strategy review (BBC, 1995) concentrates largely on extending coverage of issues, cultures and activities within the UK at the expense of international and global environmental issues.

As contextualizing programmes diminish in number and slide into less prominent late-night slots, the sustainability debate increasingly becomes, for schedulers and audiences alike, a marginal, minority or special interest issue rather than an all-encompassing and necessary process of societal change.

As Benthall (1993) suggests:

> *editors subscribe to a value system which includes a strong commit-*
> *ment to fairness, taste and ethical standards. . . . However, the value*
> *system does not appear to include a commitment to institutional self-*
> *examination, constantly reviewing how by imperceptible shifts of empha-*
> *sis the practice of the newsroom might from its position of immense*
> *influence become more rationally and equitably responsive to human*
> *need.*

Such 'imperceptible shifts' in the practices of mainstream media may be the only viable way to instigate wholesale changes in public perceptions and behaviour. Anything else, however valuable, will be working on the fringes. Yet, paradoxically, the critical audience can be an agent of such changes, and this is now examined further.

Prospects for Developing a Critical Audience Audiences are frequently oblivious to the formative influence of television's implicit assumptions and encrypted messages on their own values and perceptions. Grasping the nature and extent of the medium's influence requires the critical decon-struction of televisual artefacts and their component parts (reports, com-mentaries, captions and graphics). This creates a critical audience awareness of the criteria the media use to determine whose views count as reliable orthodoxy, whose count as deviant and whose are discounted altogether as cranky, corrupt or codswallop.

Mary Midgley (1995) argues for a kind cultural plurality which is wholly applicable to television in the context of EFS: 'If we are to keep our power of responding to what goes on, we need to be struck constantly from different angles by different aspects of the truth. We need to consult many conceptual maps — many attitudes, many ideologies — and must be ready to use one to correct and supplement another.'

Audiences often assume they get 'the whole truth' by ignoring or tacitly accepting the cultural hegemony implicit in the idea of impartial news coverage. To dispel this hegemony, the value systems that inform the editors' decision-making process need to include cultural pluralism. Reeve (1993) points out that many critics believe culturally neutral news reporting is impossible and would anyway be undesirable. As Midgley (1995) concludes, 'The reason we must be open to many kinds of messages is not that none of them are true but that they are all partial.'

Stimulating links between an informed audience and broadcasters is one way of influencing the latent hegemony of current media value systems. Many NGOs strive to promote such interaction through independent pro-duction companies and educational trusts like the International Broadcasting Trust (IBT) and Television Trust for the Environment (TVE). Such bodies often have memberships that offer enfranchisement for individuals. Most are also actively engaged in the formal education sector, stimulating participative links between young people and the otherwise 'faceless' and distant media machines in the context of development and environment education. It is important to stress the positive steps that media organizations themselves have taken. Central Television's Special Projects Department was instrumental in establishing TVE, in partnership with WWF–UK and the United Nations Environment Programme (UNEP). The BBC Multicultural Programmes Unit was set up to address cross-cultural issues, and the BBC along with other European broadcasters and IBT are closely involved in the work of the One World Group.

How far these organizations are engaged in EFS is a difficult question, but the amount of time and effort placed by, say IBT, in discussing and evaluating the messages conveyed by its documentary films, dramas and educational video packs, together with the emphasis placed on challenging audience stereotypes of developing countries and global environmental concerns, suggests that they are at least promulgating cultural pluralism, environmental sensitivity and critical autonomy.

Individuals can also exercise some limited influence on media value systems through duty officers. Telephone comments are logged and circulated quite widely within most broadcasting organizations, for example at BBC Television Centre, where a dossier of comments from the previous night's viewers lands on the desks of department heads, senior producers and staff at the *Radio Times* each morning. This relatively public airing can work for interest groups with widespread or vociferous support whether their concerns are single issues or broader.

While many development and environmental educationists blanch at the idea of sustainability being perceived as pressure-group interest, media organizations generally regard it in this light, so those engaged in EFS may need to engage in broadcaster lobbying as a strategy for change.

Conclusion Many of the dominant cultural assumptions that underlie media practice receive such widespread, uncritical acceptance that media education is a prerequisite of EFS. Yet, at the same time, so many people rely on television for their information about the world that EFS cannot take root in society without television transforming its current practices and thereby audience perception. Given the constraints on developing a more critical, more sustainability-conscious mainstream culture through and within media practice, this chapter perhaps paints a rather bleak picture. But, while the process of shifting the media towards a more holistic, even realistic agenda may be difficult, it is far from unattainable.

The radical social critic Chomsky (1992) has pointed to the power of people working locally and building up the basis for popular movements as an agent of change. Constantly updating and redrawing our conceptual map of the media is part of such groundwork. It is worth doing diligently since, if sustainability is to capture the popular imagination and change orthodox perceptions and patterns of behaviour, most people around the world are likely to encounter it either through the media, or else not at all.

Conclusion: Towards a Critical Media

In this chapter we have sketched the need for the sustainability movement to develop a critical and participative audience and have introduced some of the tensions that constrain the development of critical media. The proximity in meaning between the terms 'communication' and 'community' suggest how close and complicated are the links between mass media and processes of social change. Wholesale changes in public outlook and behaviour have been advocated in the sustainability debate. We would suggest they may occur only if EFS develops critical and systematic understanding about, within and through the mass media.

References

Abrahams, J and C Lacey (1990) *Demonstration Deception and Debate*, WWF/Kogan Page, London

BBC (1995) *People and Programmes*, British Broadcasting Corporation, London

Benthall, J (1993) *Disasters, Relief and the Media*, IB Tauris, London

Chomsky, N (1991) *Necessary Illusions*, Pluto Press, London

— (1992) in P Wintonick and M Achbar's film, *Manufacturing Consent*, Necessary Illusions Productions Inc/National Film Board of Canada

Cleasby, A (1993) *Giving the Broader Picture: BBC TV and the Wider World*, IBT, London

— (1995) *What in the World is Going On? British Television and Global Affairs*, Third World & Environment Broadcasting Project, London

Cullingford, C (1992) *Children and Society*, Cassell, London

Curran, J and J Seaton (1991) 'Mass Media and Democracy', in J Curran and M Gurevitch (eds) *Mass Media and Society*, Routledge, London

Eldridge, J (ed) (1993) *Getting the Message: News, Truth and Power*, Glasgow University Media Group/Routledge, London

Firebrace, J (ed) (1990) *Losing the Picture*, Oxfam, Oxford

Fiske, J (1987) *Television Culture*, Routledge, London

Glasgow Media Education Group (1984) *War and Peace News*, Glasgow Media Education Group, Glasgow

Hardstaff, J (1992) *Getting the Full Picture*, IBT, London

— (1993) *The Good Franchise Guide: Opportunities for Voluntary Organizations to Get Involved with ITV*, NCVO, London

Hart, A (1991) *Understanding the Media*, Routledge & Kegan Paul, London

Hastings, G (1990) 'Advertising and Young People', in J Abrahams and C Lacey, *Demonstration Deception and Debate*, WWF/Kogan Page, London

Huckle, J (1994) 'Using Television Critically in Environmental Education', *Environmental Education Research*, 1 (3)

ITC (1993) *Television: The Public's View*, ITC, London

Longman, D and C Lacey (1994) 'The Press and Public Access to the Environment and Development Debate', *Blackwell Sociological Review*

Masterman, L (1993) *Teaching the Media*, Routledge, London

Midgley, M (1995) 'Idealism in Practice', in C Thick (ed) *The Right to Hope*, Earthscan Publications Ltd, London

Midwinter, C (1994) 'Watching the World in Development Education', *Global Perspectives*

Murdock, G and G Phelps (1973) *Mass Media and Secondary School*, Macmillan, London

Orr, D (1995) 'Greening of Education', *Resurgence*, 170, Hartland, Devon

Reeve, G (1993) *Communications and the 'Third World'*, Routledge, London

Shuffel, S (1995) 'Beyond the Tear-Jerkers', *Crosslines Global Report*, April/May

Smythe, D (1981) *Dependency Road: Communications, Capitalism, Consciousness and Canada*, Ablex, New Jersey

Sullivan, E (1987) 'Critical Pedagogy and Television', in D W Livingstone et al, *Critical Pedagogy and Cultural Power*, Macmillan, London

van der Gaag, N and C Nash (1987) *Images of Africa: The UK Report*, Oxfam, Oxford

Winter, A (1991) Presentation at UNICEF Information Workshop, Nairobi, 19 June

Worcester (1993) 'Are Newsrooms Bored with Greenery?', *British Journalism Review*, 4 (3)

Part IV

Continuing Education

Progress towards sustainable development makes good business sense because it can create competitive advantage and new opportunities. But it requires far-reaching shifts in corporate attitudes and new ways of doing business. To move from vision to reality demands strong leadership from the top, sustained commitment throughout the organization, and an ability to translate challenge into opportunities.

(S Schmidheiny, *Changing Course*, Business Council for Sustainable Development, MIT Press, Cambridge, Massachusetts, 1993)

Change agents are expected to initiate a process of participatory development. They are expected to help people develop a critical awareness of their development situation which will lead to self-directed and self-determined action for change. The training process should therefore equip them for such a role. Change agents therefore need to acquire skills in areas such as awareness building, promotion of participation, analysis of local situations and group dynamics. They need to develop a sensitivity to local needs, customs and habits, limitations and opportunities. If they fail in this they will become alienated from the people and end up being barriers rather than catalysts of participatory development.

(Stan Burkey, *People First: A Guide to Self-Reliant, Participatory Rural Development*, Zed Books, London, 1993)

Sustainable development will require substantial changes in behaviour at every level, giving priority to such unfashionable ideas as planning, community and greater equality. Existing patterns of consumerism, private ownership, individualism and the free market are deeply rooted in Western society and have spread far across the globe. Attempts to uproot them seem hopelessly idealistic. But we are reaching the point where self-interest and a common interest in survival converge. Already changes are occurring in local communities, in the world of business, in national policies, and in international relations.

(Andrew Blowers, *Planning for a Sustainable Environment*, Earthscan Publications Ltd, London, 1993)

So, in the move towards a more sustainable local authority, education should achieve changes in the community which:

- lead to changes in work and lifestyles and consumption patterns which are more sustainable;
- build on people's existing knowledge, understanding and concern;
- encourage people to consider alternatives, help them to make appropriate choices and empower them to bring about change;
- encourage and enable people to take part in the decision-making process, offering them the tools (skills, values, knowledge and confidence) to be effective;
- enable people to find and use information effectively;
- give opportunities to participate — leading people to take responsibility and gain a sense of ownership;
- help people to understand the links between issues and see connections with their own lives;
- encourage principles leading to a fairer society and more equitable distribution of resources — both within and outside the authority;
- enable people to identify practices that are relevant to sustainability and to monitor their own actions in relation to them.

(Local Government Management Board, *Educating for a Sustainable Local Community*, LGMB, Luton, 1994)

Chapter 11

CORPORATE GREENING
Nigel Roome &
Andrea Oates

In the two parts of this chapter, on businesses and trade unions, we consider the changes taking place in business, labour and education as a consequence of the ideas contained in the vision and principles of sustainable development. We question the adequacy of the changes to date and the extent to which they contribute to a more sustainable society. These ideas provide a background to discussion about the contribution of education for sustainability (EFS) as it affects management and labour and, in turn, how education shapes business organizations. In the overall conclusion, we outline the need for education that is prepared to elaborate 'new' models of the world from which managers and labour can learn in order to understand and interpret change for sustainability.

Nigel Roome
Business Organizations

There are currently no business organizations, sectors of society or nations that can be held up as models for sustainability. In the case of business, there are many examples of companies involved in a process of change towards the more limited notion of improving their environmental performance (Fischer and Schot, 1993). However, few companies have distinguished between the need to improve their environmental performance and the broader notion of sustainability. Those that have made this distinction recognize that sustainability involves an organization in profound examination and change of its social and environmental identity, its purpose and its practices. Implementing these changes will take a generation or more (Eddy, 1993; Ontario Hydro, 1993; BCSD, 1993).

The implications for EFS are perhaps threefold. First, EFS should incorporate ideas and understanding about what is currently practised, but must go beyond positivist descriptions and explanations to strongly normative accounts of what ought to be practised. Second, as the meaning of sustainability is continuously unfolding, a process of continuous learning requires educators, practitioners and students to check the adequacy of their skills, knowledge, models of the world and values in contributing to a more sustainable world. Third, EFS demands profound change in the organization, structure and practice of education equal to change required in other areas of society.

Sustainability and Improving Environmental Performance The work of the Brundtland Commission (WCED, 1987) provoked a significant response from the business community in the period leading up to Agenda 21 at the 1992 United Nations Conference on Environment and Development (UNCED) and beyond. Brundtland's discussion of environment and development encouraged organizations, such as the International Chamber of Commerce (ICC), to prepare commitments to more sustainable business practice (ICC, 1992). Other business associations developed similar initiatives such as the British Chamber of Commerce's Business and Environment Forum and the 'Global Environment Charter' of the Japan Federation of Economic Organizations. Many of these built on the practices of leading companies. Other models emerged in response to specific environmental threats, such as the 'Responsible Care' programme originated by the Canadian Chemical Producers' Association and the Valdez principles which emerged in the aftermath of the *Exxon Valdez* disaster (now revised as the Coalition for Environmentally Responsible Economies (CERES) principles).

A number of important ideas shaped business thinking during this period:

■ the need for a proactive, rather than reactive, stance going beyond compliance with the environmental laws;
■ the acknowledgement that environment and sustainability are strategic business concerns;
■ acceptance of the notion of product stewardship whereby companies take responsibility for the impacts of their products throughout their life cycle from R&D, through production, transportation, use and final disposal or reuse; and
■ the importance of partnerships between business and other agents in society, whether local communities, governments or environmental interests.

Yet, as the Business Council for Sustainable Development (BCSD) observed, 'Progress towards sustainable development ... requires far-reaching shifts in corporate attitudes and new ways of doing business' (Schmidheiny, 1992). In fact, an increasing gap emerged between leading companies holding a vision for change and others in the wider business community (Six and Winsemius, 1992). Three positions can be distinguished:

- *Compliance* These businesses ask why they should take more than a compliance position on the environment when most jurisdictions around the world place fiduciary responsibilities on managers to maximize shareholder wealth. Consequently, environmental performance is not a valid concern unless it benefits this 'bottom line' or is obliged by law.
- *Stewardship* These businesses accept that there are opportunities and efficiencies to be gained in the way resources are used. Careful stewardship of resources and managing the environmental impacts of business activities, beyond legal compliance, can add to shareholder value and improve the long-term prospects for shareholders. Environmental management is justified through efficiency, long-term profitability and a continued license to operate.
- *Social responsibility* These businesses accept the idea that they are bounded by social responsibilities. Principles or ethical standards constrain or condition profit-seeking behaviour. Profit is important, but not at any cost. These businesses operate beyond compliance with the law: managers set guidelines and codes of practice to reinforce a 'culture' in the organization that is committed to striving as far as possible to meet stakeholders' (including shareholders') interests and needs.

These alternative positions are centred on notions of environmental performance. However, none of the models fully address the concerns set out by Brundtland in her call for sustainability. Sustainability is more than simply environmental protection and improved environmental performance. It is concerned to bring environmental values into economic decision-making but also to consider the needs of the future in relation to the needs of the present and to seek more equitable distribution of economic and environmental assets between members of the current generation. The problem is that conventional business decision-making and market mechanisms do not lead to this view of sustainability.

For business to incorporate notions of fairness, justice and respect into its thinking and practice, principles and values must be used to limit automatic responses to market signals in the pursuit of profit maximization. New ways of capturing the impacts that company activities have on the environment and society must be developed. This implies a more open and dynamic process of dialogue between business managers and other stakeholders and more routine application of audits of social, ethical and environmental impacts. A vision of sustainable business practice therefore obliges managers to rethink the fundamental purpose and practice of business.

Sustainability recognizes the interconnected, complex and dynamic nature of human and environmental systems. In a truly interconnected world, business is not only part of a supply chain, it is embedded in ecological, social, temporal, spatial as well as industrial networks. Some indications of the implications for practice that arise from recognition of the need to manage these relationships are provided by Carley and Christie (1993).

Beyond this, some commentators argue that it is misleading to think of sustainable organizations or sustainable technologies (Roome and Clarke, 1994). Business organizations are simply vehicles through which knowledge is combined with labour, resources and capital to provide a product or service. For their part, technologies represent knowledge in the form of an artefact — a product, service or process. More important than striving to sustain the 'organization' is the need to ensure that the knowledge represented and reproduced in the organization is used and developed in ways that maintain or add value for successive generations and the environment.

Sustainability therefore emphasizes the need for learning founded on ethics and value systems that overlay conventional (utilitarian) assumptions about the purpose of business. This perspective implies more participative business structures centred on dialogue and partnership with internal and external company stakeholders and cooperation to complement (rather than replace) competition in business and ecological networks. It involves using new tools and techniques to gauge environmental, social and ethical as well as conventional business performance.

While management education has begun to introduce the ideas and tools that enable managers to improve environmental performance it has not generally addressed this broader vision of sustainability and the sustainable enterprise. Meanwhile, a number of management approaches have developed to bridge the gap between conventional practice and improved environmental performance.

The four main approaches are:

- total quality environmental management (TQEM) which has developed as an extension of the total quality movement (TQM) (GEMI, 1991–3);
- industrial ecology, which views industrial systems as networks interconnected through the flow of energy and resources (Allenby and Richards, 1994);
- environmental management systems integrating environmental impact

assessment, environmental audits and life cycle analysis with company mission, policy, training and quality assurance (BSI, 1994; CSA, 1994);

■ eco-efficiency, first developed in the BCSD book *Changing Course* (Schmidheiny, 1992) and concerned to reduce the material intensity of products and services through such measures as better design, durability, multiple use and reuse. It has been described as involving more diverse and decentralized production strategies.

Of these, only eco-efficiency raises substantive questions about the blurred relationships between business, government and society and the folly of copying business strategies that are based on the unsustainable models of the developed world. While all recognize the importance of values and learning, they do not question the adequacy of the fundamental drivers of business in relation to ideas on sustainability as set out by Brundtland and Agenda 21. Rather they avoid this issue and, by so doing, blur the distinction between improved environmental performance and the broader goal of sustainability.

Towards EFS The move towards improved environmental performance in business is an immense challenge to the way managers and labour view the structure and activities of business organizations, and one that is only partly being anticipated by business schools. Yet, as contended above, sustainability requires a further shift — beyond improved environmental performance — in the purpose and identity of business organizations.

Sustainability will require the development of businesses that are self-regulating and constrained by principles. It suggests that organizations and institutions as well as products, services and technologies need to be checked continuously to assess their adequacy against the needs of new generations and against the context of the natural resource endowments of the earth and the accumulation and sharing of knowledge. Sustainability therefore anticipates more flexible and responsive, more diverse and devolved organizational forms than those dominant at the present stage in industrial society.

To cope with changes implied by sustainability it will be necessary for organizations, their managers and workforce to accept the importance of a 'learning' mindset in which staying attentive to the shifting needs of society and the dynamics of environmental change will be as important as staying close to the needs of customers. It requires an approach that questions the adequacy of the organization's knowledge, understanding, practices and values so that these are (re)shaped as part of increasingly sophisticated and thoughtful responses to the interconnected concerns we face.

These ideas suggest something of the paradigm of the sustainable business. They also say something to education in general and to management education in particular. Management education, which prepares managers for careers stretching to the year 2030 and beyond, must choose a fine balance between the skills and techniques needed to improve environmental performance within business today while retaining a vision of the changes required to prepare managers for the paradigm of the sustainable enterprise of the future. Part of that paradigm will involve a commitment to continual learning to welcome the challenge of change and to be able to envisage the future as well as analyse the present. It will involve appreciation of the ethical systems and values that underpin managerial decisions, an ability to gauge the values of others and to reflect on whether one's own values and images of the world are in keeping with the unfolding dynamics of a sustainable world. It will involve the development of an approach to leadership that encourages managers to listen and learn from others and from their past experiences — and to shape and communicate visions for the future to which people can assent because they are seen to hold value and because they appear to uphold justice.

Implications for the curriculum, pedagogy and the classroom process follow from these propositions, some of which have been discussed elsewhere (Roome, 1994). First, the curriculum will need to change to bring issues of sustainability and the management of environmental change into the core. For some students, an interest in specializing in this aspect of management will create a demand for electives and concentrated areas of study. Second, the management curriculum will need to become more integrated and interdisciplinary so that teaching reflects the interconnected, indeterminate nature of the open-ended, chaotic systems in which we operate. This implies the need for a better balance between the so-called hard (analytic) and soft (interpersonal) skills. Third, the curriculum will need to link theory, concept and practice through a more seamless relationship between the classroom and the world of practice. Teaching by case studies, which emphasize the perspective of a single decision-maker, will need to be complemented by stakeholder role plays and experiential learning with students working with managers in companies to address environmental/ sustainability issues.

Finally, management educators will need to forge new and potentially uncomfortable partnerships with practising managers, environmental educators and others. These will emphasize flexible, action-oriented approaches to learning. Educators will need to practise more of the principles and ideals of sustainability in the classroom and through their teaching practice demonstrate the approach to learners. Ideas of shared learning, willingness to listen and the role of faculty in facilitating the learning process are important. There should be a commitment to address ethics in the classroom and to explore normative ideas about what business organizations ought to be like rather than simply examining what they are now.

Box 11.1 MAKING PROGRESS

The application of sustainability principles within the management curriculum has been slow to take root. In the United States, the Management Institute for Environment and Business has actively promoted business and environment materials in business schools. In Europe, initiatives have largely been undertaken by individual schools such as the International Institute for Management Development (IMD) in Lausanne, the European Institute of Business Management (INSEAD) in Fontainebleau and a number of schools in the UK. Tom Gladwin at the Stern School, New York University, has been active in developing ideas on the sustainable organization, while at the University of Michigan's Corporate Environmental Management Program, strong efforts have been made to build partnerships between MBA courses and businesses. European schools, particularly those in the UK, have been concerned to develop teaching around environmental management systems, tools and techniques.

Nigel Roome's work since 1993 at York University in Toronto has been concerned to develop innovative approaches to the content and pedagogy of management education. Within the Faculty of Administrative Studies, the curriculum structure has allowed the development of a concentration in business and the environment which embraces strategy, organizational change, ethics, environmental economics and law as well as enabling the development of skills in environmental management systems, the use of environmental tools and techniques and dispute settlement. The pedagogy employs role plays and multi-stakeholder case studies as well as experiential learning through projects and consulting with companies and other organizations. In this way, students, faculty and practitioners are together learning how to improve the environmental performance of organizations and to strive towards more sustainable thinking and action.

Andrea Oates
The Role of Trade Unions

Although workers play a central role as both producers and victims of environmental damage, they remain a largely untapped source of potential knowledge and experience in addressing the changes industry will need to make in order to move towards sustainability (see above). They face major industrial and legal obstacles to playing a more active role and have therefore concentrated on 'getting a foot in the door' in areas such as cleaner technologies and resource conservation, rather than debating changing current modes of production and consumption.

In this section of the chapter I describe some of the formative initiatives unions are taking towards developing a role in sustainability and examine their educational implications.

From Safety to Sustainability 'Efforts to implement sustainable development will involve adjustments and opportunities at national and enterprise levels with workers foremost among those concerned. As their representatives, trade unions are vital actors in facilitating the achievements of sustainable development in view of their experience in addressing industrial change, the extremely high priority they give to protection of the working environment and their promotion of socially responsible and economic development' (SENSE, 1993).

So says the Scottish Environmental Network for a Sustainable Economy (SENSE), a coalition of green organizations and trade unions, and one of the few organizations actively involved in worker education on sustainable development issues in the UK.

Trade unions have a long history of campaigning on environmental issues and in achieving change in areas related to their traditional concern of health and safety, such as pesticides and asbestos. In the UK, unions including the Transport & General Workers Union (TGWU) were instrumental in achieving an effective ban on the pesticide 2,4,5,T, which is toxic not only to workers using it but also to wildlife as concentrations build up in the food chain. Transport unions also combined to ban the movement of nuclear waste at sea, with train drivers taking industrial action in refusing to take the waste on their trains; later on port workers refused to allow the unloading of toxic waste.

In addition, unions have taken an active role in the debate about the reconversion and diversification of the defence industry. The model of the Lucas Aerospace stewards committee, which developed a plan for reorientation from arms production towards socially useful products, has inspired trade unionists around the world. For example, the metal workers' union in Germany (IG Metall) has used the model to promote the idea of environmentally friendly production and environmental codetermination (joint decision-making between management and unions) with some success (Oates and Gregory, 1993).

From these fairly isolated and safety-related actions, and involvement in the debate about arms conversion, a number of trade unions have attempted to take up environmental protection as a collective bargaining issue at the workplace. Further, as the debate on sustainable development has progressed, they have tried to put themselves and the workers they represent at the heart of the debate on the environmental challenge and sustainability in the workplace.

Trade unions have responded to employer organizations' statements about the need for change. For example, in response to the Business Council on Sustainable Development's view that: 'Sustainable development is about redefining the rules of economic game in order to move from a situation of wasteful consumption and pollution to one of conservation and from one of privilege and protectionism to one of fair and equitable chances to all. No one can reasonably doubt that fundamental change is needed,' unions have argued that they, and the workers they represent, can play an important role in realizing such change.

The Manufacturing, Science and Finance Union (MSF), for example, argues that meeting the environmental challenge will be one of the most important issues facing industry in the years ahead, and that its membership's skills should be put to use. Its *Action on the Environment* pack, produced to help its members take up environmental issues at work, outlines the constructive role the union can play in helping to bring about change through engaging the expertise of its membership of thousands of scientists, designers and technologists in the public and private sectors.

The Trades Union Congress (TUC) argues that 'Trade unions are on the frontline when it comes to the impact of work activities on the environment and have the organization, experience and commitment to both identify the problems and seek practical solutions' (TUC, 1993).

Trade unions recognize that it is in their interest to be involved in issues that go beyond the workplace at a time when membership in the UK has fallen to the extent that only around one third of the workforce is now unionized. Sociologist André Gorz points out that the changed nature of work means that many workers no longer identify with their professional occupation or work role and this 'requires that unions be not centred exclusively on defending people as workers at the places of work. It requires unions to take into account the needs, aspirations and interests and for workers to develop as persons, citizens, dwellers, parents, consumers etc beyond their places of work' (Gorz, 1993).

Sustainable development therefore provides opportunities as well as challenges for the trade unions:

> *Bringing environmental issues on to the bargaining agenda in a positive way can also open up potential opportunities for trade unions. For example, it can open up new avenues to discuss related issues associated with investment, site location and corporate planning and employee training. It can facilitate closer links with the local community and other outside groups; and make a positive contribution to the union's image and recruitment. Taking up the environmental challenge can also*

> *harness the skills and interest of members who hitherto have not participated in union activities.*

> (TUC, 1993)

Such possibilities are endorsed by a German researcher who recently argued that unions could link the traditional struggle for reduction in working time with opportunities for environmental training, or discussion on changing the structure of jobs having negative environmental impact (Marien, 1995).

Obstacles to Change However, union activity on environmental issues has remained fairly low and unions have had little success in translating national policies and initiatives into collective action at the workplace. Although part of the problem in unions failing to take up environmental issues at the local level is no doubt due to fears about the impact of environmental protection policies on jobs in particular cases, there are major legal and industrial barriers to union involvement.

At present, union representatives have no legal right to participate in the changes that will be required to move towards sustainable development. Employers have generally been hostile towards union attempts to negotiate collective green agreements that accept a joint management/union approach to environmental challenges and give workers the right to participate in environmental decision-making and to attend environmental training courses. A 1991 Labour Research Department survey of trade union representatives in over 400 workplaces, showed only 7 per cent of employers involved unions in their environmental audits (LRD, 1991).

The Confederation of British Industry (CBI) has expressed reservations about a distinctive new role for trade unions in partaking in environmental decision making, based on the provision by companies of information on their environmental performance (CBI, 1991). It sees this as a 'green trojan horse' and argues that if that role is achieved, the unions' longstanding industrial relations objective of a wider collective bargaining agenda as well as involvement in companies' decision-making will have been achieved.

The current Conservative government has brought in a number of pieces of legislation aimed at reducing the role of the trade unions rather than enhancing it. However, environmental training has been endorsed in a number of governmental policy statements since Agenda 21.

While unions, including the public sector union UNISON, MSF and the general union GMB have all run training courses for their representatives on environmental issues, the government and employers' organizations have ignored the TUC's calls for roundtable discussions on the need for employee/trade union involvement in environmental training, environmental audits and the employment dimension of environment policies.

In contrast to the situation with regard to health and safety — where trade unions have proved they have a major role to play — there is no right for trade union representatives to receive paid time off for environmental training, although this has been one of the central demands in 'green' collective agreements put forward to employers by unions like the GMB.

Trade union education in areas such as health and safety aims not only to give workers technical, scientific and legal information, but also to build confidence and improve negotiating skills to enable them to effect change in the company. The need for a similar kind of education on sustainable development issues is vital for helping workers and their representatives participate in the necessary changes in industry.

Positive Initiatives to Build On Despite the barriers to union involvement in such changes, industry will need to move towards sustainability, using fewer resources and producing less waste. A number of examples of initiatives in the UK and other parts of Europe demonstrate that unions and the workers they represent do have an important potential role in the greening of industry, and some of these are reviewed below.

Involvement in clean production MSF sees clean production as a key part of reorienting manufacturing industry towards sustainability, involving new methods of production and consumption that are inherently cleaner, use much less energy and do not generate harmful by-products.

Its publication *Clean Production: From Industrial Dinosaur to Eco-Efficiency* (Gee, 1994) says that evaluation of a number of clean production projects has shown that 'Company-focused, face-to-face contacts were the best methods of transferring clean production technology to other companies' and asserts that unions are well placed to offer this kind of service to companies and their employees. It also outlines the largely untapped potential of employees, saying that there is currently insufficient encouragement to employee creativity in solving environmental problems.

The report asserts that 'Clean production is about involving people in questioning the way their work is organized. It is people at the sharp end who know how work is done in practice (as opposed to the theory) and who are in the best position to identify the waste minimization possibilities.' This statement is backed up with a series of examples showing how employee involvement in waste minimization has saved companies millions of pounds. For example, 3M's Pollution Prevention Pays programme, which is based around employee involvement, has generated over 3000 initiatives that have prevented more than $1.5 billion of polluting emissions and saved the company over $500 million.

By showing how environmentally friendly production could save industry £300 million a year, the MSF report challenges the view that taking the environment into account costs jobs, thereby raising awareness among its own membership that clean production can actually save and create jobs. The union has followed up its publication by including environmental awareness and clean production in its education courses for union representatives.

In Denmark, a more cooperative style of industrial relations and greater acceptance by employers and the government of the role of unions and workers has lead to more worker and union participation in environmental issues at the workplace. One of the conclusions of a recent research project on employee participation in the introduction of clean technologies was that 'Employees and their elected representatives have an important role to play when it comes to developing cleaner technologies' and that their exclusion from such a role will undoubtedly reduce the potential efficiency of the effort (Lorenzten, 1995).

Box 11.2 *LEARNING FROM DENMARK: THE SUBSPRINT PROJECT*

The Subsprint project is a good example of how trade unions have been involved in the education of print workers, including practical demonstrations by print workers already using cleaner technology, to enable others to change to more environmentally friendly production.

The print union GPMU, as well as the British Printing Industry Federation, has been involved in this technology transfer project which is part-funded by the European Union (EU) and aims to transfer the Danish unions' experience of substituting petroleum-based organic solvents with vegetable-oil-based solvents in the wash-up process of the printing industry to other EU countries.

Petroleum-based organic solvents are volatile, that is they evaporate rapidly into the air. Many solvents currently used in the printing industry have a high volatile organic compound (VOC) content. VOCs contribute to stratospheric ozone depletion; some are carcinogenic and most contribute to the formation of ground-level ozone and thus photochemical smog. So in addition to the health hazards they pose to printers working with them (the Danish government recognized that organic solvents can cause brain damage) there are also serious environmental concerns.

In Denmark, as a result of campaigning by the trade unions about the hazards of organic solvents, 90 per cent of the paints used in the construction industry are water-based rather than petroleum-based organic solvents, and one in three printers now use vegetable-oil-based solvents for wash-up.

In 1993, the Department of the Environment issued guidance on the reduction of solvents in the UK which will require the UK print industry

---

> *to reduce its solvent emissions from 42 kilotonnes in 1988 to 28 kilotonnes in 1999, a 33 per cent reduction.*
>
> *The UK Subsprint project aims to increase the use of vegetable cleaning agents to 10 per cent of print works through raising awareness about the health and environmental benefits and training printers and others in the use of the vegetable-oil-based cleaning products. The project recently reported that one of the largest UK print firms, Express Printers, which produces some 7 million copies of daily newspapers has been using vegetable-oil-based wash-up successfully since 1994. The firm's production director told a Subsprint seminar in Manchester that the estimated extra costs of moving away from using petroleum-based solvents, anticipated at no more than 15 per cent, were acceptable for providing a healthier workplace and improving the environment.*
>
> *(DALTON, 1993)*

Involvement in environmental management systems The European Eco-Management and Audit (EMA) regulation was adopted in July 1993 and member states were required to set up a voluntary scheme for participation by companies with industrial sites by April 1995. In addition, the British Standard BS7750 Environmental Management Systems was produced in 1994 with requirements compatible with those of the EMA.

Many UK companies have started to carry out environmental audits and implement environmental management systems in line with these two schemes in order to reduce their environmental impact. The TUC sees environmental audits as the key area in which trade unionists can become involved in environmental issues at the workplace.

Although unions have expressed concern about moves towards self-regulation, there are reasons why trade unions may welcome such systems. According to Charlie Clutterbuck of the TUC Education Service in Blackburn, they provide a systematic way of dealing with environmental matters and offer an opportunity for unions to negotiate change within companies if they are involved in the process.

A pilot scheme in Blackburn — one of the areas targeted by the government through the Groundwork Trust and funded by the Commonwealth Trade Union Council — in 1994 was the first trade union education course on environmental management systems. Some 22 local companies signed up to BS7750, or the European EMA regulation, and the TUC Education Service responded to these developments by running a ten-day course on environmental management systems, which local companies allowed trade union representatives to attend.

The tutors claim that the course was successful in helping union members understand the process of eco-management and auditing schemes, but said that without legal protection, consultation rights and adequate back-up unions will find it difficult to become fully involved.

The Implications of Sustainability for Trade Union Education The above examples demonstrate that trade unions and the workers they represent can have a role in realizing the changes necessary to move towards sustainable development. But these examples are still the exception rather than the rule and there is a long way to go before trade unions can be said to be playing a part in the societal transformation towards more sustainable development.

For trade unions and workers to be able to participate more fully, legal rights are obviously important, not least in relation to the right to education and training. However, while rights for trade union representatives to receive paid time off to attend union training courses are important, there is also a need for trade unions to put more resources into environmental education and training for their representatives on sustainable development. There are only a few examples of unions that have dedicated significant resources to environmental action. Only UNISON has a full-time environment officer post, although other unions have extended their health and safety support to additionally cover environmental issues.

Sustainability presents a challenge to the unions to represent their members' interests in a more holistic way. It requires patterns of production and consumption to change so that they remain within the earth's natural boundaries. At present, however, any trade union involvement in environmental issues is at the very beginning of the necessary changes towards sustainable development. They are involved in areas such as reducing energy and water consumption, substituting chemicals and recycling resources rather than changing the fundamental way of producing in society or at company level, questioning the societal use value of the products being produced. Beyond this, they need to be involved in the continuous learning processes which will be at the heart of sustainable business practices.

If workers and their representatives are able to overcome some of the barriers they face in participating in improving the environmental impact of their company, industry may be a step further on the road to sustainability.

Corporate Greening

In this chapter we have described the response of business organizations, management and labour to the developing agenda of sustainability. We have suggested that there are many approaches under the banner of sustainability and that these are dominated by the idea that improving environmental performance is synonymous with sustainability. It is argued that sustainability goes beyond the improvement of environmental performance and that business organizations cannot seek sustainability unless they redefine their purpose, reassess their relationships with the social, physical and biological environment and continuously reshape organizational boundaries and practice.

It is suggested that the education provided for management and labour has tended to follow the practice set in organizations. It has not been complemented with a forward-looking, normative, holistic and change-oriented vision of sustainability. As a result education is not yet helping to lead us towards sustainability, yet it could become a leading force for change. Education has a critical role to play in putting forward alternative notions of sustainable business as well as describing and analysing leading approaches to practice, which will help management and labour to contribute to the more sustainable world of tomorrow.

References

Allenby, B and D Richards (1994) *The Greening of Industrial Ecosystems*, National Academy Press, Washington DC

BCSD (1993) *How Can Business Contribute to Sustainable Development? Getting Eco-Efficient*, Business Council for Sustainable Development, Geneva

BSI (1994) *Specification for Environmental Management System BS7750*, British Standards Institute, Milton Keynes

Carley, M and I Christie (1993) *Managing Sustainable Development*, University of Minnesota Press, Minneapolis

CBI (1991) *Employment Affairs Report*, 30 April, Confederation of British Industry, London

CSA (1994) *Guidelines for Voluntary Environmental Management System*, Canadian Standards Association Z750, Toronto

Dalton, A J P (1993) *The Greening of the UK Print Industry*, Centre for Industrial & Environmental Safety & Health, London

Eddy, E B (1993) *A Question of Balance: First Status Report on Sustainable Development*, E B Eddy Group, Espanola, Ontario

Fischer, K and J Schot (1993) *Environmental Strategies for Industry*, Island Press, Washington DC

Gee, D (1994) *Clean Production: From Industrial Dinosaur to Eco-Efficiency*, MSF, London

GEMI (1991–3) *Corporate Quality Environmental Management*, Reports of the Global Environmental Management Initiative Conferences, Washington DC

Gorz, A (1993) 'Working Less: Post Industrial Society', quoted in SENSE, *Economics for a Sustainable Future: Environmental Economics for Trade Unionists and Environmental Campaigners: A Pack of Adult Education Materials*, Scottish Environmental Network for a Sustainable Economy, Edinburgh

ICC (1992) *The Business Charter for Sustainable Development*, International Chamber of Commerce, Paris

Lorenzten, B (1995) 'Employees, Trade Unions and Environmental Protection', Paper prepared for the International Conference on Action Research, Copenhagen, Denmark

LRD (1991) *Bargaining Report Magazine*, 108, April, Labour Research Department, London

Marien, S (1995) 'The Discussion about Environment and Employment in the United Kingdom and the Possibilities for Creating Jobs by Job Creation Schemes with Environmental Issues', working paper, London

Oates, A and D Gregory (eds) (1993) *Industrial Relations and the Environment: Ten Countries Under the Microscope*, vols 1 and 2, European Foundation for the Improvement of Living and Working Conditions, Dublin

Ontario Hydro (1993) *A Strategy for Sustainable Energy Development and Use for Ontario Hydro*, Ontario Hydro, Toronto

Roome, N (1994) *Environmental Responsibility: An Agenda for Further and Higher Education: Management and Business*, Pluto Press, London

Roome, N and S Clarke (1994) 'Designing the Sustainable Enterprise: A Journey Through Theory and Practice', paper presented to Greening of Industry Network Conference: From Greening to Sustaining Transformational Challenges for the Firm Greening of Industry Network, Copenhagen

Schmidheiny, S (1992) *Changing Course*, MIT Press, Cambridge, Mass

SENSE (1993) *Economics for a Sustainable Future: Environmental Economics for Trade Unionists and Environmental Campaigners: A Pack of Adult Education Materials*, Scottish Environmental Network for a Sustainable Economy, Edinburgh.

Six, F and P Winsemius (1992) *The Response of European Firms to the Environmental Challenge*, McKinsey & Company Inc, The Netherlands

TUC (1993) *Greening the Workplace: A TUC Guide to Environmental Policies and Issues at Work*, Trades Union Congress, London

WCED (1987) *Our Common Future*, Oxford University Press, Oxford

Chapter 12

LOCAL GOVERNMENT's EDUCATIONAL ROLE in LA21

Julian Agyeman, Jane Morris & Jeff Bishop

The 1990s have seen an increasing and widespread recognition of the fundamental (and potentially creative) role of local authorities in managing, raising popular awareness of and stewarding the local environment. This has culminated in them playing a pivotal role in the delivery of local sustainability through, more often than not, a consensual approach to Local Agenda 21 (LA21) involving local stakeholders. Tuxworth and Carpenter (1995) have shown that 71 per cent of UK local authorities state their commitment to participating in the LA21 process.

Education, information and awareness are integral parts of any authority's moves towards advancing sustainability through LA21. However, as this chapter shows, the rhetoric of public commitment only rarely matches up to the depth and consistency of action on the ground — despite the enthusiasm and action of staff in a number of highly imaginative and creative authorities. At this moment, the 'whole' of what exists is clearly 'less than the sum of the parts', and yet a number of significant opportunities are now in place to bring consistency and coherence to this important area of work. The authors remain uncertain as to whether such opportunities will be seized by enough people and authorities to shift practice to the higher levels.

The National Policy Context

Developments in local environmental action, and latterly, sustainability, have taken place in the context of a central government lacking a coherent national environmental or sustainability strategy (such as that of The Netherlands) and operating only selectively reactive approaches to given issues. Two factors underpin this selective reactivity. First, the tradition of voluntarism in environmental regulation in the UK, which produces a *laissez-faire* attitude to environmental protection. Second, the ideological commitment to non-interventionism, privatization and deregulation, which was the focus of the Thatcher administration and which continues to dominate government policy today. This makes central government vulnerable in the face of the emerging international environmental and sustainability agenda to which ever increasing numbers of local authorities, NGOs, not-for-profit organizations and businesses are subscribing. In particular, there is bemusement and alarm in Whitehall at the growing confidence in those local authorities responding enthusiastically to the new agenda. The policy initiative is clearly not in central government hands. In addition, the critique of existing government policy from local and European tiers of government is both echoed and further developed by a vast network of independent environmental organizations, protest groups and direct action specialists who are better informed, networked, resourced and more media-wise than ever before. This is unique in Europe and a clear strength for the UK.

Growing Local Authority Confidence: The Late 1980s

The origins of the recognition and confidence in the environmental role of local authorities can be traced back in particular to three events in the late 1980s:

■ Friends of the Earth's (FOE) Environmental Charter for Local Government;
■ mounting public and political environmental concern; and
■ the development of environmental coordination mechanisms by the local authority associations and the Local Government Management Board (LGMB).

FOE produced its specimen charter in 1988 and invited all local authorities to adopt (and adapt) it, thereby challenging them to face up to their wider environmental responsibilities, that is those beyond their (limited) statutory role. At around the same time public concern and awareness about the environment were mounting, manifested in soaring memberships of environmental organizations and the dramatic 'green' vote in the 1989

European Parliament elections. Margaret Thatcher's apparent 'conversion' to environmentalism provided further impetus to local authorities to think seriously about expanding their environmental responsibilities. In response, a slowly increasing number began to:

- appoint environmental coordinators;
- draft environmental charters, statements and policies (often within local plans and structures);
- hold green fairs;
- set up environmental fora with interested parties or 'stakeholders' in the local community; and
- develop awareness and education initiatives aimed at local communities and schools.

Local authority associations were keen to set up mechanisms to deal with this burgeoning policy area. In 1989, the Association of Metropolitan Authorities (AMA) appointed an environmental policy officer who coordinated the first joint environmental publication between the three major associations in England and Wales: the AMA, the Association of County Councils (ACC) and the Association of District Councils (ADC). This publication was entitled *Environmental Practice in Local Government* (1990). In 1991, an environmental advisor was appointed to the LGMB and this specialist appointment marked a departure for it. One of the adviser's first tasks was to work closely with the associations, to update *Environmental Practice in Local Government*, with funding from the Department of the Environment and the EU (through the General Directorate for the Environment, known as DGXI).

As with any such advocacy from the centre, however, the baton was not taken up by all authorities — though those that did were not always those most usually associated with innovation and progressive thinking.

LA21 and the Challenge of Sustainability

The groundwork of the late 1980s ensured that most local authorities in the UK were at least in a position to respond dynamically to the opportunity presented by the Rio Earth Summit in 1992. They did this through lobbying central government for recognition of the role local authorities could and should play in the delivery of local environmental improvement. This was reinforced by efforts by local government worldwide to ensure that the national governments involved in the Rio process (and subsequent agreements) formally recognized local government as a major group that would have to be mobilized if sustainable development at a local, national and global scale was to be achieved.

The International Council for Local Environmental Initiatives (ICLEI) was instrumental in ensuring that local government was written in to Agenda 21 and proposed the text for Chapter 28: 'Local Authorities' Initiatives in Support of Agenda 21'. This states that 'because so many of the problems and solutions being addressed by Agenda 21 have their roots in local activities, the participation and cooperation of local authorities will be a determining factor in fulfilling its objectives.' Also, part of Chapter 28 was a rallying call; a challenge to local government to live up to the role it claimed for itself: 'By 1996, most local authorities in each country should have undertaken a consultative process with their populations and achieved a consensus on a Local Agenda 21 for the community.'

In 1994, the LGMB developed a step by step guide to LA21. In essence, it suggested that authorities should manage and improve their own environmental performance; integrate sustainable development aims into their own policies and activities; develop awareness raising and educational activities; consult and involve local people; develop local partnerships for environmental action; and measure, monitor and report on progress towards sustainability. It was no coincidence that an educational role was listed here because education, information, awareness, empowerment and capacity building were (like community participation) all integral — not optional — components of the sustainable development thinking that informed LA21.

At the same time as Agenda 21 was being agreed by national governments at Rio, the EU was drawing up its Fifth Environmental Action Programme (subtitled 'Towards Sustainability'), which runs from 1992 to the year 2000. The programme also takes on board the new vocabulary of sustainable development and recognizes the need to mobilize all sectors within society — including local government — to deliver what Agyeman and Evans (1994) have called the 'new environmental agenda': the linking of environmental, social and economic concerns.

Despite the UK government's mealy-mouthed endorsement of sustainable development (as seen in 1994 in the DoE document *Sustainable Development: The UK Strategy*), the new legitimacy accorded to local government in helping to implement sustainable development struck a chord with many local authorities in the UK. They had long been used to having their role and responsibilities diminished by a central government intent on curbing local services and democracy through increasingly draconian centralizing powers.

With further help from the local authority associations and the LGMB a cross-sectoral LA21 steering group has been formed and a range of guidance materials for local authorities produced. A recent series of round-table guidance notes includes two directly relevant here: on education for sustainability (EFS) and community participation. A database of all the environmental coordinators in the UK has been produced, and regular mailshots of information/guidance are sent to database contacts. An annual forum is held to facilitate networking and information exchange between authorities. Two recent initiatives are the development of a journal, *Local Environment*, which aims to link academics with practitioners in local authorities, and an electronic networking project, which aims to encourage coordinators to join GreenNet (a global environmental, peace and human rights network with gateways to the Internet). All are seen explicitly as supporting the educational effort within LA21.

Environmental Coordinators and EFS

Environmental coordinators are a new breed of local government officer. They come from a variety of backgrounds and bring a wide range of skills in, among other things, nature conservation, community development, planning, environmental health, the voluntary sector and teaching.

They play two major roles. One is to ensure that environmental (and now sustainability) issues are integrated into the corporate workings of the authority. The other is to develop interaction not only with other officers and elected members in their authority, but with the wider community, including businesses and, increasingly, multi-stakeholder partnerships. Environmental coordinators therefore have a significant role to play in EFS in both their internal and external activities. Yet, despite the centrality of educational themes, this area has not been addressed clearly in developing and supporting the activities of the ever-increasing number of coordinators.

Internally, coordinators provide information and run training courses for other officers and elected members to ensure that the local authority does what it can to get its own house into environmental order and to ensure that sustainable development aims are integrated into the authority's policies and activities. In terms of the external role, the government Panel on Sustainable Development (1995, paragraph 11) 'recommends that the Government should develop a strategy for environmental education and training to cover both formal and informal education and to bring in the wide range of related activities by official and voluntary bodies, industry and commerce, and local communities'.

To achieve this, it is essential that *all* the information and skills found within a local authority are used to consult, raise awareness, educate and ultimately empower the wider community, with a view to giving it the skill, will and confidence to take individual and/or collective action. This may in turn ultimately lead to more popular input into local decision-making processes — ie linking back directly to community participation. This is also, at least in principle, a two-way process, with feedback from the community on local issues and on peoples' attitudes to them being of increasing importance in developing authority-wide consensus.

As well as substantive or content-based education on issues such as pollution control, recycling or nature conservation, coordinators have a role to play both internally and externally in developing capacity, skills, attitudes, values and confidence. There is in fact a vigorous history of this kind of capacity building in local authorities, located particularly with the many educationally active planners of the 1970s and early 1980s. Linked to the post-Skeffington community participation theme, the urban studies movement grew out of the TCPA's education unit and focused attention on critical decision-making aspects of the local environment at a time when many students were only undertaking field trips to distant and often rural locations. Practical projects such as 'Planawaydays', town trails and simulated public enquiries were the regular result of teacher–planner collaborations over this period. In this respect, it is sad to see the continuity broken, for few of today's local authority planners are picking up and developing their wider educational role, even within LA21. The support this might give to environmental coordinators is therefore missing.

One problem with the wide remit of environmental coordinators and the demands of a fast changing policy agenda is that unless they (or a senior officer or member) are personally committed to an educational role, it can often fall down the list of priorities for action. Tuxworth and Carpenter (1995) note that 62 per cent of local authority respondents to their survey stated that their authority provided support for environmental education. The real meaning of this figure becomes clearer when one notices that the same survey revealed that the large majority of local authorities had seen no reason to adapt their consultation procedures to accommodate the demands of LA21.

This lower priority reflects not only the daunting nature of the task of educating for sustainability, but also in part the demise of the local education authorities' role in advising schools and teachers. Few educational advisers now have this as a sole role; their concentration is more commonly on being inspectors. Consequently, the environmental coordinator receives far less educational support than he or she may have done previously. This, and the demise of planner support, has led to a situation in which there is no single emerging model for EFS among environmental coordinators, only a set of local approaches (some of which are described in a later section).

This is further exacerbated by a prevailing perception that education means only work within the formal education sector, ie predominantly with children and schools. Though undoubtedly influenced by the growth of narrow, instrumental initiatives within the territory of 'training', and the apparent uncertainties of 'action learning', the widespread failure to see education as a *lifelong*, open, developing process for *everybody* is clearly limiting the conceptual frameworks of EFS and hence the breadth and depth of action on the ground.

These problems ought to be even more surprising and worrying given the wide range of officers within a local authority who have environmental/ sustainability skills that could (and should) be utilized to greater effect in the educational process, and the strong tradition of training and professional development within local government. It could be argued that local government today represents the greatest repository of such skills in the UK. As well as the educationists and planners already mentioned, there are environmental health officers, architects, landscape architects, horticulturalists, waste management officers, recycling/waste reduction officers, arboriculturalists, park managers, ecologists, community development workers, community health specialists, housing managers, equal opportunity officers, purchasing officers, PR specialists and energy managers. All these have a part to play in developing individual and collective empathy with the educational aims of sustainability, as well as coordinating the implementation of sustainable development. Indeed, many individuals keenly wish to be able to take on such a role, but constraints of time, finance, priorities and organizational culture make it difficult.

Apart from the skills of their often keen employees (most of whom would need careful support in taking forward an educational role), local authorities also have another great resource: extensive information about the locality. This can range from detailed information on geographical information systems (GIS) about the state of the local environment (for example fauna, flora and geology) and pressures on that environment (for example traffic flows and air quality) to more basic leaflets, policy reports and committee minutes. Sadly, much of this material is in a format that is inaccessible to the general public, so imaginative ways need to be found of presenting it to those outside the authority. At the same time, it is also true that providing open access to information (as legislated for in a 1992 EU directive) is a prerequisite to developing community capacity. Care is needed, however, because the simple provision of information is in no way the same as empowering people to understand and utilize it.

Case Studies of Good Practice

It has not been easy to locate coherent, rounded examples of good practice of local government officers enabling sustainable thinking and action through educational work. In part this is because of the relative novelty of sustainability and in part because of the relentless attack on the role and funding of local government in recent years. We have chosen to focus here on specific LA21 initiatives, but before examining these it is important to acknowledge other more general developments.

Local authority environmental coordinators and external consultants regularly run awareness-raising and training courses for their own officers, some of which address the need to promote and develop effective working practices with schools and local communities. Developments in Devon County and the London Borough of Redbridge illustrate how knowledge, skills and even raised commitment can be 'cascaded' through authority teams. Some authorities (for example the London Borough of Croydon) run courses for members of the public who wish to take sustainability issues into their own neighbourhoods, and a number of different short courses on LA21 for environmental coordinators have been run through a mutually supportive network which includes the LGMB, the Royal Town Planning Institute, the Environment Council and the Association of Community Technical Aid Centres. A recent initiative by LGMB has brought together a team of trainers first to run a series of regional day courses for elected members and then to prepare a 'distance-learning' pack for use by in-house training teams. This successful initiative is already moving on into related areas.

Moving to a more direct interface between local authority staff and the general public, we find initiatives like that in Luton, which has grown out of Bedfordshire County Planning Department's ongoing work with teachers and local communities (Young, 1995a, 1995b). This initiative seeks to involve the Pakistani community in the LA21 process through formal and community education in ways that are informed by similar initiatives in Peshawar. It will promote mutual awareness and education, which are features of a number of other LA21 'launch' events elsewhere. In the case of Sutton, a remarkably wide mix of over 120 people spent all of a Saturday and most of a Sunday together learning about and discussing sustainability issues both generally and locally, before moving on to set specific targets and priorities for a balanced programme of shared local action. On reflection from all such events, it is difficult to say whether they were 'education', 'training' or 'action' because, in essence, they demonstrate how it is possible to merge all three productively.

Complementing the 'get-together' model of workshops is an approach initiated by Scottish Natural Heritage (SNH). It has produced a 'signposting' pack for local communities, the *Environmental Community Chest*. Whereas most packs either generate their own material or adapt from those produced by others, SNH's pack simply assembles pre-existing guidance (for example from Wastewatch on community recycling or from the Wildlife Partnership on wildlife gardening) and accompanies this with a signposting handbook. The handbook helps local communities ask themselves the necessary questions about the most relevant projects for them, then points them straight to the relevant material.

Getting nearer now to 'recipes' — ie more coherent approaches — are two broad-ranging initiatives in Reading and Leicester aimed directly at supporting local community involvement in the eventual formulation of LA21s. The work in Reading is funded by the Reading Borough Council and the WWF's education department. The aims are to work with the communities in a series of neighbourhoods to:

- stimulate their awareness of aspects of sustainable development;
- trigger some community-led action on prioritized issues;
- start work on area-wide sustainability plans; and
- work with other communities to contribute to the Reading LA21.

WWF has provided a full-time officer based in the council offices who works alongside other LA21 officers. It has also brought in the expertise of the Community Education Development Centre to advise on appropriate approaches and to front some of the early events. At this stage, activity has moved ahead well in the first two selected neighbourhoods. It is now the intention to start in another two areas, learning from the professional team's experiences, but also putting the new communities in touch with those in the first study area for mutual support.

Activity has followed a familiar community education and development mode. Initial networking enabled contact with currently and potentially motivated people and groups, and their commitment was used as the base for some opening events to which all in the neighbourhood were invited. At the opening event emphasis was placed — through participative techniques — on problem-raising and general awareness. An informal local group was formed, further meetings were held and the emphasis shifted from problems to priorities and possible actions. From within the very wide range of issues generated at the outset, three main priorities have now been agreed for further action.

Monitoring and evaluation are seen as important and are already under way, leading to a realization that this approach to bottom-up action will need to be complemented by a parallel top-down approach by the local authority, not just by those managing LA21 but by all professions, groups and elected members. There is a recognized limit to how far any single local community, or even group of communities, can go before being thwarted should they fail to meet the authority coming towards them. Nevertheless, positive outcomes, even at this stage, have led WWF to set up further projects with the authorities in Bradford, Coventry, Dorset and Walsall. Materials (such as a video and training pack) based on experiences in the pilot projects are being produced and should be available in early 1996.

The approach in Leicester is different. A few years ago the city council assisted in setting up a limited company — Leicester Promotions — to promote the city and support Environ, an NGO which coordinates the BT Environment City initiative. This has been extended into Blueprint for Leicester, its local title for LA21. The city also has an established neighbourhood environmental appraisal scheme which started with an attitudinal survey of 100 randomly selected households in each of its eight wards to obtain information on key concerns in the neighbourhoods. Events followed the survey to encourage local people to explore solutions.

These pre-existing initiatives, and a general climate of consultation were a great advantage when it came to move forward on LA21. Positive relationships already existed with local people and the Blueprint partnership deliberately tried to avoid prescribing solutions for local people. An early scheme used a short questionnaire to find out what people thought of Leicester now, what they hoped it might be like 20 years hence, and what might usefully change and stay the same. Before moving forward from this they were careful to locate existing organizations and key target groups. Rather than inviting people to new meetings, they ensured that they were invited to established meetings to put across the scope and content of LA21. A pack has been produced to help local groups.

The Leicester work has placed emphasis on quality of life (rather than environment) and on action learning — the integration of awareness raising with training and the balance of individual, community and overall authority-wide initiatives. This appears to us to be a hint at how to move forward more broadly.

Developing the Potential

While the case studies all show what can be done (given the constraints on local government officers), they give no indication of how widespread 'good practice' is. From our experience, the local government officer who 'does education' in addition to his or her other duties, often by default rather than by design, is still the most common model. This must change. Agyeman and Evans (1994) and the Panel on Sustainable Development (1995), among others, have all argued that a comprehensive educational programme is a vital tool in achieving sustainability.

A recent report by Lancaster University (1995) on behalf of Lancashire County Council tried to understand what factors might influence public understanding and responses to 'sustainability indicators' in Lancashire. Through 'focus group' discussions, the researchers found that:

■ Lancashire's sustainability indicator initiative is only partially accepted by the public largely because of lack of trust in government and business;
■ people's sense of agency (ie the ability to do something about what they know to be damaging) is not purely related to *extra* information. It is more related to trust in the information provider and the need for empowerment;
■ sustainability is regarded by many as an expression of self-interest on

behalf of official bodies, thus alienating people even further; and

■ there is widespread anxiety and pessimism about current social trends (crime, increasing job insecurity among higher socio-economic groups and continued unemployment among the already unemployed) and local people feel that politicians are either unable or unwilling to do anything about these issues.

This scepticism about such a central democratic process demands a vigorous and radical response from all areas of local and central government; such a gulf cannot be bridged by minor adjustment in existing patterns. It is our view that attention to educational issues is a classic means to expose the areas of local and central government ideologies, thinking and practice which must be addressed if real progress is to be made towards sustainability. Concerns which need to be addressed include:

■ narrow subject, departmental and professional thinking that still equates 'sustainable development' solely with 'environment' — and then only certain aspects of environment;
■ thinking that assumes that 'development' can only be delivered through physical growth and building, ignoring the human and social dimensions of 'personal development' inherent in sustainability;
■ the desperate clinging by some professionals to traditions of professionalism, and particularly the superficially controllable areas of technical skills and knowledge;
■ traditional assumptions of top-down management, paternalism and control, denying the two-way, bottom-up value of progressive and critical educational approaches;
■ a remarkable lack of creativity in developing new ways of thinking and working, most dramatically expressed in the way few environmental coordinators even bother to take advantage of the educational and training skills within their own organizations;
■ a steadfast refusal to acknowledge that sustainability demands radical cultural and structural change; and
■ the apparent contradictions between environmental and sustainability initiatives and, for example, the development of major roads by some authorities.

Despite such cautions, a number of positive signs can be identified for the future:

■ like it or not (for some), sustainability discussions are bringing unusual assemblies of people together, often in unlikely settings, and issues of democracy, access, social justice and equity are being raised;

■ even the most mixed groups, including members of the public traditionally resistant to spending money on airy-fairy things such as monitoring, are now agreeing that it is essential not only to collect baseline data but to establish and operate indicators and targets to show the move towards sustainability (or otherwise);

■ there are beginning to be a number of examples of educational courses and programmes that specifically address aspects of process rather than product and bring together new ways of working. Notable within this is the attention being paid to partnership — a more established concept — but, more significantly, to consensus building between often opposing groups, and to community participation; and

■ in relation to the latter, it is now being realized that the so-called developed world — the North — has much to learn from the less developed world — the South. For many years now, small, quiet, low-resource, high-quality sustainable schemes have been advanced in the South, and all within a framework of integral community participation built from continuing education.

The key problem now being faced is how to mobilize the gathering momentum and enable it to work coherently rather than in isolation or even against itself. No model yet exists, but a recent study by BDOR (not yet published) for Scottish Natural Heritage on *Educational Support Material for Communities on LA21* pointed the way.

The study report aimed to build on several positive (and potentially positive) features in Scotland at the time of writing (early 1995). First, there was the new role being given to community councils (the Scottish equivalent of parish councils) under the forthcoming local government reorganization. Community councils would be able to secure training for themselves and local people, and the more proactive councils had already identified sustainability as the core theme of their training.

Second, Scotland is fortunate in still retaining the basis of a nationwide system of local community education workers. With such a network, a community council would have speedy access to a professional to help it identify its training needs and then to assist in delivering the training. Community education workers themselves have highlighted the centrality of sustainability.

Third, there is still a strong tradition in Scotland of environmental education, not just in schools but lifelong. A recent report — *Learning for Life* — identified six areas of educational focus: education at school, at work, in the home, at leisure, in post-school situations and in the general environment. (Unusually, this report took the wider view of education commented on earlier.)

The report then went on to suggest the need for two intertwined strategies for moving forward in this basically supportive context. It argued that success can come through a structured programme of *education for participation*, but only if this is developed closely with developmental (and still partly educational) work to help create a strong *community infrastructure* to mobilize learning fully. The two are interdependent though one may advance ahead of the other (for example when a local authority is not active on LA21). Education for participation, though implicit in *Learning for Life*, requires further work if it is to move beyond environment into sustainability, and beyond substantive content into processes.

Education for participation in LA21 will also only achieve its potential when it is targeted as much at community and environmental professionals as at communities themselves. It must be a two-way process.

Developing community infrastructure requires an approach that engages a wide range of local people from the outset, trains them and supports them as they consolidate their learning into action in their local communities. The necessary training and support requires a combination of:

- a publicly shared commitment by key agencies;
- formal training events;
- the involvement of community councils and community education workers;
- a computer-based networking system; and
- a resource pack of easily adaptable 'tricks and techniques'.

Prognosis

As implied in the case studies section above, there is already a reasonable range of challenging, enjoyable and informative methods in use to bring people into LA21 processes, but some important gaps remain to be filled. In this chapter we have also commented cautiously on the growing momentum within local authorities — especially among environmental coordinators — to look more seriously at their educational role.

Because, as in the SNH model, many of the elements of the proposed structure already exist and are proven, the main task now is to make the whole greater than the sum of its parts — ie to work on the recipes rather than the ingredients, and on the supportive organizational context rather than just getting the odd keen officer in post. If SNH or others fully adopt the proposed approach — and it is one in which resources and commitment are shared very widely between all sectors (including local authorities) — we could begin to look forward to a coherent, wide and inclusive model for a sustainable educative community.

On reflection there is some cause for optimism as new ingredients appear to emerge almost daily from creative practice around the country, new people are drawn in, new links are made and the total national resource of skills, experience, enthusiasm and techniques grows. At the same time local government faces new pressures — again almost daily. With the increased emphasis on direct, measurable, short-term performance indicators, it seems unlikely that those committed to a liberating philosophy of open and lifelong education for all will be able to produce the hard evidence of progress before the district finance officer's axe is finally sharpened for the inevitable next round of cuts. At this moment the future of EFS lies very much in the balance

References

Agyeman, J and B Evans (eds) (1994) *Local Environmental Policies and Strategies*, Longman, London

Lancaster University (1995) *Public Perceptions and Sustainability in Lancashire*, Centre for the Study of Environmental Change, Lancaster

Panel on Sustainable Development (1995) *First Report*, HMSO, London

Tuxworth, B and C Carpenter (1995) *Local Agenda 21 Survey 1994/5*, LGMB, Luton

Young, J (1995a) *A Change of Plan for Teachers*, WWF, Godalming

— (1995b) *A Change of Plan for Planners*, WWF, Godalming

Part V

Making Progress Towards Sustainability

Chapter 13 | DEVELOPING STRATEGY
Stephen Sterling

Education for change has always been marginal to mainstream thinking and practice. But if the objective of 'a sustainable society' is to move from rhetoric towards reality, EFS has to become a central function of that society. Work on or from the margins is no longer adequate — although it may still be necessary to ensure that a radical leading edge is maintained. How we get from the periphery to the centre, from a state of poor EFS to universal richness of thinking and practice, is inevitably a question of strategy, as the *ad hoc* growth in incidence and quality of education for change that has taken place in the past will be too slow and ineffective for the future. A strategic approach, I will argue, is relevant at all levels from international and national to local and personal. However, while multilevel strategies are vital, and strategy theory is simple, implementation — paradoxically — is difficult and challenging if done well, and invariably raises many important issues.

While every chapter in this book is in some way concerned with strategy for EFS, this chapter focuses directly on the meaning of strategy, and reviews the strengthening mandate for a strategic approach, basic strategy theory, contesting approaches and critical questions arising from strategy, and a limited number of case studies to indicate lessons and issues. National strategies are the main theme, but many of the points raised are relevant at any level of work.

A Growing Mandate

In relation to environmental education in particular, the idea of *planning* change, rather than merely calling for 'more and better' environmental education, has emerged strongly since the beginning of the 1990s and particularly since the publication of *Caring for the Earth* (IUCN/UNEP/

WWF, 1991) and Agenda 21 (UNCED, 1992). International opinion, both at NGO and intergovernmental level has increasingly reflected a view of environmental education as a key ingredient of social change. The quotes introducing Part V illustrate this growing mandate.

International endorsement has led to a number of countries engaging in a process of developing environmental education strategy, often as part of an environmental strategy, or strategy for sustainable development. This trend has been strengthened through the Commission on Sustainable Development, set up after the Rio Earth Summit conference of 1992, which has required signatory countries to Agenda 21 to produce national plans for sustainable development. In addition, a number of countries have been encouraged to produce national environmental action plans under World Bank directives, including countries in eastern and central Europe which are producing them as part of the Environment for Europe agenda set by interministerial meetings held in Lucerne in 1993, and Sofia in 1995. Meanwhile, IUCN, particularly through its Commissions on Education and Communication (CEC) and on Environment and Strategic Planning (CESP) have taken a lead in bringing together leading players, particularly from NGO and government agencies, to share experience and promote strategy development to support these trends (Hulm, 1994).

What is relatively new about this activity is the linking of environmental policy on the one hand and environmental education and public participation on the other (IUCN/CEC, 1995). Whereas this association had been made before in the UK (notably in the post-Stockholm UN Conference flush of environmentalism in the early 1970s), recent governmental endorsement of the link between environmental policy and education and participation began with the White Paper *This Common Inheritance: Britain's Environmental Strategy* (HMG, 1990), which stated that 'It is essential, if environmental policies are to achieve their objective, that there is wide public awareness of the issues at stake and their importance to the future of the planet and to subsequent generations.'

This paper and its ensuing annual updates devoted chapters to education and training but, despite the government's claim to 'place the environment at the centre of its new initiatives in training, in education and research' (HMG, 1991), there was little evidence of strategic review and systematic thinking in developing environmental education and public awareness. Despite a long history of dialogue between government and NGOs pressing for environmental education (Sterling and EDET, 1992; Sterling, 1992; ESF, 1993) and the UK government's own *Sustainable Development: The UK Strategy* (HMG, 1994), which reasserted that 'education and training are crucial to the achievement of sustainable development', little genuine progress was made until the independent British Government Panel on Sustainable Development (BGPSD), set up by the government's UK strategy, recommended that 'Government should develop a comprehensive strategy for formal and informal education and bring in the wide range of related activities by official and voluntary bodies, industry and commerce, and local communities' (BGPSD, 1995). By mid-1995, a government review of its strategy in relation to environmental education and training was under way.

Meanwhile, spurred on by international endorsement and perhaps a growing realization that key environment and development issues can no longer be addressed by central 'command and control', an increasing number of countries have begun the process of strategy development for environmental education and public participation. It is probably true to say that a number of the countries that have taken a lead, such as Finland, Norway, The Netherlands, Nepal and the Czech Republic, dissimilar in many respects, have in common a pressing concern for environmental quality and this is often quoted as a key part of the rationale in strategy documents.

The environmental agenda has thus been a spur to planned change in educational provision and systems, which it is hoped will in turn have a positive effect on environmental quality. As the debate has developed, the concern has broadened from environmental policy to sustainable development and in turn — although more slowly — attention to environmental education has also begun to broaden to encompass development education and EFS. What is still rare, however, is a full appreciation of the necessary complementarity of EFS and progress towards sustainable modes of living in society as a whole, that one cannot satisfactorily advance without the other. Too often, education and its role in relation to environment and development is still narrowly conceived even when the rhetoric suggests otherwise. To understand this issue, it is necessary to examine some of the values and assumptions that accompany strategy work.

Instructive and Constructive Strategies

Environmental and sustainability imperatives are exerting pressure for change in educational systems, and this is leading to an emerging international consensus on the need for a strategic response. While the current debate rightly calls for a whole response, emphasizing multilevel responses and the building of cross-sectoral partnerships, there is at the same time a need to bring to light underlying tensions resulting from different assumptions and ideas if real change is to be achieved.

Two different approaches to strategy, which are partly complementary and partly contesting, may be characterized by the following models:

Strategy I: 'instructive' In this approach, education, training and public participation are seen as important to the implementation of environmental policy. Education is regarded as an instrument or tool of public policy alongside (though qualitatively different to) other instruments such as regulation and economic incentives. Essentially, the public and other sectors (target groups) are recipients of a message, knowledge or information generated by professionals, which needs to be communicated and understood, primarily to generate awareness and secondarily, it is hoped, to induce behavioural change. If this succeeds, it will be easier for the centre to adopt progressive environmental policy. Real power and control is maintained at the centre, while there are exhortations for 'environmental responsibility' among individuals. The engine of change is perceived by target groups as being external to themselves. Change in values and behaviour, where it occurs, can be fast, particularly when supported by other policy instruments, but tends to be shallow and impermanent. This approach might be termed 'education *about* sustainability'.

Strategy II: 'constructive' In this approach, the emphasis is on environmental policy being shaped, negotiated, owned and enacted at local level as far as possible, often in relation to personal, social and economic needs and concerns, through the medium of learning and the educational process. People are engaged in all aspects simultaneously and there is no hard distinction made between making policy decisions and learning for change. The emphasis is on capability and confidence-building, participation, ownership, empowerment and the generation of meaning (such as local sustainability indicators). Participants' perceptions, values and concerns are the starting point for any change, which may be structural as well as individual, and people feel themselves to be the initiators and owners of such change. The process is inherently flexible and integrative. The role of the centre is facilitation; power and professionalism are released and transferred rather than guarded. Change tends to be slower and more difficult, but deeper and more permanent. Any two or more strategies are likely to be different — reflecting local circumstances. This approach is 'education *for* sustainability', or more radically perhaps 'education *as* sustainability'.

The first approach is essentially technocratic and transmissive, centring on awareness and behavioural change, and is most commonly associated with a top-down process with intended and preconceived outcomes. The latter is essentially participative and transformative, centering on capacity building and self-organization and determination, and is most commonly enacted through a bottom-up process. The outcomes are open-ended and spring from the concerns of the participants. The first approach is often concerned with environmental education and training, quantity and teaching in a broad sense; the second is concerned with learning, quality, EFS and democratization. Either may be concerned to strengthen values, knowledge, information, skills and institutions, but the approach to and interpretation of them differs.

These are different strategies (which I call Strategy I and Strategy II) and relate to different ideological roots as have been discussed in other parts of this book. However, it should be stressed that these models are not entirely exclusive in practice, that they can be understood as two ends of a spectrum of practice and that elements of both may often be observed in strategies at different levels. It will also be noticed that they apply as much at local and institutional level as at national level.

In a period when market philosophy and management principles are dominant in many spheres of life, some may see any strategy as part of this management culture and therefore irredeemably technocratic. However, I argue that a strategic approach is valuable at every level and that a mixture of Strategy I and Strategy II is often needed, depending on circumstances (Stapp and Crowfoot, 1980). Strategy II is the more radical model and is more conducive and appropriate to strong sustainability modes (see Chapter 1), particularly since these require a rejuvenation of democracy and a reinvention of community.

While elements of Strategy I, such as information campaigns, may be needed in the short term, perhaps for example where sustainability policies are perceived by people as being against their short-term interests, educators and societies as a whole need to work towards a situation where Strategy II is predominant because only this is socially sustainable in the longer term. It is interesting to note that progressive thinking and practice in business relate more to Strategy II than old management styles (Lynch and Kordis, 1989; and see Chapter 2 of this book). From an educational point of view, these strategy styles may be seen as directly linked with, or indeed an expression of, contesting positivist and critical educational paradigms (see Chapter 2) and related 'propositional' and 'constructivist' learning strategies (Wals, 1994; Mrazek, 1993). Local Agenda 21 (LA21) work exhibits elements of both and, often, tension between them (see Chapter 12), yet there is a clear and encouraging commitment — reflected in national and local documents — to working through Strategy II approaches (LGMB, 1994; and see Chapter 9).

Differences between these approaches remind us to use key words such as 'strategy', 'empowerment' and 'participation' with care and to be critical about how language is employed, wittingly or not, for different ends. Pretty (1995) has constructed a typology of seven modes of participation relating to development programmes (but relevant to this chapter) ranging from 'manipulative and passive participation, where people are told what is to happen and act out predetermined roles, to self-mobilization where people take initiatives largely independent of external institutions'.

Strategy Building

While some form of strategy is often better than none, it does not necessarily follow. It may be well done or badly done. Some clarity about strategy principles can help here, starting with the reason for strategy. Essentially, strategy is about reducing the uncertainty of attaining an agreed goal. Done well, it can:

■ identify needs;
■ clarify objectives and build consensus;
■ relate educational work to other policy areas;
■ promote communication and cooperation between actors;
■ build on existing work, reduce duplication and increase synergy; and
■ allow progress to be monitored and evaluated.

One of the myths surrounding strategy theory is that it is abstruse. On the contrary, the principles are simple, and revolve around four key questions:

■ Where are we now? (assessment);
■ Where do we want to be? (objectives);
■ How do we get there? (implementation); and
■ How do we know we are getting there? (evaluation).

These questions can be applied at any level, from international policy to change in the classroom. At a personal level, strategy is employed informally every day, most obviously in planning a journey. In group strategy building, however, answering these four questions is very much more involved than posing them.

Task 1 involves generating information to assess the current state of play, including strengths and weaknesses (strategies must be grounded in reality) and should be associated with 'constituency building'. Task 2 involves setting and prioritizing objectives that will guide the strategy. Task 3 involves designing and putting into operation a programme of activities that will move the group closer to the goal. Task 4 involves setting success criteria or indicators, monitoring and evaluation to ensure that real progress is occurring and making adjustments to the strategy as required. These may relate to sustainability indicators and/or social learning indicators (see Chapter 2).

Frequently, this planning cycle is repeated in the strategy building process, and includes mini-planning cycles and feedback loops within it. Indeed, strategy should be seen as a continuous way of working, rather than as an isolated event.

Important, but difficult qualities to ensure include:

- setting the right objectives (by asking appropriate questions first);
- causally linking objectives at different levels so that achievement of one will also help achieve others higher up the hierarchy (vertical integration). This point also relates to the need to integrate strategies at different levels, for example national, regional and local. Critical to this is continuous feedback and revision;
- promoting synergy rather than dysfunction between work in different sectors (horizontal integration); and
- choosing appropriate tools and meaningful indicators for evaluation.

All this requires consultation, negotiation and consensus among all groups that have something to gain and/or lose (stakeholders) if it is to work, and it is this that makes strategy a participative, evolving and often difficult process and not a one-off technical exercise: 'The objectives determine the participants and the participants determine the objectives' (Carew-Reid et al, 1994).

The emphasis therefore should be on *process*, on strategy and capacity building and on gaining a broad mandate, rather than exclusively on a *product* such as writing a strategy document. The latter is undoubtedly important as a consultative and communicative tool, as a guide, symbol and benchmark, but can be useless if not won through a consultative strategy-building process. There are many examples of strategy documents, carefully written by experts, that never proceed beyond the policy stage. This distinction between product and process reflects a further difference of emphasis between Strategy I and Strategy II approaches.

There are two spectra which define the style of any strategy (see Figure 13.1):

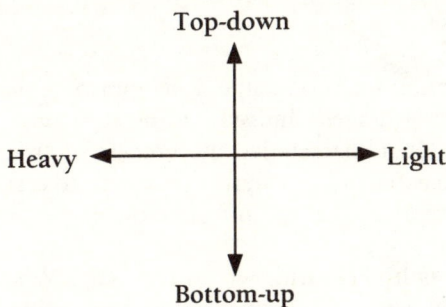

Figure 13.1 The Spectra of Strategy Styles

- *Heavy* — detailed, directive, versus *Light* — outlined, flexible;
- *Top-down* — written and disseminated by elite group, versus *Bottom-up* — generated by local groups.

Each of these has clear disadvantages where taken to extremes and advantages where more balanced. Where a particular strategy should locate itself in relation to these spectra and the Figure 13.1 axes depends on local circumstances. Strategy II type strategies, however, usually have more local detail and are more bottom-up the more locally-based they are. The desired relational state between strategies and substrategies at different levels, if it can be achieved, appears to be 'unity in diversity'. Whereas there is no off-the-peg formula because each situation is different, there appear from experience to be a number of factors that determine the success of strategy.

For example:

- strategies must build on previous and existing initiatives;
- strategies should be tailored to local conditions, needs and priorities;
- objectives should be realizable;
- governments and authorities should play a key support and facilitation role;
- participation, alliance and capacity building are essential elements;
- conflict resolution is a central element;
- efforts must be made to attain coherence between strategies at different levels; and
- communication between participants is vital.

(CESP, 1994; Carew-Reid et al, 1994)

Useful as such checklists are, it is important to recognize critical questions that arise in any strategy process.

Critical Questions

Strategies for education for sustainable development — from local to international level — raise issues. Indeed, airing tensions, negotiation and conflict resolution often characterize the process of strategy building and must proceed or accompany any agreed and effective strategy. Typically, questions concern such areas as meaning and ownership, for example:

- Whose strategy is it? For, with whom and why? Where is the locus of facilitation or energy? Is it exclusive and controlling or inclusive and empowering?
- Who or what is likely to benefit from the strategy exercise and in what way? Who might feel threatened?

- What concept of environmental education or EFS is being advanced here? Is it narrowly or broadly drawn? (Often governmental strategies lean towards a narrow, instrumental 'Strategy I' view of environmental education, although this is not always the case.)
- How far are stakeholders using the same words but attaching different meanings — whether these are environment or development education, EFS, or keywords such as ownership, participation and empowerment?
- What is the overriding goal? How has it been decided and in relation to whose needs?
- Are the goal and objectives supported or supportable, realistic, achievable or measurable?
- To what extent does the exercise take full account of all other related factors that may hinder or help its success?
- Who decides what the indicators of success will be and how are they decided?

Lastly, it is important to remember that there is no simple and direct relationship between improved EFS through strategy and social change in a linear cause-effect sense (although this thinking often lies behind strategy initiatives). If done well, the two dynamics merge as part of the same process.

National Case Studies

Box 13.1 THE NETHERLANDS

In The Netherlands, there have been three national plans for environmental education. The first, resulting from a plan developed by two key ministries between 1988 and 1990, had limited impact, partly because other target ministries did not fully understand the relevance of it to their own areas. The second plan resulted from a request from Parliament to government in 1990 to provide 70 million guilders (about US$ 31 million) for a Formal Education Plan for 1991–4. The responsibility was spread over six ministries with the Ministry of Education coordinating. The plan was aimed to integrate environmental education both into school subjects and into school organization and policy, and covered primary, secondary, vocational and agricultural school sectors. Many projects were funded including regional workshops, pilot projects in schools and cooperative projects between schools and NGOs. The strengths of this Formal Education Plan were political commitment from the top, availability of finance, and external (non-government) executive managers, funding of local activity and the involvement of individual

---

schools and local environmental education networks. A weakness perhaps was that the plan was not preceded by an analysis of the situation or of needs of schools and learners, nor by an analysis of possible desired contents and approaches in environmental education.

A third national plan (Concept Plan for Environmental Education) to develop environmental education in non-school situations was begun in October 1993 in response to a request from the Dutch parliament. Inspired by Caring for the Earth *and* Agenda 21, *and subtitled 'To make sustainability a second nature', the plan is subsequent to the National Environmental Policy Plan of 1989, which adopts sustainable development as a policy objective. Consequently, the concept plan (later called the Framework Plan) sought a broader definition and understanding of environmental education which it saw as 'helping individuals and groups in society to learn to apply the principle of sustainability to all public and individual decisions and activities' (Huitzing, 1994). In the light of experience, some changes in approach were made too: the seven ministries were involved in analysing the relevance of environmental education to their own policies; there was concern to integrate better the work of government departments; bottom-up approaches were seen to be as important as top-down ones and therefore there was determination to discuss the framework with implementing groups; it was felt that it was important to involve non-environmental as well as environmental groups and to expand public participation; and there was a desire to improve the quality of and synergy between environmental education activities.*

The plan is in two stages: a development stage (1994–5) based on elaborating the objectives and framework of the plan in cooperation with environmental education actors; and an implementation stage (1994–9) where agreements regarding responsibilities reached in the development stage are put into operation. As Bos (1993) writes: 'This agreement is the crucial element of this strategy. We are not really interested in non-committal statements about the usefulness of cooperation.'

Agreement in the first stage has been sought through interviews, round-table discussion, conferences and workshops, and communication carried out by contracted managing organizations. A strength of this open process has been building consensus and commitment among players; an inevitable weakness has been some lack of clarity regarding outcomes as these evolve from the process.

The Framework Plan adopted four 'activity profiles' or foci which will be used to structure environmental education programmes. This is based on the idea that people have different roles in different settings:

- ■ *the local environment (home and neighbourhood);*
- ■ *leisure and recreation;*

- *work situation; and*
- *lifestyle and consumption.*

While it is too early to evaluate the course of the Plan, it appears that The Netherlands has achieved a remarkable mix of Strategy I and Strategy II approaches, with strong central — and often local — political support and funding, and a high degree of regional and local participation by acting bodies and groups. Dozens of NGOs, 12 provinces and numerous local councils have been involved. This momentum, together with an emphasis on practical activity and determination to monitor the process, appears to be paying off.

Box 13.2 SCOTLAND

The Scottish experience has some parallels with that of The Netherlands, but also some strong differences. Opportunities presented by an 1989 conference in Scotland of the Northwest European Committee of IUCN's Commission on Education and Communication were used to initiate consultations with the Scottish Office as a result of which the Secretary of State for Scotland set up a working group on environmental education in 1990. This group quickly became aware of the importance of the process of strategy development as well as the product. The final report, Learning for Life, *was presented to government in April 1993. Environmental education was broadly defined to encompass the principles of* Caring for the Earth *(IUCN/UNEP/WWF, 1991). This holistic view led the group to set up six subgroups representing the main contexts in which they felt learning occurs — paralleling the 'activity profiles' of The Netherlands strategy. These were: the home, the community, leisure and recreation, school, post-school education and training, and the workplace. Additional subgroups were concerned with important outside influences such as government, the media and advertising. These were critical to the success of the assessment phase of the process, which identified the state of environmental education in Scotland across all sectors.*

A second and related strand in the group's approach was to involve as many players as possible. As well as discussion, questionnaires and conferences, a series of intersectoral workshops were held on relevant topics involving government departments and agencies, local government, formal education, business, professional institutes, and voluntary, community, religious and youth organizations. This promoted exchange of information, communication and networking, and a sense of owner-ship in the strategy process. This consultation was extended before the final draft of the report was prepared, by discussion with the main organizations likely to be involved in implementation.

As well as generating a wealth of information and a database, the consultation generated new working relationships that promised new initiatives beyond the life of the working group. Unlike The Netherlands situation, the Scottish working group neither had a large budget to carry out the strategy building process, nor could count on resources to fund recommendations. While some of the recommendations do require extra funding, many do not but require changes of policy and commitment at many levels of society.

After the report was published, it was widely disseminated in Scotland and abroad, and generated further significant support and influence on groups' activities both in Scotland and elsewhere. In the government's response of June 1995 (Scottish Office, 1995), the Secretary of State for Scotland welcomed the report, stating that 'He intends to adopt it as the foundation on which developments in his policy will be based' but the tone of the response is one of qualified endorsement, limited imagination and commitment and no new funds.

The Scottish experience is one that proves the importance of process; of involving as many groups as possible both before and after publication of the report as it is the involvement generated in this way that is likely to have the more lasting effect, compared with any late and lukewarm endorsement by government. In Scotland and elsewhere in the UK, the healthy local responses to sustainability issues such as those stimulated by LA21 were early on outpacing any central response (see Chapter 12; UNA–UK, 1995).

Box 13.3 FINLAND

In Finland, a national strategy for environmental education was produced in 1991, but this proved to have little direct effect, although it did lay the ground for later developments. It was written by government officials and international experts. Consultative seminars were centrally organized and there was little sense of ownership of the strategy. In 1993, however, in the wake of Agenda 21, the Finnish National Com-mission on Sustainable Development (FNCSD) was set up, with a subcommittee on environmental education and training representing a broad section of society. After Agenda 21 was sent out to over 1000 groups for comment, the commission produced an action plan based on Agenda 21 (FNCSD, 1995). As in The Netherlands, the emphasis is on partnership and, where possible, devolving responsibility to local implementers. This is now the subject of discussion and consultation, and newly established regional environmental centres are being strengthened to support regional networks and strategies for environmental education. Meanwhile, a number of sectors and ministries have worked on complementary strategies defining their own role in relation to sustainable development.

Conclusion

While in this chapter I have concentrated on strategy at the national level and in a limited number of countries in Europe, what emerges from reports of strategy building at any level, from local group to international level and in virtually any cultural context, is that there are a number of generic principles of what works. How the principles apply in practice can vary considerably, however, and taking full account of these differences is critical to success.

It is difficult to say whether governmental and international interest in strategy for EFS represents a gradual transformation of mainstream thinking and practice, both in education and public life, as it appears in The Netherlands, or whether the mainstream is largely accommodating the radical as seems more the case in the UK. Barriers to advancement remain strong in many countries, and include lack of political will and vision, lack of funds, lack of expertise and poor cross-sectoral communication. However, there is a growing casebook of success stories and international cooperation in strategy work, and IUCN's Commission on Education and Communication is working to share experience (Sterling, 1995). Meanwhile, UNED–UK is involved in preparing a paper to be put to the Commission on Sustainable Development in its review of Agenda 21 scheduled for 1997, which aims to get 'the education community' recognized as a major group in the Agenda 21 process (ESF/UNED–UK, 1995). If this succeeds, EFS may receive a major boost towards wholesale educational reorientation in the way envisaged in Agenda 21.

The urgency of sustainability requires a strategic response at all levels. We can expect government and policy-making bodies' responses to be primarily of the Strategy I type, and there is often a place for this reactive 'information and provision' approach in the short term. But this is essentially a shallow, non-participative and insufficient response and tends to lead to superficial and impermanent change — as is often demonstrated in other areas such as health campaigns. As suggested in this book, sustainability is a deeply cultural issue rather than a technical challenge, and therefore EFS must be transformative.

The problem, as Pretty (1995) suggests, is that authorities both need and fear people's participation. Strategy I responses by authorities must increasingly shift towards encouraging and facilitating Strategy II approaches at local levels to allow the growth of deeper, flexible and owned change, to allow real 'stakeholding'. This appears to be a lesson that is being learnt (Macnaghten et al, 1995), ie strategies for EFS must themselves be sustainable. If this shift occurs widely — and it appears to be happening in some localities and countries — it will be a profound change, with implications for democracy, politics and social organization in resonance with and contributing to the emergence of constructive postmodernism in a postmodern world (see Chapters 1 and 2; and Hutton, 1995).

The sustainable society, by definition, will be a learning society. We need to start by seeing education as an essential and inseparable element of sustainable development. As a letter received from a Finnish correspondent in connection with this chapter says: 'The process is very dynamic and, I would say, everlasting too' (Nikulainen, 1995).

References

BGPSD (1995) *First Report*, Department of the Environment, London

Bos, P (1993) 'Strategic Planning of Education in The Netherlands', paper presented to IUCN conference on Strategic Planning in Environmental Education, Bergen, The Netherlands, 1–3 November

Carew-Reid, J et al (1994) *Strategies for Sustainable Development: A Handbook for their Planning and Implementation*, IUCN/IIED/Earthscan Publications Ltd, London

CESP, (1994), 'Strategies for Sustainability', *Environmental Strategy*, Newsletter of the IUCN Commission on Environmental Strategy and Planning, 8, Sacramento, USA

ESF (1993) *The Role of Education for Sustainability: A Submission to Government*, Education for Sustainability Forum, London

ESF/UNED–UK (1995) *Strengthening the Role of the Education Community*, Education for Sustainability Forum/United Nations Environment and Development–UK, draft

FNCSD (1995) *Finnish Action on Sustainable Development*, Finnish National Commission on Sustainable Development, Forssa

HMG (1990) *This Common Inheritance: Britain's Environmental Strategy*, HMSO, London

— (1991) *This Common Inheritance: The First Year Report*, HMSO, London

— (1994) *Sustainable Development: The UK Strategy*, HMSO, London

Hulm, P (ed) (1994) *Report of IUCN–UNESO Meeting: National Strategies for Environment and Development Education in Europe*, IUCN Commission on Education and Communication, Gland, 15–17 November

Huitzing, D (1994) 'Concept Plan for Environmental Education 1993–1999', paper for Nature Management and Fisheries, Ministry of Agriculture, Wageningen

Hutton, W (1995) 'Take a Stake in the Nation's Real Wealth', *Guardian*, London, 26 July

IUCN/UNEP/WWF (1991) *Caring for the Earth: A Strategy for Sustainable Living*, IUCN/Earthscan Publications Ltd, London

IUCN/CEC (1995) *Communication: An instrument of Environmental Policy*, IUCN Commission on Education and Communication, Gland

Lynch, D and P Kordis (1989) *Strategy of the Dolphin*, Arrow Books, London

LGMB, (1994) *Local Agenda 21 Roundtable Guidance Notes: 'Community Participation'*, Local Government Management Board, Luton

Macnaghten, P et al (1995) *Public Perceptions and Sustainability in Lancashire: Indicators, Institutions, Participation*, Lancaster University/Lancashire County Council, Lancaster

Mrazek, R (1993) *Alternative Paradigms in Environmental Education Research*, North American Association for Environmental Education, Troy, Ohio

Nikulainen, T (1995) Correspondence about strategy for environmental education in Finland, May

Pretty, J (1995) 'The Many Interpretations of Participation', *Tourism in Focus*, 16 (summer issue), Tourism Concern, London

Scottish Office, (1995) *A Scottish Strategy for Environmental Education: The Statement of Intent by the Secretary of State for Scotland*, The Scottish Office, Edinburgh

Stapp, W and J Crowfoot (1980) *Suggestions for Developing a National Strategy for Environmental Education: A Planning and Management Process*, UNESCO, Paris

Sterling, S, (1992) 'Environmental Education and Environmental Policy: A Good Alliance?', paper presented to World Congress for Education and Communication on Environment and Development, Toronto, October

Sterling, S and J Baines (eds) (1995) *Planning Environmental Education in Europe*, European Committee for Environmental Education, IUCN, Gland

Sterling, S and EDET (1992) *Good Earth-Keeping: Education, Training and Awareness for a Sustainable Future*, UNEP–UK, London

Wals, A (1994) *Pollution Stink! Young Adolescents' Perceptions of Nature and Environmental Issues with Implications for Education in Urban Settings*, Academic Book Centre, De Lier, The Netherlands

UNA–UK Sustainable Development Unit (1995) *Towards Local Sustainability*, UNA–UK/Community Development Foundation, London

UNCED (1992) *Agenda 21*, Regency Press, London

Chapter 14 | THE POLITICIANS RESPOND

Ken Collins MEP
Chairman, European Parliament's Committee on the Environment,
Public Health and Consumer Protection

In certain economic theories absurdities abound which can make a nonsense of real life. Take the recent Kobe earthquake in Japan as an example. According to WWF, statisticians have calculated that Japan will actually make a profit from the earthquake: 5500 people were killed, 33,000 were injured and the bill for damage has already exceeded US$ 110 billion. However, the income generated by the rescue and clean up efforts means that calculations based on GDP show a slightly positive result on balance for the 'well-being' of Japan. This is quite astonishing and renders some economic theory entirely meaningless. It is also a very vivid illustration of why environmental education should be an integral part of the learning process.

A parallel problem existed until relatively recently at EU level. However, in 1987, the Single European Act declared that environmental concerns should be considered in all other policy areas. This was greatly strengthened in the Treaty on European Union (Maastricht Treaty) and in the Fifth Environmental Action Programme, which establishes community environment policy up until the millennium. This programme specifies policy sectors where environmental concerns must be given higher priority; industry, energy, transport, agriculture and tourism. Too often in the past, policy-making has been entirely divided into separate departments. It has meant, for example, that there has been little cooperation between those responsible for transport policy or agricultural policy and those responsible for environment policy. For example, it is essential for DG VII (Transport) to know what DG XI (Environment) is doing to curb vehicle emissions to tackle air pollution. It is important for DG VI (Agriculture) to know what DG XI thinks about pesticide use yet often this cooperation and contact has simply not been present to any great extent.

In such circumstances, it is clearly difficult for coherent policies to emerge. However, this state of affairs is beginning to improve gradually, environmental concerns having filtered slowly into the consciousness of European decision-makers (apart from those directly involved in environment policy of course who have long had the foresight to advocate wholesale integration into all policy areas).

This same integration process should occur in education policy so that the consideration of environmental aspects of economics or sociology are integral to courses in these subjects; when students examine the economic gain from industrial production they should always consider the environmental costs that industry inevitably carries.

However, achieving this degree of integration is not without its problems as the Parliament's Environment Committee discovered only recently. We held a conference with WWF and the Club of Rome on the subject of 'taking nature into account' in systems of national accounting such as GDP. We highlighted the importance of reforming accounting such as GDP. We highlighted the importance of reforming these indicators since they represent only what a country has produced in terms of its economic output and fail to take into consideration socio-economic and environmental factors. That being the case, they are in no way a measurement of that country's well being, but they are universally presumed so to be. Yet even if we agree that these types of indicators need to be accounted for, it is less clear how monetary value can be assigned to some of the environmental and socio-economic costs that we need to measure. That is why environmental education is so important; we need to establish a clear link in people's minds between their actions and their environmental impacts at as early a stage as possible.

European commitment to environmental education has been part of EU environmental policy since the first action programme was adopted in 1973. When the fourth programme was adopted by the council in October 1987, it was expressly mentioned as a priority field of action. This attention was carried through into the fifth action programme too. Pilot projects have taken place throughout the EU. A budgetline was established in 1988 and, in 1993, EU spending on environmental education amounted to 1 million ecu. Today, immediate priorities can be gleaned from the most recent call for tenders from the commission; these focus on teacher training and the design of appropriate teaching materials on a Europe-wide basis.

European Commission initiatives to promote environmental education throughout the EU have always been warmly welcomed and firmly supported by the European Parliament as an institution. What is more, through the direct contacts with school pupils and teachers that MEPs enjoy, we can play a particular role in seeing that plans are put into action and by helping to ensure that younger generations know why natural resource management matters.

The Rt Hon John Gummer MP
Secretary of State for the Environment

Sustainable development will have to be at the core of our economic, social and political thinking, if we are to make the most of our opportunities without jeopardizing the capability of future generations to enjoy their own lives. In particular, we must guide young people into an understanding of this concept from their earliest days. This, the Department of the Environment is seeking to do. But we cannot do so successfully without many partners in the endeavour, both as regards the formal education process and informal exercises concerned with raising awareness.

I have no intention of interfering with the content of the national curriculum, particularly in view of the extended period of uncertainty which preceded the revised version to which schools are now working. I said as much at a seminar in February 1995, hosted jointly by my department and the Department for Education (as it was then). But I am concerned that the environmental components of the revised curriculum should be delivered to the best effect, and this is the remit of a DfEE taskforce. It is giving advice to industry and other providers of environmental curriculum materials about how best to prepare them so that they can be used effectively in (and outside) the classroom; it is exploring the possibility of preparing a database of good material, easily accessible by teachers, and it is to seek out and publicize examples of good practice by schools in using such materials. The voluntary sector, in particular WWF, has been a pioneer in the development of environmental teaching materials and I expect to see many examples of its work in the results of the taskforce's deliberations.

I believe the environment should not be a stand-alone subject in the curriculum. That could lead to compartmentalizing and marginalizing — perhaps to its being one of those subjects which at a certain stage is no longer compulsory. The environment *is* compulsory — it is always with us. I look to see young people's attention being drawn to the environmental inferences to be drawn from the whole curriculum — and also from the rest of their daily lives.

The essence of sustainability, our proactive response to the environment, is that all the partners in our society should aim to work together to achieve it. This means cooperation between sometimes unfamiliar partners, both nationally and locally. Our Round Table on Sustainability, which I chair jointly with Professor Sir Richard Southgate, has representatives from industry, education, the voluntary sector, environmental groups and local authorities.

At the local level, it is the local authorities themselves which have made great strides, for example in developing Local Agenda 21 programmes, which set out, again, to engage the whole local community in these efforts. And a vital part of any local community is its schools, colleges and universities. I launched the 'Going for Green' campaign earlier in 1995, as another means by which these local enthusiasms can be brought together. Its purpose is to promote those actions and choices by which each individual can make a personal contribution to sustainable development. 'Going for green' is in turn to run the Eco-Schools project. This will involve children in examining the environmental impact of their school and its surroundings, the exercises all being designed with the curriculum in mind.

I am particularly concerned about the dual task of preparing young people, whether school leavers or university graduates, for the world of work, while ensuring that they have a proper perception of environmental matters. I am not alone in this: the Advisory Committee on Business and the Environment, which is appointed jointly by myself and the Secretary of State for Trade and Industry, has expressed concern about the perceptions of young people, potentially their new recruits, about the general place of industry in our society, and their perceptions about industry and the environment. I believe that the same highly trained, skilled people we will need for our economies to remain competitive are essential to meet the complex environmental challenges of the future.

Industry may indeed have an impact on the environment, for example in extracting and processing raw materials. But it is also industry which has developed the techniques and skills to deal with the environmental problems of an industrialized society. We need industry to create the wealth without which our striving for sustainability will be fruitless. And in turn, to remain competitive in today's world it needs both proper educational provision for its potential recruits and the proper training programmes which will provide continuing professional development for its employees.

There is a challenge implicit throughout this review, and that is to the teachers — and of course in turn to the teacher trainers themselves: are they attuned to the delivery of these messages? I look forward to the follow-up of the Toyne Committee's 1993 Report on the place of the environment in FHE as a whole. In particular, though, I commend WWF in its identification of the education challenge. Its support of courses at Jordanhill and of the new MSc in environmental education at South Bank University are very valuable.

WWF has made an irreplaceable contribution to the cause of environmental education in this country. I applaud it for this and look forward to being able to support it in more developments in the future.

Jean Lambert
Green Party

This is probably the first generation where we, as parents, teachers and politicians, cannot honestly say the future will be better for young people. They already know that. They know about the vast environmental problems we face on a global basis; they know that employment prospects are uncertain and that life is tough. They are therefore looking for honesty about the future and a range of skills and ideas that will help them to look forward positively. This puts an enormous responsibility on educators who are faced with a system which appears to be growing ever more rigid in its content, unimaginative in its goals and increasingly under-resourced.

So, what must be done to help us face the future with greater confidence?

In the short term, education for sustainability means building on the work already done in the formal sectors so that students have a thorough understanding of the effects of the way we currently live. This has particular implications for education in economics, where the valuable work being done by green economists must become an integral factor. There is a great deal of work to be done in questioning current economic orthodoxies about the inherent values of trade and increased production. Consumer education has to embrace the option not to consume as well as how to consume wisely in environmental as well as economic terms.

Despite commitments to the cross-curricular nature of environmental education, much of it still takes place in subject 'boxes', failing to make the links between what we learn and what we do. The importance of understanding how food is grown, its impact on the land and on energy consumption, for example, is given very little place in education. Many people have no link at all with growing food and there is little time or place for this in schools. Yet this is fundamental to the issue of sustainability. The priorities of the national curriculum are real barriers to developing useful education and either need overhauling or the whole thing should be scrapped.

In many parts of the country, valuable resources such as environmental study centres face uncertain financial futures. Local management of schools and increasing government requirements of our educational institutions mean that schools are often unable to plan far ahead financially. So, many of the means of providing direct experiential education are becoming optional and we are all the losers. It is not every family or community that can make up this shortfall, which ought to be part of a universal education. National government needs to provide longer-term funding guarantees so that educators can plan ahead.

However, sustainability is about process as well as content.

Local Agenda 21 makes it clear that participation is essential to clear understanding and committed action. Therefore students, in whatever area of formal or informal education, need to be able to experience, question, discuss and solve things. Active citizenship is essential, yet political education is often poorly handled and participation is too often viewed as opposition. It is essential that we learn the skills of democracy — how to listen constructively, how to negotiate, how to come to a communal decision and how to handle dissent positively. These are not just skills for the school or workplace but for handling change and government.

This has enormous implications for organization and resources. Institutions which are being pushed towards 'teaching for tests' and delivering a set curriculum, find it increasingly difficult to set time aside to go into topics in depth, and in a rounded cross-circular way. Few schools do their own environmental audits on any regular basis, involving students, staff and parents to take just one basic example. We still fail to make full use of the enormous skills and resources in our wider community or even in our local councils. Local Agenda 21 has yet to make an appearance in most schools and colleges and yet the views of young people are seen as essential to its progress.

Sustainability is also about goals — and currently our educational goals are about training for work and helping the nation's competitiveness. The goals for sustainability are about learning to live in harmony with our planet and with each other — about learning to live fruitfully with 'enough'.

If we are to attain education for sustainability, it can only be done if we change the aims of our education system and resource it adequately. This applies to both the formal and informal sectors.

Teachers may sigh deeply at the thought of further changes, but at least education for sustainability can free creativity and imagination to pursue discovery and provide a sense of joy, confidence and purpose in our lives. It is a form of cooperative education from which we all benefit.

The Rt Hon Joan Ruddock MP
Shadow Minister for Environmental Protection

The air we breathe, the water we drink, the land we inhabit, the countryside we enjoy: these are fundamental issues that affect us all. In short, the fate of the environment is about the wellbeing of people. That is why Labour believes that the environment must be placed at the heart of all areas of policy. Labour is committed to the principle of sustainable development, accepting the Brundtland definition as 'development that meets the needs of the present generation without compromising the ability of future generations to meet their own needs'.

Labour recognizes the importance of education in progressing sustainable development. In order to meet our environmental responsibilities, radical change is necessary. We cannot go on living as if there were no tomorrow: using up raw materials without developing alternatives, creating waste which cannot be disposed of safely, and endangering the stability of the global climate. If we are to achieve sustainability, we must take into account the social and environmental, as well as economic, impact of decisions. Yet in order to make such evaluations, people need to have a greater awareness and appreciation of environmental issues. Labour is committed to ensuring that the environment is part of the school curriculum, part of workplace education and part of continuing education in the community. Labour will aim to raise environmental awareness so that people are empowered and motivated to protect the environment.

Education for sustainability chimes fundamentally with Labour's concepts of citizenship and community. Labour believes that active citizenship complements active government. Central government alone cannot achieve a sustainable society. What is required is partnership, between individuals, companies, government at all levels and international institutions. Choices and decisions made in each home, each school, each workplace, each locality and each country can all make a real difference to our future.

Labour proposes a charter of environmental rights, which will be legally enforceable. Enhanced environmental awareness achieved through better and more widespread environmental education will enable citizens to exercise their new environmental rights, and to take on the environmental responsibilities that go hand in hand with those rights. Labour will give people a right to clean air and clean water, a right of access to common and open country, mountain and moorland, a right to compensation for environmental damage, a right to consultation on local environmental issues and on environmental issues in the workplace, and a right to environmental information.

But environmental rights must be set alongside environmental responsibilities. Labour will look to individuals and communities to take on environmental responsibilities and work together towards a sustainable society. The environment cannot fend for itself; it is something we all share and from which we all benefit. If our environment is damaged, we are all diminished. Yet no one person can save the environment. Unless we share responsibility for the protection and enhancement of the environment, each of us and all of our children will be the losers.

Education for sustainability includes, but goes beyond, environmental education. It also includes education about development issues. Crucially, it encourages people to think about how they live their lives, and how their actions, behaviour and forms of organization can help or hinder progress towards a sustainable society. Labour is committed to ensuring that Britain plays its part in achieving global sustainable development. The developed world's grip on the terms of international trade and widespread dumping of agricultural surpluses mean that many developing countries are forced to degrade their environment to survive. Acute poverty forces many individuals to destroy their environment. Yet all countries have a common interest in the global environment. Labour believes respect for the environment should be a fundamental consideration in international trade, and aid and debt relief should be linked to environmental protection. Education for sustainability will help people to develop a greater understanding of these complex issues.

The importance of environmental education has been increasingly recognized in recent years. The first report of the British Government Panel on Sustainable Development, published in January 1995, identified environmental education as an issue of long-term significance for sustainable development (and one of the first two such issues which the Panel chose for study.) They made four recommendations relating to environmental education and training. The House of Lords Select Committee on Sustainable Development report, published in June 1995, also looked at the issue of environmental education, and made a recommendation to government. Labour broadly endorses both reports.

Although the present government claims a commitment to environmental education, Labour believes it has not gone far enough. The current status of environmental education within the national curriculum is uncertain, giving rise to understandable concerns among environmentalists and educationists alike. Furthermore, the crisis over lack of resources in the state education system is felt particularly acutely in cross-curricular 'themes' such as environmental education, as the Department for Education tends to direct resources towards the core curriculum. At present, educational materials on the environment are largely provided by environmental organizations, statutory bodies and educational private companies. While the involvement of such organizations in environmental education is welcome, the government should take greater responsibility in ensuring that educational resources on the environment are accurate, balanced and of high quality.

Labour does not believe that education for sustainability should begin and end at the school gate. Environmental education is far more than a single school project or a set of facts to be memorized and tested. The challenge for government is to enable people of all ages, in all communities, inside or outside the formal education system, to learn more about our shared environment, so that they can fully exercise their environmental rights as citizens, and understand their environmental responsibilities. Labour looks forward to taking on that challenge.

Matthew Taylor MP
Liberal Democrat Environment Spokesperson

This book makes an important contribution to improving environmental understanding across society — an understanding necessary to real environmental sustainability. The Liberal Democrats believe strongly in environmental education. Education and the environment are key priorities for us and we welcome the use of one to benefit the other. Frankly, society cannot be expected to move towards more environmentally sustainable development and behaviour without adequate education.

At present few people, even some of those who consider themselves to be 'environmentally friendly', are actually prepared to take positive action to change their lifestyles. Such action may simple mean walking or cycling more or minimizing waste produced by their households or businesses. However, a survey during the recent air pollution smogs showed that few people are prepared to shift to alternative forms of transport or even reduce their time on the roads. This problem highlights the need for more effective policies, regulation and education.

Education empowers individuals to take control of their lives. By providing environmental education people are given the knowledge to take responsibility for their actions and the effect they have on our air, land and sea. Environmental education must combine the theoretical with the practical — how each individual can take action towards sustainability.

Within this it is also important that we do not aim environmental education only on certain groups in society. This is something we are all involved in: the young and old, the rich and poor, businesses, local government, men and women. As such, every individual can play a part in improving the environment if given the understanding and the know-how to do so. We therefore need to educate not only the next generation but also our businesses, media and government bodies, both nationally and locally, to promote sustainable development.

The fact is that without sensible, long-term and far-reaching environmental policies, economic development is likely to be shortlived. We should never lose sight of the alternative to promoting more sustainable behaviour — the cost to jobs and livelihoods of failing to take action. Take the example of overfishing: ask the 40,000 Newfoundland fishers and fish workers who lost their jobs when cod stocks collapsed from overfishing and the Canadian government was forced to close the fishery. The truth is that the alternative to sustainable management of the fishing industry is no fishing industry at all. The Newfoundland fishers know only too well the cost of inaction.

In the 1990s it is widely accepted that our environment is under threat and that we need to promote more sustainable development. For example, the recent controversy over the disposal of the Brent Spar oil platform showed that abandoning waste at sea is no longer acceptable and that public opinion is turning strongly against polluters. This widespread consensus is the success of years of hard work and campaigning. However, with this success came a new problem — the need to find and introduce effective solutions.

Our society has changed drastically over the past few decades. Twenty years ago only 20 per cent of children were taken to school by car; this figure has now risen to 80 per cent There are more than 20 million cars on Britain's roads today. One in seven children suffers from asthma — exacerbated by air pollution — and there is a growing disparity between the rise in asthma suffering and the increasing numbers of young adults who want cars of their own.

The time has therefore come for us to move away from rhetoric about environmental sustainability and concentrate our efforts on actually implementing solutions and actively changing our society for the better. We must not only create better legislation and tougher national targets; we must improve environmental education.

It is crucial that we improve our understanding of the environment around us — that is the only way we will guarantee the survival of the world as we know it. Today 80 per cent of the world's population consumes more than 20 per cent of the world's natural resources. If developing countries follow the same path as industrial countries have, any gains we make in combating our environmental problems will be quickly offset.

However, the developing world has a right to develop its economies and to expect to improve its standard of life. This means that we cannot simply take enough limited action to clean up the environment in order to protect our lifestyles in the West — and assume that the world's poor will stick with theirs. We need to work in partnership on an international level, as well as cooperation within Britain, to ensure that development the world over becomes both economically and environmentally sustainable.

The interests of us all will be best served by clean air, unpolluted oceans and ecosystems that have supported life for thousands of years. We must all work together to find and put into action the best solutions or we will lose that treasure. This book will, I hope, contribute to that goal.

Chapter 15

A VISION of a 21st-CENTURY COMMUNITY LEARNING CENTRE

Shirley Ali Khan

Martin Luther King said that 'If you want to move people, it has to be towards a vision that's positive for them, that taps important values, that gets them something they desire — and it has to be presented in a compelling way that they feel inspired to follow.' The development of a positive vision of a sustainable future is a way of getting people motivated and activated in the pursuit of sustainability. When trying to visualize the future, people tend to think in terms of what life will probably be like, as opposed to what they would prefer it to be like. This is essentially a passive and fatalistic process. It reflects a common view that one is relatively impotent in helping to create a more preferred future.

We must lift our eyes above 'the probable' and engage in envisaging our preferred future. Such an approach will be immediately branded by cynics as creating a 'wish-list', without any sense of reality. I would argue that envisaging a preferred sustainable future has everything to do with the reality of living on a planet which has finite resources and a limited capacity to absorb human waste. Such a vision could not be arrived at merely by extrapolating existing trends. The vision that follows does not provide a detailed analysis of how change from an unsustainable present to a sustainable future comes about. Technology is mentioned as one agent of change, but the forces that direct its use are not discussed. The vision should be judged by its internal consistency, its ability to motivate and inspire, and its possibility.

We are approaching the millennium, which makes it a good time for envisaging the future. The motto of the Australian Commission for the Future is an appropriate preface to the vision of a twenty-first century community learning centre. It states:

■ the future is not some place we are going to, but one we are creating;
■ the paths to it are not found but made; and
■ the making of those pathways changes both the maker and the destination.

Box 15.1 THE CHANGE

Although there had been many calls for a more locally based, locally relevant, locally interactive further and higher education system throughout the twentieth century, the change came — as changes often do — out of necessity.

A widespread recognition that the use of the private car had to be reduced in the interests of environmental and public health, lead to a whole package of incentives and disincentives from a number of agencies to reduce mobility while maintaining access. Encouragements for home-working, teleconferencing, tele-meeting, home shopping and local learning, enabled the rebirth of a new type of local community. Eco-taxes on fuel also played a significant role. These initiatives, together with the general decline in the power of central government and the ascendancy of the local context, had the unplanned consequence of beginning the restoration of social cohesion and a sense of place.

People began, once again, to inhabit (by which I mean live in an intimate, organic, mutually nurturing relationship with place) rather than merely reside in their local communities. A resident, if you remember, was one who put down few roots, investigated little, knew little and often cared little for the immediate locale beyond its ability to gratify.

The Buildings and Surroundings *The Greentown Community Learning Centre is a good example of a new generation of locally distinctive buildings, built with local materials and designed to last 1000 years. Architects realized that it is more conserving of resources to build once, well, rather than repeatedly and badly. No one will be surprised to hear that this building did not cost 50 times more than a similar building designed for a 20-year life.*

Much use has been made of solar energy. Photovoltaic panels are worked into the facades and decorative details of the building. The primary heating and cooling systems consist of insulation and passive

---

ventilation. The whole site is designed to live within its own energy cycle budget. The surrounding land of the centre is used multifunctionally and managed in accordance with sustainable development principles — there is a reed-bed sewage system, some food is organically grown for use in the centre's kitchen, some areas are managed to enhance local bio-diversity and others are managed to enhance local community enjoyment. All areas are used for learning.

Inside, the centre is not so much decorated as landscaped. Research revealed that the long winter months of indoor living could be made much pleasanter if the indoor environments were richly textured, varied, colourful and alive. The centre's internal landscape makes use of stone, wood, bricks, plants, water, gravel and rocks, with an accent on local materials. The living decorative elements provide important indoor air quality services and a subtly changing environment as seasons change.

Good Housekeeping *The waste bins and recycling containers, so common in the twentieth century, are fewer and farther between. Recycling is a standard part of institutional life, but more significantly, much has been done to reduce waste at source. For instance, food services use only durable cutlery and crockery and organic materials are composted. The use of paper has been substantially reduced and electronic messaging, information storage and movement substantially increased. Many learners use portable computers.*

As far as possible, goods and services are purchased locally in order to assist the local economy. The centre, the local hospital and a few local companies have formed a local purchasing consortium which has been instrumental in establishing local storage facilities and a brokering centre for local producers. There is limited parking at the centre, which is much more easily visited by bicycle or by public transport. Vegetarianism prevails and smoking is now considered unacceptable in terms of personal health and polite company.

Inefficient and ineffective management practices including poor communication, weak strategic planning, perverse systems of accounting, provocative decision-making, failure to value the creative contributions of individual institution members — which, in turn, resulted in wasted money, wasted resources and pollution — have been replaced by a collective self-management system.

Community Focus *When Greentown locals were consulted at the design stage of the centre, they made it clear that they wanted all the centre buildings to be beautiful, special and 'people friendly'. Their wishes were granted. One of the most striking buildings is the universal hall which is used, as the name suggests, for all sorts of community* *activities from dances to public meetings. It possesses the beauty of the bioregion from which it is made, the specialness of a church in its 'heyday', and the friendliness of a corner shop.*

Local people feel that they belong to the Greentown Universal Hall in the same way that people used to feel they belonged to the church — reflecting a shift from a confidence and dependence on the wisdom of religious and political leaders to a greater confidence in common sense and a rediscovery of community values.

The centre is a place where local people, from different walks of life, can meet up to discuss common problems and to celebrate positive solutions. Citizen information and involvement in local decision making is delivered and facilitated through a citizen cable television channel, which is managed by the centre. The emphasis is not necessarily on bigger databases and better statistics, but on information flowing in new ways, to new recipients. The centre is part of a regional, national and global centre network linked by computer.

Global, national and local sustainability indicators are broadcast regularly. Creative techniques are used to make progress towards sustainability targets easily understood by all ages — for instance through animation. There is also a permanent interactive exhibition in the centre linking local and global issues which includes access to 'live' local, national and global data. Network links with other centres, regionally, nationally and globally are used continuously.

Day-to-Day Working *As far as the day-to-day work of the centre is concerned, things have changed a bit since the days of the old universities. Disciplines such as science, history, English and geography have become part of much broader educational domains which better reflect life — such as housing, food, energy, waste management, recreation and leisure. These domains include both disciplinary and interdisciplinary studies and value both. The environment is not a separate educational domain, rather, it is the context which weaves through all educational domains.*

The value of the redefinition of the domains lies in the new contexts provided for disciplinary enquiry. For instance, within the educational domain of housing, scientists and social scientists can both make unique contributions to improving energy efficiency in the home and to facilitating learning in relation to this topic.

This leads on to another change in the system. The emphasis has shifted from 'learning to know' to 'learning to do', and so research and teaching have become much more purposeful. Yes, there is always a place for whimsy and the pursuit of anomalies — but still the main work of the centre is geared towards enriching and improving local community life by enabling people to learn what they want to learn. Informed learner demand and learner autonomy are the hallmarks of today's local learning centres.

One of the most popular centre programmes at the moment is a series of ten community stories, developed and presented by artists, poets and experienced story-tellers, featuring the community's natural, economic and social history and development with contributions from local people. The stories are told on significant community days at a variety of locations. This approach is in keeping with learner preference for pedagogic approaches that are inspiring.

The balance between theory and practice is much more even than used to be the case in the late twentieth century. The valuation of practical 'real life' learning has led to a dynamic interactive relationship between the community and the centre, which has enabled the untapped teaching and learning potential of local people to be released. Learning facilitators, both part- and full-time spend as much time working in the community as they do in the centre.

The centre is appropriately located in the centre of the community. It has many 'front' doors, making it like a semi-permeable membrane which allows the free movement of local people in and out. It has fewer lecture rooms than twentieth-century colleges and more meeting rooms. Lectures are still used, but more for inspiration and providing synthesis and analysis than for the communication of information which is delivered in other ways, such as IT-based distance learning packages.

Most learners are involved in some IT-based learning, which they may do either at home or in one of the many community work rooms in the centre. These rooms provide a communal working and learning environment for community members. The distinction between working and learning is not as great as it used to be.

The general acceptance of the theory of multiple intelligences has helped to reduce the arrogance of those with high, narrowly defined IQs and has given permission and approval for pedagogic experimentation. The perennial question of whether intelligence is more or less dependent on nature or nurture, while still unanswered, is considered less important. More important is the general agreement that any measure of intelligence relates to both individual competencies and their application. The CV has been replaced by the learning intelligence profile (LI).

There is still much to discover about how different types of people can learn best and about what things are most useful to know and be able to do. This said, Greentown is already well on the way to becoming a learning community and its community learning centre is at the heart of this development.

A Conclusion — Or Beginning

This is not a utopian vision — rather it is a vision of a possibility which can be made real if enough people want it and work towards it.

■ *Acronyms and Abbreviations*

3M	Minnesota Manufacturing and Mining Company
3WE	Third World and Environment Broadcasting Project
ACC	Association of County Councils
ADC	Association of District Councils
AMA	Association of Metropolitan Authorities
ATEE	Association for Teacher Education in Europe
AUDES	Association of University Departments of Environmental Science
BBC	British Broadcasting Corporation
BCSD	Business Council for Sustainable Development
BEE	*Bulletin of Environmental Education*
BGPSD	British Government Panel on Sustainable Development
BS	British Standard
BSI	British Standard Institute
BT	British Telecommunications
BTEC	Business and Technical Education Council
CADISPA	Conservation and Development in Sparsely Populated Areas
CBI	Confederation of British Industry
CD-ROM	compact disc read only memory
CDP	Committee of Directors of Polytechnics
CEC	Commission on Education and Communication
CEE	Council for Environmental Education
CEED	Community Environmental Education Developments
CERES	Coalition of Environmentally Responsible Economies
CERI	Centre for Education, Research and Innovation
CESP	Commission on Environment and Strategic Planning
CFC	chlorofluorocarbon
CHE	College of Higher Education
COPERNICUS	Cooperation Programme in Europe for Research on Nature and Industry through Coordinated University Studies
COSHH	Control of Substances Hazardous to Human Health
CSA	Canadian Standards Association
DE	development education
DfE	Department for Education
DfEE	Department for Education and the Environment
DGXI	General Directorate for the Environment
DoE	Department of the Environment

DSP	dominant social paradigm
EDET	Environment and Development Education and Training Group
EE	environmental education
EFS	education for sustainability
EMA	Eco-Management and Audit
E-mail	electronic mail
ENSI	Environment and School Initiatives
ESRC	Economic & Social Research Council
EU	European Union
FE	further education
FHE	further and higher education
FNCSD	Finnish National Commission on Sustainable Development
FOE	Friends of the Earth
GDP	gross domestic product
GEMI	Global Environmental Management Initiative
GIS	geographical information systems
GNP	gross national product
GNVQ	General National Vocational Qualification
HMSO	Her Majesty's Stationery Office
IBT	International Broadcasting Trust
ICC	International Chamber of Commerce
ICLEI	International Council for Local Environmental Initiatives
IIED	International Institute for Environment and Development
IMD	International Institute for Management Development
INSEAD	European Institute of Business Management (France)
IT	information technology
ITC	Independent Television Commission
ITV	Independent Television
IUCN	International Union for Conservation of Nature and Natural Resources
LA21	Local Agenda 21
LAMB	Lloyds and Midland Boycott
LETS	local exchange trading system
LRD	Labour Research Department
MBA	Master of Business Administration
MSc	Master of Science
MSF	Manufacturing, Science and Finance (Union)
NAEE	National Association for Environmental Education
NCC	National Curriculum Council
NEP	new environmental paradigm
NGO	non-governmental organization
NUS	National Union of Students
NUSSL	National Union of Students Services Ltd
NVQ	National Vocational Qualifications
NYA	National Youth Agency
NYB	National Youth Bureau
OECD	Organization for Economic Cooperation and Development
OFSTED	Office for Standards in Education
OPCS	Office of Population Censuses and Surveys
PE	physical education
PgDip	Postgraduate Diploma

PR	public relations
PRA	participatory rural assessment
R&D	research and development
RRA	rapid rural assessment
RSA	Royal Society of Arts
SATIS	Science and Technology in Society
SENSE	Scottish Environmental Network for a Sustainable Economy
SME	small- or medium-sized enterprise
SNH	Scottish Natural Heritage
TCPA	Town and Country Planning Association
TEC	Technical Education Council
TELI	Tufts Environmental Literacy Institute
TEMPUS	Trans-European Mobility Programme for University Studies
TGWU	Transport & General Workers Union
TQEM	total quality environmental management
TQM	total quality movement
TUC	Trades Union Congress
TVE	Television Trust for the Environment
TVEI	Technical and Vocational Education Initiative
UETP-EEE	University Enterprise Training Partnership in Environmental Engineering Education
UK	United Kingdom
UN	United Nations
UNCED	UN Conference on the Environment and Development
UNED–UK	United Nations Environment and Development–UK
UNEP	United Nations Environment Programme
UNESCO	United Nations Educational, Scientific and Cultural Organization
UNICEF	United Nations Children's Fund
USA	United States of America
VOC	volatile organic compound
WCED	World Commission for Environment and Development
WCS	World Conservation Strategy
WWF	World Wide Fund for Nature

■ *Index*